Microsoft® Word 2000
QuickTorial®

Patricia Murphy

St. Thomas Aquinas College
Sparkill, New York

VISIT US ON THE INTERNET
www.swep.com

South-Western Educational Publishing
an International Thomson Publishing company I(T)P®
www.thomson.com

Cincinnati • Albany, NY • Belmont, CA • Bonn • Boston • Detroit • Johannesburg • London • Madrid
Melbourne • Mexico City • New York • Paris • Singapore • Tokyo • Toronto • Washington

Managing Editor: Carol Volz
Project Manager: Dave Lafferty
Marketing Manager: Larry Qualls
Design Coordinator: Mike Broussard
Development and Production: Thompson Steele Production Services, Inc.

I(T)P®
South-Western Educational Publishing is a division of International Thomson Publishing, Inc. The ITP logo is a registered trademark used herein under license by South-Western Educational Publishing.

The names of all commercially available software and other products mentioned herein are used for identification purposes only and may be either trademarks, registered trademarks, and/or copyrights of their respective owners. South-Western Education Publishing disclaims any affiliations, associations, or connection with or sponsorship or endorsement by such owners.

Microsoft® and Windows® are registered trademarks of Microsoft Corporation.

Microsoft and the Office logo are either registered trademarks or trademarks of Microsoft Corporation in the United States and/or other countries. South-Western Educational Publishing is an independent entity from Microsoft Corporation and not affiliated with Microsoft Corporation in any manner. This text may be used in assisting students to prepare for a Microsoft Office User Specialist exam (MOUS). Neither Microsoft Corporation, its designated review company, nor South-Western Educational Publishing warrants that use of this publication will ensure passing the relevant MOUS exam.

Open a Window to the Future!

With these _exciting new products_ from South-Western!

Our exciting new **Microsoft Office 2000 QuickTorial®** books will provide everything needed to master this software. Other books include:

NEW! **Microsoft® Word 2000 for Windows® QuickTorial** by Murphy
15+ hours of instruction for beginning through intermediate features

0-538-68849-1	Text, Soft Spiral Bound
0-538-68850-5	Text, Perfect Bound, packaged with Data CD-ROM
0-538-68851-3	Electronic Instructor Package (Manual and CD-ROM)
0-538-68939-0	Testing CD-ROM Package

NEW! **Microsoft® Excel 2000 for Windows® QuickTorial** by Murphy
15+ hours of instruction for beginning through intermediate features

0-538-68853-X	Text, Soft Spiral Bound
0-538-68855-6	Text, Perfect Bound, packaged with Data CD-ROM
0-538-68854-8	Electronic Instructor Package (Manual and CD-ROM)
0-538-68939-0	Testing CD-ROM Package

NEW! **Microsoft® Access 2000 for Windows® QuickTorial** by Murphy
15+ hours of instruction for beginning through intermediate features

0-538-68857-2	Text, Soft Spiral Bound
0-538-68858-0	Text, Perfect Bound, packaged with Data CD-ROM
0-538-68859-9	Electronic Instructor Package (Manual and CD-ROM)
0-538-68939-0	Testing CD-ROM Package

NEW! **Microsoft® PowerPoint 2000 for Windows® QuickTorial** by Murphy
15+ hours of instruction for beginning through intermediate features

0-538-68861-0	Text, Soft Spiral Bound
0-538-68862-9	Text, Perfect Bound, packaged with Data CD-ROM
0-538-68863-7	Electronic Instructor Package (Manual and CD-ROM)
0-538-68939-0	Testing CD-ROM Package

NEW! **Microsoft® Office 2000 for Windows®, Introductory Course** by Pasewark & Pasewark
75+ hours of instruction for beginning through intermediate features

0-538-68824-6	Text, Hard Spiral Bound

NEW! **Microsoft® Office 2000 for Windows®, Advanced Course** by Cable, Morrison, & Skintik
75+ hours of instruction for intermediate through advanced features

0-538-68828-9	Text, Hard Spiral Bound

A new feature available for these products is the **Electronic Instructor**, which includes a printed Instructor's manual and a CD-ROM. The CD-ROM contains tests, lesson plans, all data and solutions files, SCANS correlations, portfolio analysis, scheduling, and more!

South-Western
Educational Publishing

Join Us On the Internet **http://www.swep.com**

APPROVED COURSEWARE

What Is Certification?

The logo on the cover of this book indicates that these materials are officially certified by Microsoft Corporation at the **core** user skill level for Word 2000. This certification is part of the **Microsoft Office User Specialist (MOUS)** program which validates your skills as knowledgeable of Microsoft Word.

Why Is Getting Certified Important?

Upon completing the lessons in this book, you will be prepared to take a test that could qualify you as a **core** (or proficient) user of Microsoft 2000—which can benefit you in many areas. For example, you can show an employer that you have received certified training in Microsoft Word 2000 or you can advance further in education or in your organization. Getting this certification makes you more competitive with the knowledge and skills that you possess. It is also personally satisfying to know that you have reached a skill level that is validates by Microsoft Corporation to help meet your personal and professional goals.

You can also be certified as an **expert** user of Microsoft Word. The difference between **expert** and **core** users is the level of competency. **Core** users can perform a wide ranges or basic tasks. **Expert** users can do all those same tasks, plus more advanced tasks, such as special formatting and features.

Where Does Testing Take Place?

To be certified, you will need to take an exam from a third-party testing company called an **Authorization Certification Testing Center.** Call **800-933-4493** to find the location of the testing center nearest you. Learn more about the criteria for testing and what is involved. Tests are conducted at different dates throughout the calendar year.

South-Western Educational Publishing has developed an entire line of training materials suitable for Microsoft Office certification. To learn more, contact your South-Western Representative or call **800-824-5179.** Also, visit our web site at **www.swep.com.**

What's New in Word 2000

Microsoft Word 2000 includes the following new features:

- Microsoft has improved the installation process in Word 2000 so you get the program you need when you need it. The Detect and Repair command on the Help menu will reinstall files that are missing or corrupted. Your system administrator can configure your user profile to travel with you to make logging on and working from remote locations easy.

- Menus and toolbars are set up to take up less space on the screen and are personalized to display the commands you use most often. The Windows taskbar displays an icon for each open document. The new Open and Save dialog boxes make locating files much easier than ever before.

- The Office Assistant uses less space, can take you to the Web for more information, and can be quite entertaining. AutoCorrect is more powerful and there is a new Thesaurus.

- You can nest tables within other tables and align text vertically and horizontally.

- You can use the Web Page Wizard to start creating a Web site and use the Web Folders feature to manage your files stored on a Web server. You can collaborate with others via the Web in real time as if everyone were in a meeting in the same room. You can even send your Word document as an e-mail message in HTML format.

Start-Up Checklist

HARDWARE

Minimum Configuration

- ✓ PC using 486 processor operating at 25 MHz
- ✓ 8 Mb RAM
- ✓ Hard disk with at least 30 Mb free disk space
- ✓ VGA monitor with graphics adaptor
- ✓ Mouse or tablet
- ✓ Printer

Recommended Configuration

- ✓ PC using 486 or Pentium processor operating at 66 MHz
- ✓ 16 Mb RAM
- ✓ Hard disk with at least 91 Mb free disk space
- ✓ CD-ROM drive, 2x or faster
- ✓ VGA monitor with graphics adaptor
- ✓ Mouse or tablet
- ✓ Printer

SOFTWARE

- ✓ Microsoft Windows 95 or 98
- ✓ Microsoft Office 2000 or Microsoft Word 2000

PREFACE

To the Learner

Word 2000 is one of Microsoft's word processing programs and a component of the Microsoft Office 2000 suite. This book assumes that you have already learned to use your computer and that you have learned to use Windows, Microsoft's operating system for the personal computer. This book also assumes that Word is installed on your computer and is set to work with your printer.

It is very important that you watch your screen carefully as you go through the exercises in this book. If you click the mouse or press keys without understanding what is happening, you will miss a great deal. It is also important that you work through this book in the order presented. Each lesson builds on what you learned in previous lessons, so you may find yourself missing a lot if you skip through a lesson.

Every effort is made throughout this book to use Microsoft Word terminology when working with the program to help you to access Help files. Once you work through this book, you will be able to use many of Word's features to create professional-looking documents quickly and easily. The first few times you use a feature, you may have to use this book or the Help system to refresh your memory about the steps involved. For features you seldom use, you might always need to use Help.

You can do as many or as few of the exercises at the end of the lesson as you like or are assigned in class. The exercises concentrate on the main points covered in the lesson and provide good practice.

Conventions Used in This Book

Each topic includes brief explanatory text on using the particular Word feature and includes screen captures to help learners understand what should happen on their screens. Whenever a toolbar button is mentioned for the first time, the term is in boldface type and often the button is displayed nearby. Information useful to the learner but not appropriate in the explanatory text is entered in a Hot Tips, Important, Concepts Builder, Did You Know?, Teamwork, Extra Challenges, Note and Internet boxes. Terms that appear in the Glossary are shown in boldface type in the text.

The Step-by-Step exercise that follows each small group of topics allows the learner to use the features just covered. The numbered steps in the exercises begin by telling the learner what is to be accomplished in that step.

Menus, commands, file names, and toolbar buttons the learner is to click during the exercises, and short entries the learner is to type are shown in boldface type.

When more than one key is to be pressed at one time, the learner will be asked to hold one key and press the second.

The word *mouse* is used to refer to any pointing device learners may be using (IntelliMouse, trackball, pen, etc.). You will use the mouse rather than keystrokes whenever possible to accomplish tasks. You should know the following mouse definitions:

- *Point* means to move the mouse until the pointer is in the appropriate position on the screen.

- *Click* means to press the left mouse button with a quick motion. Always click the left mouse button unless you are directed to click another button.

- *Double-click* means to click twice without hesitating between clicks.

- *Drag* means to hold down the mouse button while you are moving the mouse.

About the Author

Pat Murphy has been teaching computer applications in corporate and educational environments since 1980. Pat was teaching at The Berkeley College in New Jersey when she founded Abbott Institute in 1982. She was president until she sold Abbott in 1994. Pat has been developing, licensing, and delivering end-user computer training for major corporations and colleges for all those years. She has often been a featured speaker at national and regional conferences. South-Western Educational Publishing Company has now published 22 of her books.

Acknowledgments

Thanks to Dave Lafferty and Carol Volz at South-Western for their support throughout the Office project. Thanks to Elinor Stapleton and Thompson Steele for their editorial input and for the book's production.

Once again, I must thank my husband, Mike, my children, Michael, Patti and Mark Schuette, and Kathleen, my mother, Lily Hough, my sister Mary O'Callaghan, and many other relatives and friends who have been supportive throughout. A big thank you to the community that is St. Thomas Aquinas College for making so much of what I'm doing possible. Thanks also to Larry Luing and The Berkeley College where I was teaching when first introduced to computers.

The biggest thank you of all, however, goes to Abbott Institute's corporate clients—at among others, Exxon, Warner-Lambert, RJR Nabisco, Morgan Bank, and Olsten Services—whose insistence on top-quality end-user training shaped my ability to develop instructional materials for computer applications.

Patricia Murphy
St. Thomas Aquinas College, Sparkill, New York

How to Use this Book

W hat makes a good applications text? Sound instruction and the most current, complete materials. That is what you will find in *Microsoft Word 2000, Quicktorial.* Not only will you find a colorful, inviting layout, but also many features to enhance learning.

Microsoft Office Certification– This icon is shown wherever a criteria for Microsoft Office User Specialist (MOUS) certification is covered in the lesson. A correlation table with page numbers is provided in the Electronic Instructor.

SCANS– (Secretary's Commission on Achieving Necessary Skills)– The U.S. Department of Labor has identified the school-to-careers competencies. The five workplace competencies and foundation skills are identified in the exercises throughout the text.

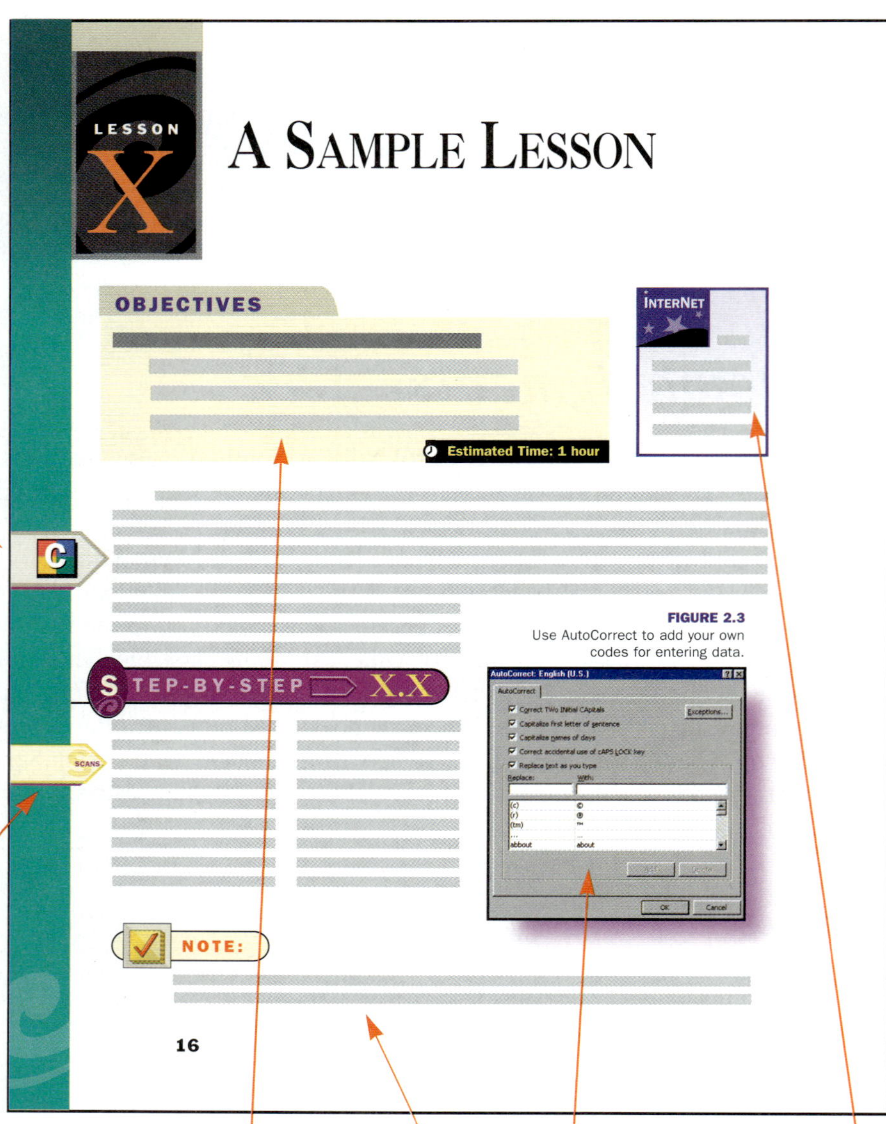

Objectives– Objectives are listed at the beginning of each lesson, along with a suggested time for completion of the lesson. This allows you to look ahead to what you will be learning and to pace your work.

Notes– These boxes provide necessary information to assist you in completing the exercises.

Enhanced Screen Shots– Screen shots now come to life on each page with color and depth.

Internet– Internet terminology and useful Internet information is provided in these boxes located throughout the text.

Important– These boxes provide important information about Word.

Marginal boxes– These boxes provide additional information for Hot Tips, fun facts (Did You Know?), Concept Builders, interesting Web sites, Extra Challenges activities, and Teamwork ideas.

Tables– These may appear in a lesson to help clarify and/or summarize key ideas and application functions.

Summary– At the end of each lesson you will find a summary to prepare you to complete the end-of-lesson activities.

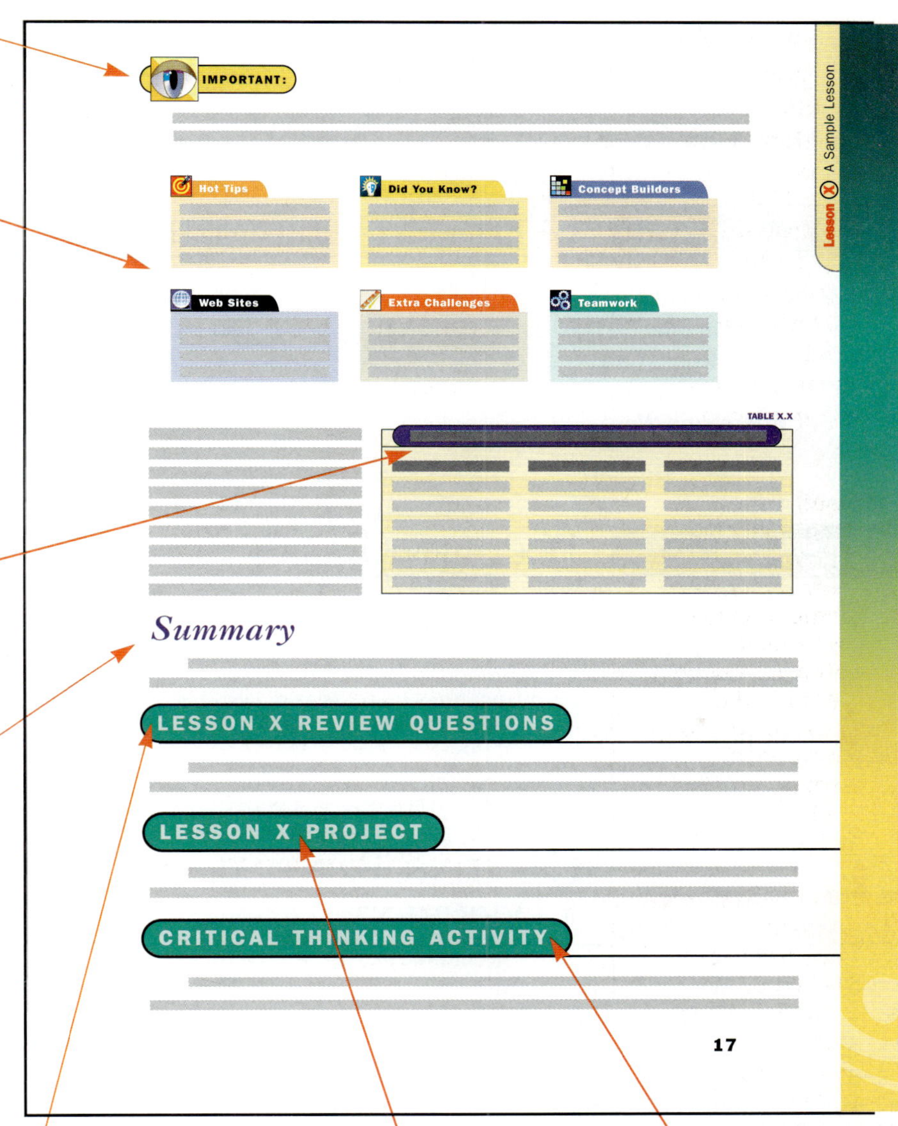

Review Questions– Review material at the end of each lesson enables you to prepare for assessment of the content presented.

Lesson Projects– End-of-lesson hands-on application of what has been learned in the lesson allows you to actually apply the techniques covered.

Critical Thinking Activity– Each lesson gives you an opportunity to apply creative analysis to situations presented.

Table of Contents

Getting Started with Word

LESSON 1 — Document Basics

LESSON 2 — Creating, Printing, and Sending a Document

LESSON 3 — Working with Basic Writing Tools

GETTING STARTED WITH WORD

When you complete this lesson, you will be able to:

- Start Word and exit from Word.
- Identify parts of the Word screen.
- Work with menus and dialog boxes.
- Customize Word.
- Use Help.
- Use the Internet and the World Wide Web.
- Manage documents and files.

 **Estimated Time: 1½ hours**

Introduction

Word 2000 is a word processing application that you can use with the Windows 95 operating system or later or Windows NT Workstation 4.0 with Service Pack 3.0 or later installed. You can use Word on its own or as part of the Microsoft Office suite of applications. You can prepare letters, reports, memos, invoices, newsletters, and even home pages for the Word Wide Web. You can use information or graphics from other Microsoft Office applications—Excel (spreadsheet), PowerPoint (presentation), and Access (database)—as well as from other applications in your Word documents. You can use the hyperlink feature to create links to Microsoft Office, HTML, or other files.

In this lesson you will reset your Word application so your settings match the default settings used in this book, and you will learn the basics so you can get started using word processing features.

Starting Word

The large area you see when you start Windows is the **desktop.** To start Word, use the Start button on the Windows **taskbar,** choose Programs, and then choose Microsoft Word on the Programs submenu (see Figure GS.1). If you are using the Microsoft Office 2000 suite,

Concept Builders

There are other ways of starting Word, but we will work with the two mentioned.

1

you can also use the Microsoft Word button on the **Office Shortcut bar** (see Figure GS.1). The Office Shortcut bar lets you quickly open Office applications.

Click on one of the marked areas to start Word.

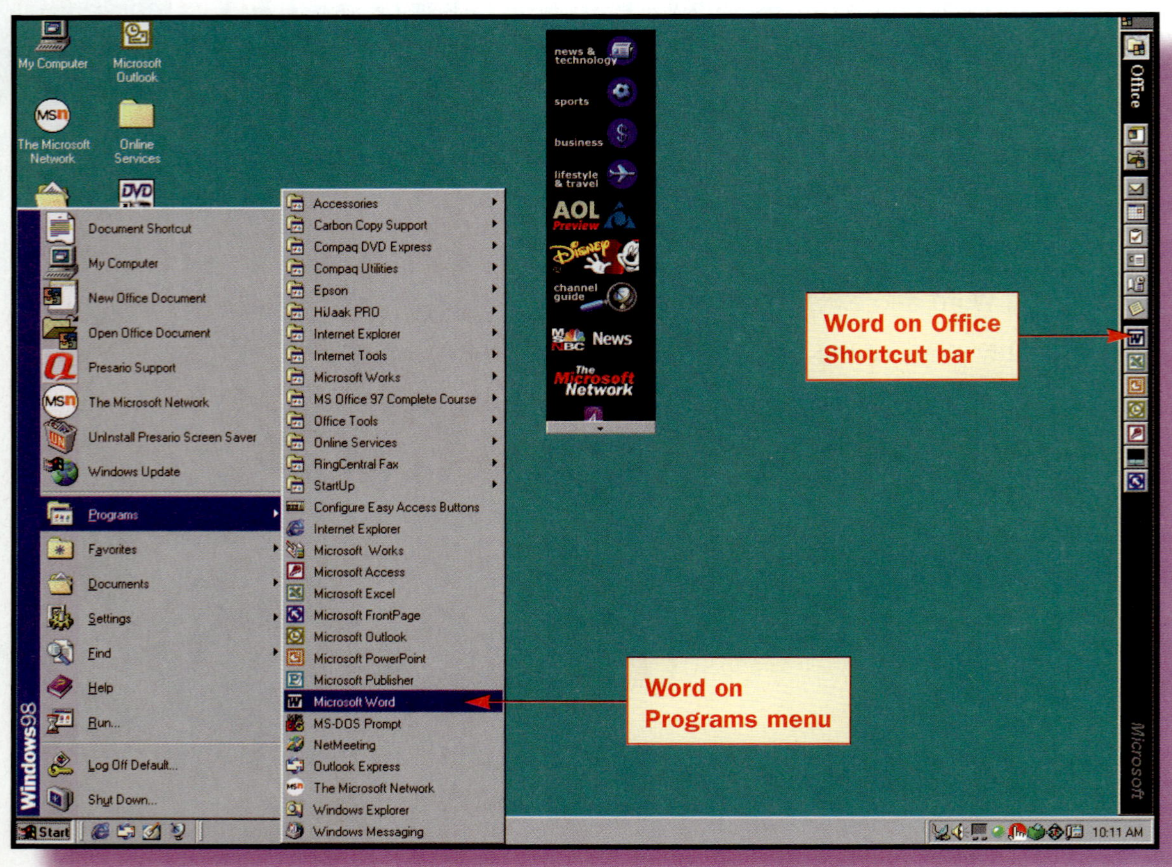

NOTE:

Your Office Shortcut bar may be on the right side of the window or across the top.

Identifying the Parts of the Word Screen

When you start Word, you will see a screen similar to the one in Figure GS.2. If you have used another Windows application, you will notice that the Word screen has many of the same components you saw in the other Windows application. There are many common elements in Windows applications that make it easy for users to learn and adapt to new applications.

Listed below are the components of the Word screen:

- *Title bar*—shows the name of the application and the document in use.

- *I-beam*—position the insertion point by moving the beam and clicking (when there is existing text in a document).

2

FIGURE GS.2
Parts of the Word Document window and Windows desktop.

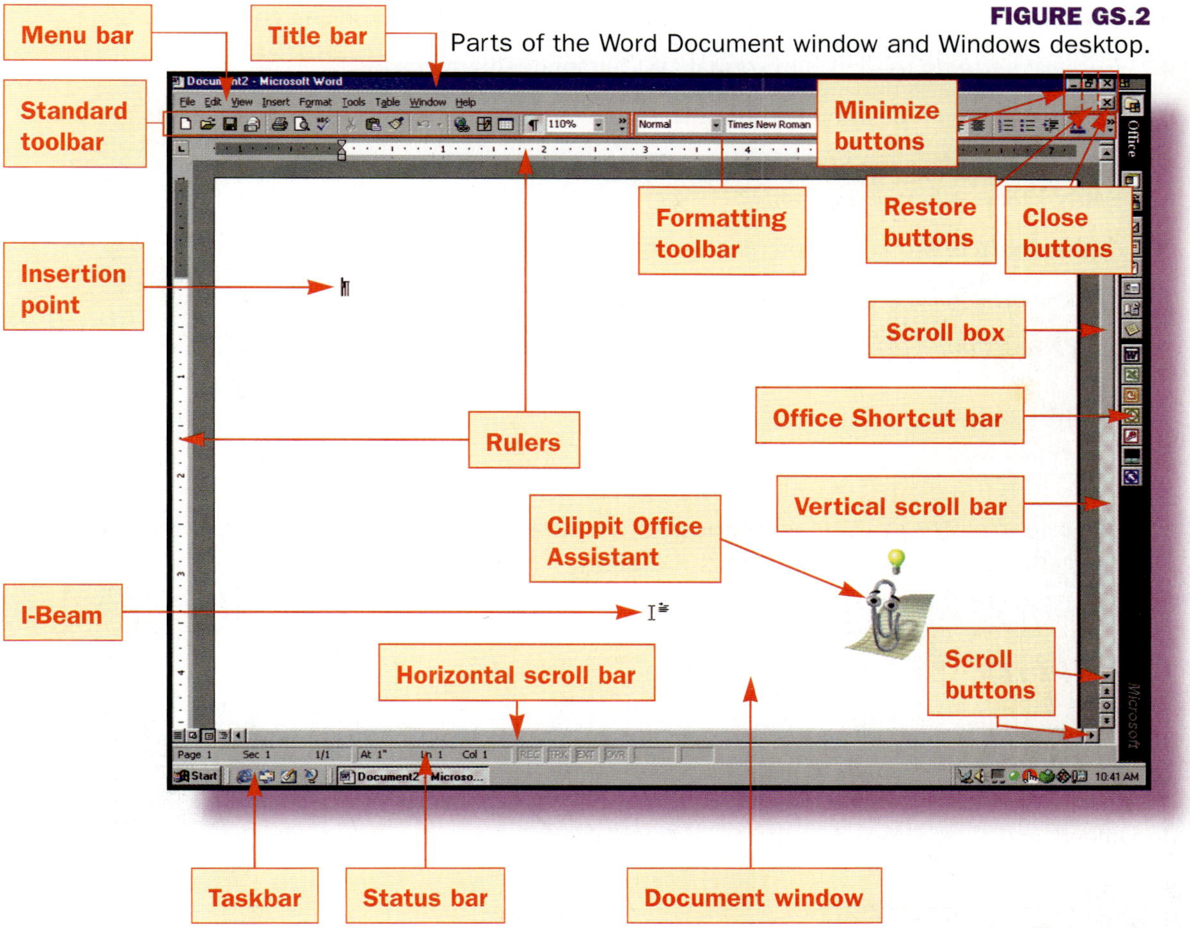

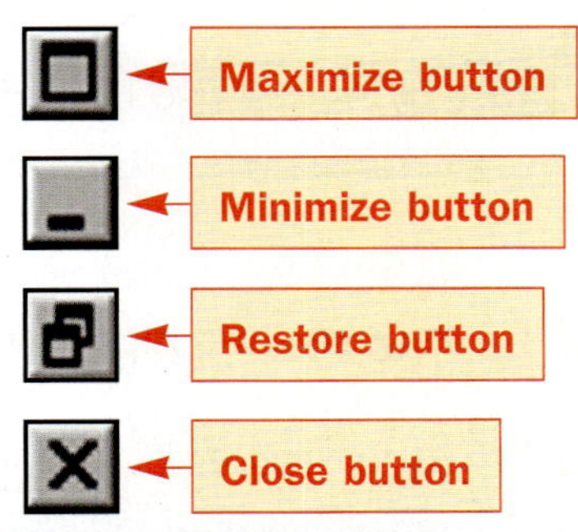

- *Insertion point*—blinks as a vertical bar displaying the position where information you type appears.

- *Menu bar*—shows the names of drop-down menus.

- *Status bar*—displays information about current settings.

- *Maximize button*—enlarges the window to fill the screen and then changes to a Restore button.

- *Minimize button*—reduces the window to a button on the taskbar.

- *Restore button*—returns the window to its previous size.

- *Close buttons*—close the window or application.

- *Scroll bars*—let you move through documents.

- *Scroll buttons*—let you move the display up or down one line.

- *Scroll boxes*—let you move to a position by dragging the scroll box until Word displays the page you want.

Hot Tips

Notice you sometimes have size/close buttons for both the application and the open document.

Concept Builders

The Close button on the menu bar is called the Close Window button.

- *Standard toolbar*—contains shortcut buttons for commonly used menu commands.

- *Formatting toolbar*—lets you format text without using menus.

- *Rulers*—help you position text or objects and let you set margins, tabs, and indents.

- *Taskbar*—displays the Start button and buttons representing open applications so you can easily access other applications.

- *Office Shortcut bar*—lets you quickly switch between Office applications.

- *Document window*—shows where you enter and edit text.

- *Office Assistant*—offers tips and lets you ask questions about using Word.

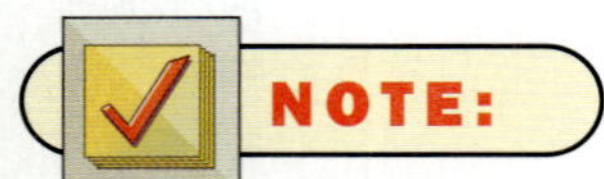

NOTE:

You will learn later in this lesson how to use the Office Assistant and how to remove the Office Assistant from the display.

Exiting from Word

You exit from and close the Word application by clicking the Close button on the Title bar or choosing the Exit command on the File menu.

When you exit from the Word application, Word prompts you to save any unsaved changes in documents and closes open documents. You will learn to save documents later in this lesson.

IMPORTANT:

You should always use the Shut Down command on the Windows Start menu on the taskbar when turning off your computer. It is good practice to exit from open applications before using the Shut Down command.

STEP-BY-STEP GS.1

1. To start Word, click the **Start** button, click **Programs** and click **Microsoft Word.**

2. To familiarize yourself with the names of various parts of the Word window, carefully look over your screen and Figure GS.2. Your Word window may not look exactly like the one shown in Figure GS.2.

3. To exit from Word, click the application **Close** button on the title bar.

4. To start Word again, click the **Start** button, click **Programs,** and click **Microsoft Word.**

Working with Menus and Dialog Boxes

You use menu commands and dialog boxes to let Word know how you would like to work with the application.

Using Menus

Drop-down **menus** display commands (see Figure GS.3). You click the menu name on the Menu bar—the bar below the title bar—to see its commands.

Word displays a menu in collapsed form when you first click the menu (see Figure GS.3). After a short delay, or if you click the expand button at the bottom of the menu or double-click on the menu, the entire menu appears (see Figure GS.4). Only the most often or recently used commands are shown initially.

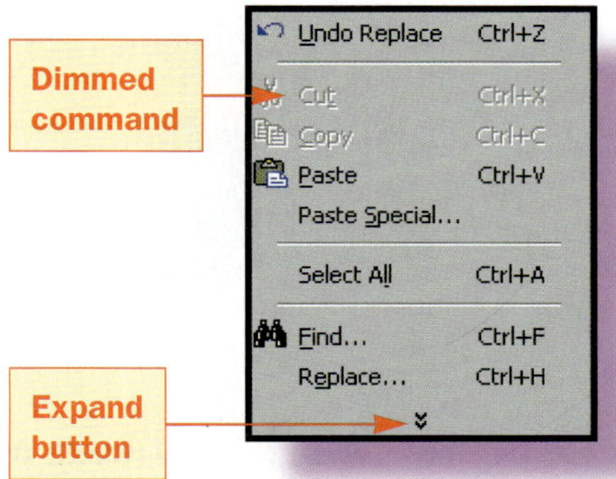

FIGURE GS.3
You can see a collapsed menu.

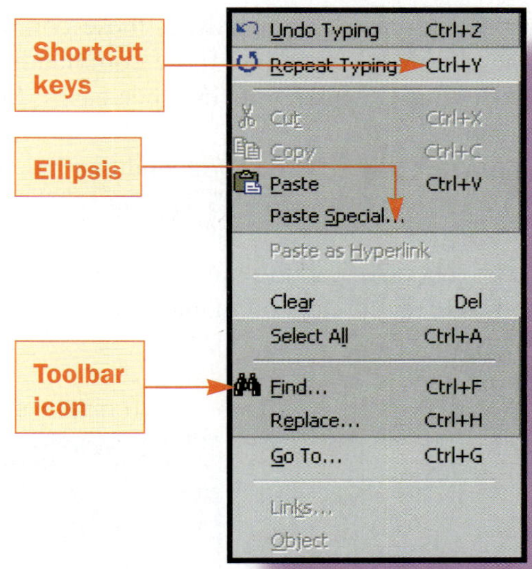

FIGURE GS.4
Menus contain related groups of commands, and Word expands the contents of menus to coincide with the work you do.

When there is no possibility of using a command, Word dims its name. In Figure GS.3, for example, because nothing is selected in the document, the Cut and Copy commands cannot be used at the moment, and Word dims the command names.

You can close a menu without selecting a command by clicking on a blank part of the window or by pressing the Esc (escape) key on the keyboard twice

Some menu commands display **shortcut keys**—keystrokes you can use instead of opening the menu—to the right of the command (see Figure GS.4). If you find you often use a command and would prefer to use keystrokes, check the menu to see if the command has shortcut keys. You will not use them in the exercises in this book.

Some commands, such as the Find command (see Figure GS.4), display icons to the left of the command names. These icons may also appear as buttons on a **toolbar.** It is easier to use toolbar buttons than it is to open menus and make selections there. You will use toolbar buttons whenever possible in the exercises in this book.

You can also open a menu by pressing the Alt key and then typing the underlined letter in the menu name. You can then execute a command by typing the underlined letter in the command name.

Some commands have right-pointing arrows displayed to the right of their names. If a menu command, such as the Toolbars command shown in Figure GS.5, has a right-pointing arrow next to its name, a **submenu** with more choices is available. To select a command from a submenu, click the desired command.

Some menu commands display check marks in boxes to the left of the command (see Figure GS.5). If the check mark is displayed, these commands are turned on. You can toggle these commands on or off by clicking the boxes or, in other cases, by making another selection.

When you select a command that has an **ellipsis** (…) after it (see Figure GS.4), you will see a dialog box such as the one shown in Figure GS.6. You can accept or enter additional information that Word needs to execute the command in a dialog box.

Some menu commands display submenus.

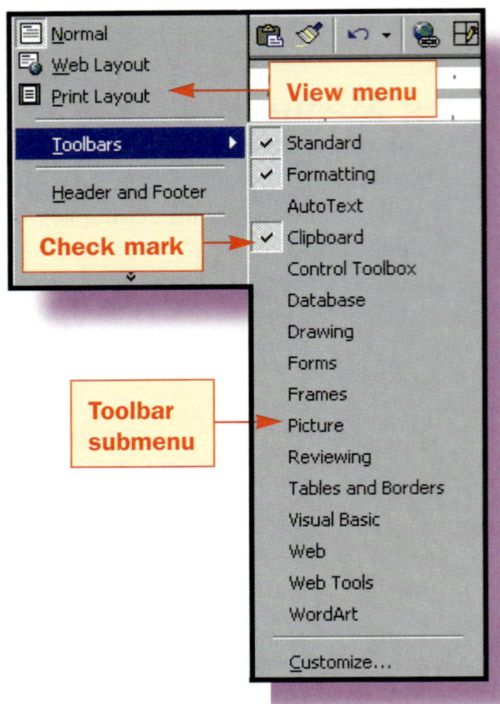

Word displays a dialog box when you can change or add information.

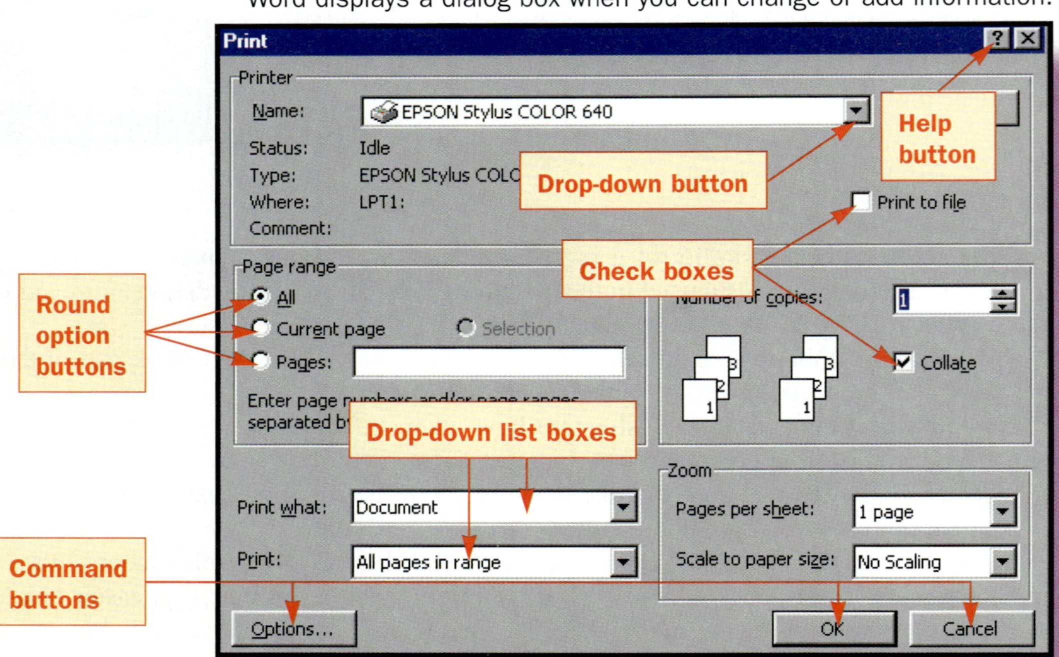

Using Dialog Boxes

Word displays a **dialog box** when you can add additional information or change information that Word needs to carry out a command. Table GS.1 describes how to work with various parts of dialog boxes.

Dialog boxes also contain **command buttons** (see Figure GS.6). The command buttons you will see most often are the OK button to carry out choices you make in the dialog boxes and the Cancel and Close buttons to close dialog boxes without making changes.

When you want to see a brief explanation, called a ScreenTip for a part of a dialog box, click its Help button, and then point to the part of the box and click to display the ScreenTip (see Figure GS.7). ScreenTips are available for commands, various parts of dialog boxes, and other screen areas.

FIGURE GS.7
You can see a ScreenTip explaining an option in a dialog box.

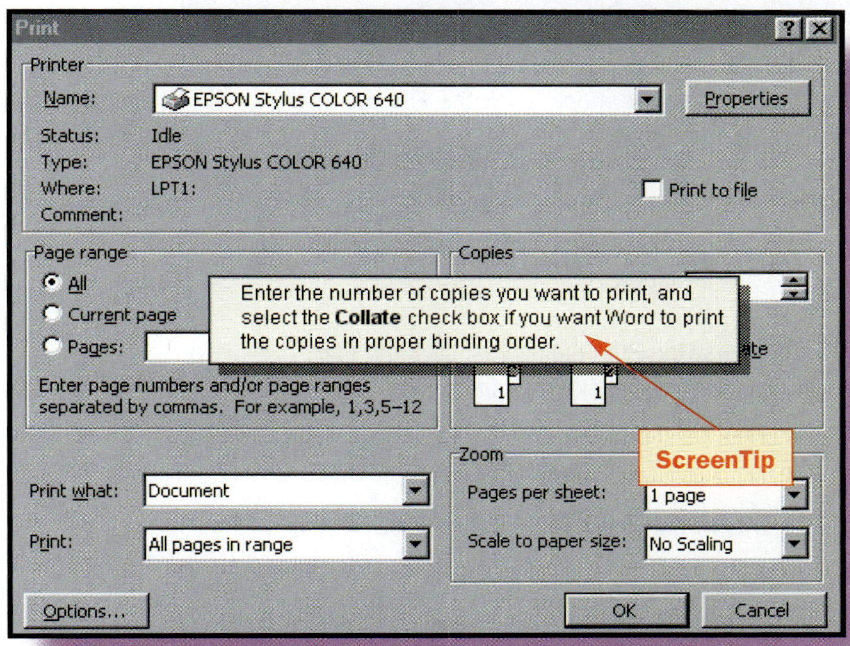

TABLE GS.1

SELECTING OPTIONS IN DIALOG BOXES	
TO SELECT/CLEAR	**CLICK**
Tab in a dialog box	Tab name
Option in a round option button or in a check box	Button or box
Number in a spin box	Up or down button until the number you want appears
Item in a drop-down list	Down button to display the list and then the item you want
Icon option	Icon

Many frequently used menu commands are also available on **shortcut menus** (see Figure GS.8). Shortcut menus are function-specific. That is, a shortcut menu displays commands that are frequently used at the location where you access it. To display a shortcut menu, simply point at the area with which you want to work, and click the *right* mouse button.

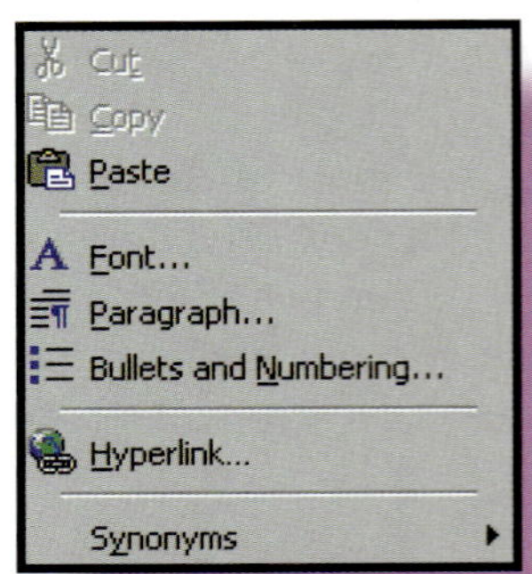

FIGURE GS.8
Word displays a shortcut menu when you right-click in your Word window.

S TEP-BY-STEP ⟹ GS.2

1. To open the File menu, click the **File** menu on the menu bar.

2. To close the File menu without making a selection, click a blank space anywhere in the Word window.

3. To display the Print dialog box, click the **File** menu and then click the **Print** command.

4. To display information about the Properties button, click the **Help** button at the top right of the dialog box, and then click the **Properties** button.

5. To close the dialog boxes, click the **Cancel** button in each box.

Customizing Word

Because Word makes it easy to set up the application to suit your own needs, your screens may not look exactly like the ones shown in this book. Whenever you start Word, it opens with the settings that were used during the last session.

If others are using your computer, you may have to change these settings each time you start a lesson so that your display matches the one shown in this book. Even if your screen display matches, you should go through the exercises on customizing Word so you become familiar with the various options and commands available to you.

Using the Full Screen Command

If the last user turned on the Full Screen command, you may not see the title bar, toolbars, scroll bars, or status bar on your screen. The Full Screen command on the expanded View menu lets you display as much as possible of your document without the other parts of the window that are usually displayed.

If you do not see anything but your document and the Close Full Screen button, you can click the Close Full Screen button to return to a different view. You can also press the Esc key to close Full Screen view.

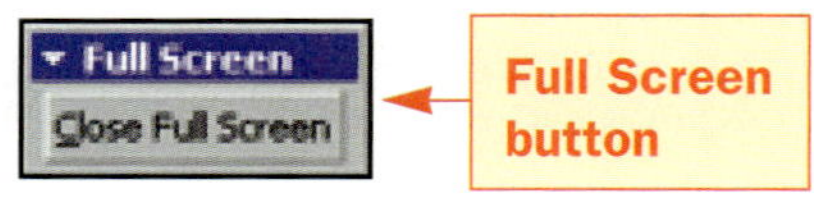

Maximizing Your Windows

When you start Word the first time, or if Word used less than the full screen to display documents during the last session, you might find the Word window does not fill the screen. You can use the **Maximize button** to enlarge the window. You can use the **Minimize button** to reduce the window to a taskbar button. Sometimes there are Maximize buttons for both the application and document windows.

Using the Zoom Command

You can use the Zoom command on the View menu to open the Zoom dialog box (see Figure GS.9). You can set greater or lesser degrees of magnification on your screen. Word displays a preview of the character size that will appear. You can also opt to see the entire width of the page, the whole page, or more than one page. You can also click the Zoom button on the Standard toolbar to see a drop-down list of Zoom settings.

If the last user changed the Zoom settings and did not return to the 100% view, the text in your document may appear to be smaller or larger than that in the figures in this book.

FIGURE GS.9

The Zoom dialog box displays options for viewing the document.

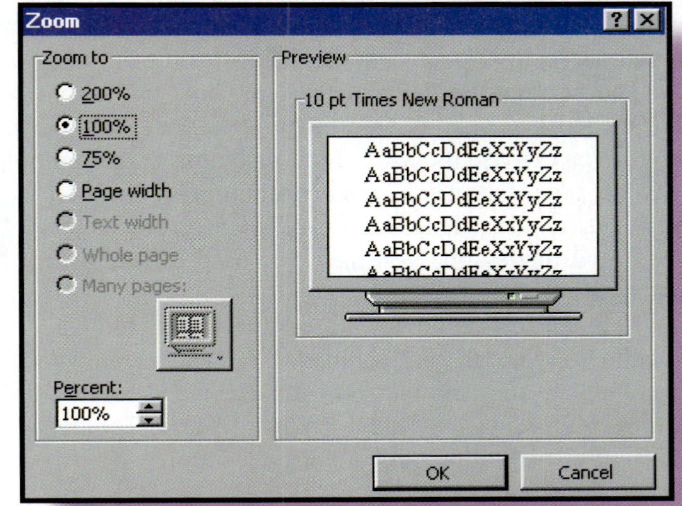

Using the View Menu

The View menu provides several view options. A list of the most commonly used follows.

- *Normal view*—displays text continuously.

- *Web Layout view*—displays the page as it will appear on the World Wide Web or on an intranet.

- *Print Layout view*—displays the page as it will print, including headers, footers, footnotes, and graphics.

- *Outline view*—displays the structure of your document in classic outline format.

You will most often use the default Print Layout view with the exercises in this book.

An intranet is is a private organization's network that uses Internet technologies but is separated from the rest of the Internet by a firewall. A firewall is a hardware and software combination that prohibits unauthorized access to the intranet. An intranet is used by just the people within the organization and is generally not available to those outside the organization.

You can also use the View buttons on the left side of the Horizontal scroll bar to switch easily among these four views. You will learn more about these and other Word views throughout this book.

You may see the Document Map displayed on your screen. The Document Map divides the screen into two panes to allow you to navigate through a document. You will learn more about the Document Map command in Lesson 10.

Word also provides you with the option of using a ruler to help you position text and graphics on your page. To display the ruler, be sure the Ruler command on the View menu has a check mark, as shown in Figure GS.10.

Using Toolbars

As you already learned, toolbars contain buttons for commonly used commands. You can click a toolbar button to use a menu command without having to open the menu. When you slide the mouse pointer over a button, a ScreenTip appears that identifies the button.

The Standard and Formatting toolbars are displayed by default. They are docked side-by-side below the Menu bar. When toolbars are docked, you can use the More Buttons button at the right of each toolbar to display other buttons. If you use a button on the More Buttons drop-down list, Word puts that button on the toolbar and moves one you have not used to the More Buttons list.

You saw earlier in the lesson the list of toolbars available to you on the Toolbars submenu. You will sometimes see other toolbars on your screen because Word displays toolbars appropriate for the Word features with which you are working. Use the Toolbars command on the View menu (see Figure GS.11) to display other toolbars or to customize toolbars so they contain buttons for commands you most often need.

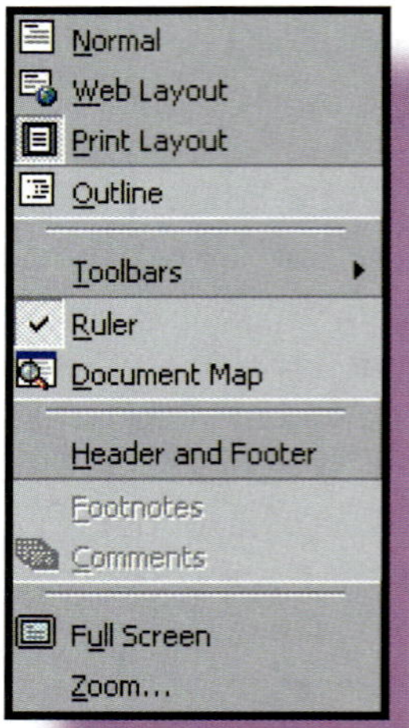

Print layout view and the ruler are in use.

NOTE:

Don't worry if your toolbars do not match exactly.

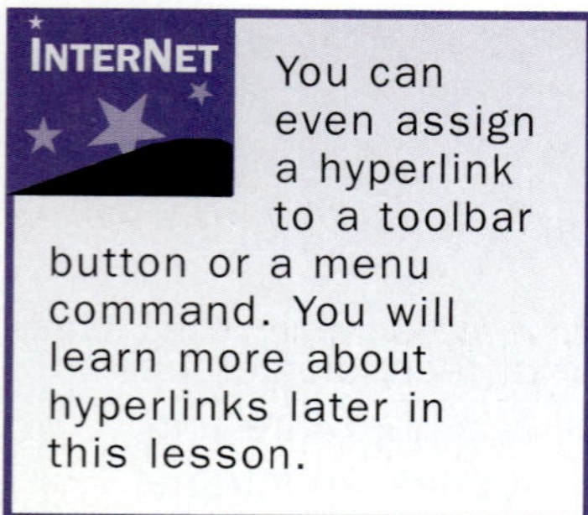

FIGURE GS.11

Use the Toolbars submenu to turn toolbars on or off.

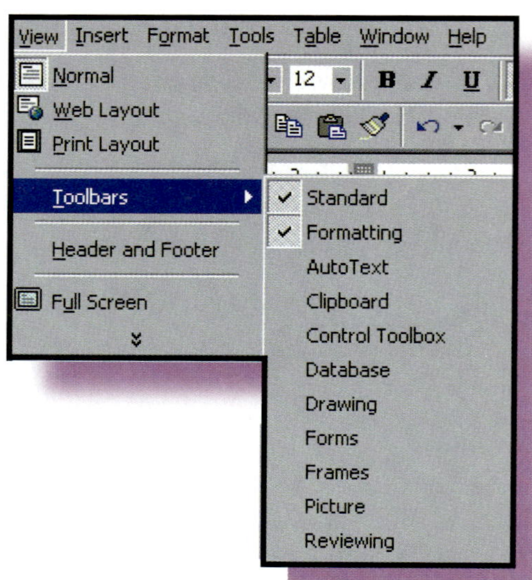

S TEP-BY-STEP ▷ GS.3

1. To return to a different view if your screen has a Full Screen button (pictured earlier) displayed, click the **Full Screen** button.

2. To maximize your display if your Word window and document do not fill the entire screen, look for one of the **Maximize** buttons (pictured earlier), and click it.

3. To check the settings in the Zoom dialog box, click the **View** menu and click the **Zoom** command. If 100% is not selected, click its Round Option box. Then click the **OK** button. If 100% is selected when the Zoom dialog box opens, click the **OK** or **Cancel** button.

4. To use Print Layout view, click the **View** menu, and click the **Print Layout view** button. If the Print Layout view is already

pushed in, Print Layout view is already selected, and the view will not change.

5. To be sure the ruler is displayed, click the **View** menu, and if the **Ruler** command does not have a check mark next to it, click its box.

6. To display the Standard and Formatting toolbars, click the **View** menu and click the **Toolbars** command. If you do not see check marks in the boxes next to both **Standard** and **Formatting,** click the box that does not have a check mark. You may have to again click the **View** menu, click the **Toolbars** command, and click the second box if both toolbars were turned off. If you see check marks in the boxes next to any other toolbar names, repeat the procedure to turn them off.

Using the Customize Command

You can use the Customize command on the Tools menu to customize toolbars, commands, and other options, such as shortcut keys. If you find your menus or shortcut keys are different from the ones used in this book, you may be able to return to some of the original settings with the Reset My Usage Data button in the Customize dialog box.

To be sure the exercises in this book work on your computer, you need to match the default settings.

Using the Options Command

The Options command on the Tools menu lets you change the default settings for many of Word's features.

You will use the Options command to match your system's setup to the default one used in this book. Many of the selections in the Options dialog boxes will be covered in later lessons.

In the following exercise you will look at each of the tabs in the Options dialog box and will make sure the settings match those shown in Figures GS.12 through GS.21.

1. To display the Options dialog box, click the **Tools** menu and click the **Options** command.

2. To check the settings on the View tab, click the **View** tab, and compare the settings to those in Figure GS.12. Make any necessary changes.

View options affect how Word displays your document.

General options cover miscellaneous settings.

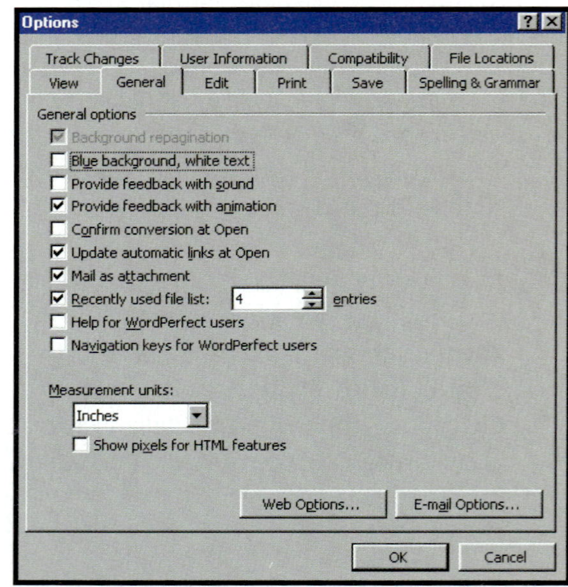

3. To check the settings on the General tab, click the **General** tab, and compare the settings to those in Figure GS.13. Make any necessary changes.

4. To check the settings on the Edit tab, click the **Edit** tab, and compare the settings to those in Figure GS.14. Make any necessary changes.

Edit options affect how you enter and edit text.

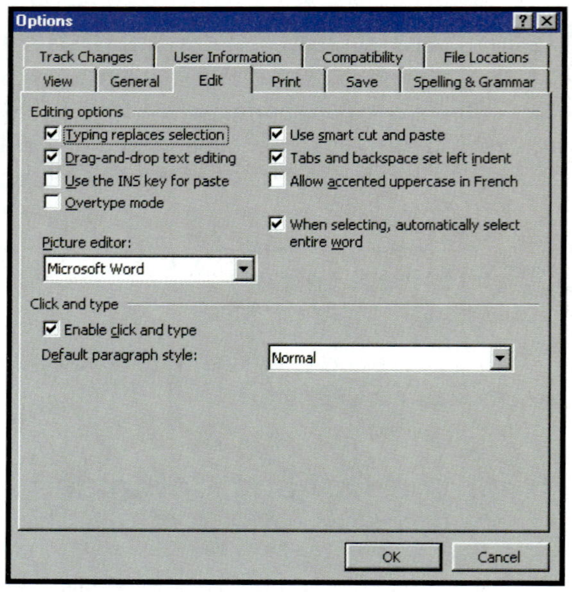

5. To check the settings on the Print tab, click the **Print** tab, and compare the settings to those in Figure GS.15. Make any necessary changes.

6. To check the settings on the Save tab, click the **Save** tab, and compare the settings to those in Figure GS.16. Make any necessary changes.

Print options control various elements of your printed documents.

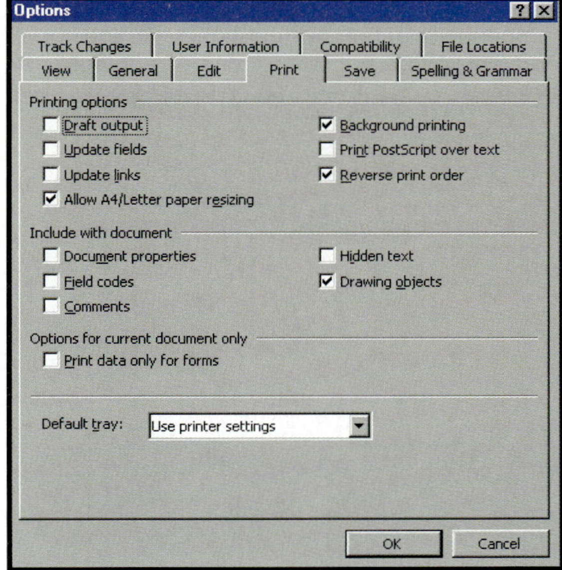

You can designate various options for saving documents.

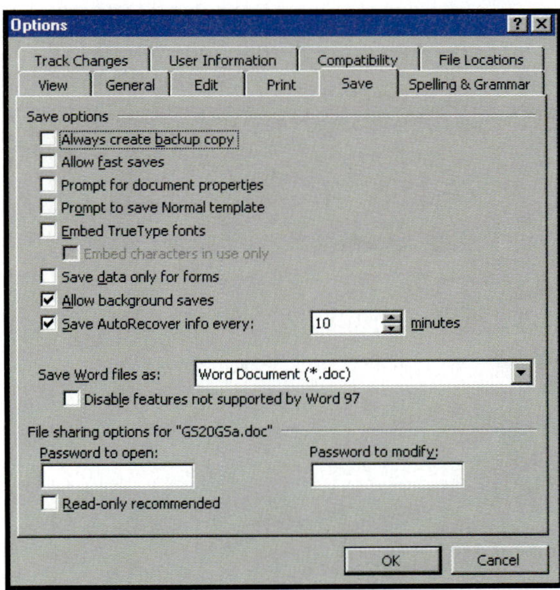

7. To check the settings on the Spelling & Grammar tab, click the **Spelling & Grammar** tab, and compare the settings to those in Figure GS.17. Make any necessary changes.

Spelling and grammar options affect how the spelling and grammar features work.

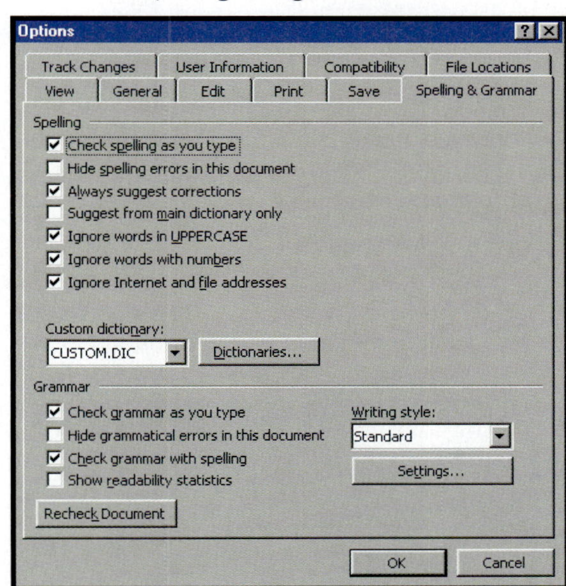

8. To check the settings on the Track Changes tab, click the **Track Changes** tab, and compare the settings to those in Figure GS.18. Make any necessary changes.

You can choose from a number of ways to track changes in a document.

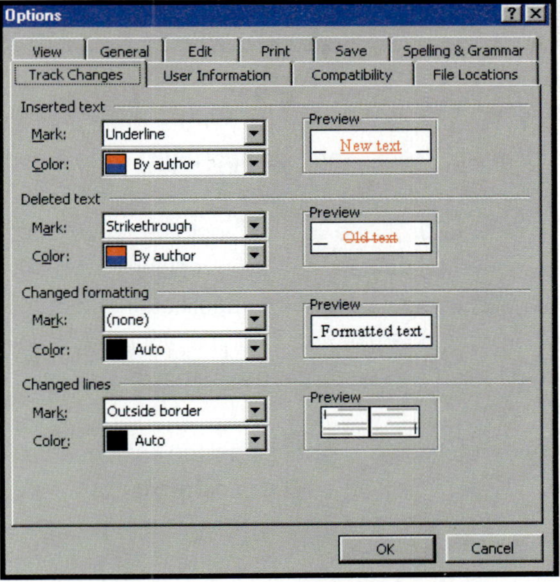

(continued on next page)

1 3

9. To check the settings on the User Information tab, click the **User Information** tab (see Figure GS.19). If you are using your own computer and would like to change the user information, do so. If you are using a classroom computer, the settings should probably not be changed.

FIGURE GS.19

Word will sometimes use information in the User Information dialog box to save you time.

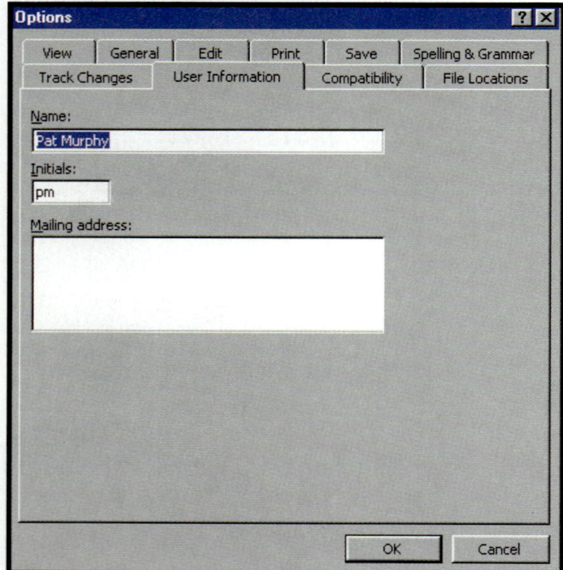

10. To check the settings on the Compatibility tab, click the **Compatibility** tab, and compare the settings to those in Figure GS.20. None of the options should be turned on now, but if you regularly exchange documents with other applications, use the drop-down box to find the application you need and display other settings.

11. To check the settings on the File Locations tab, click the **File Locations** tab, and compare the settings to those in Figure GS.21. If you are using a classroom computer and your instructor followed the suggestions for this book, the location for

FIGURE GS.20

Compatibility options affect how your document translates to other word processing programs.

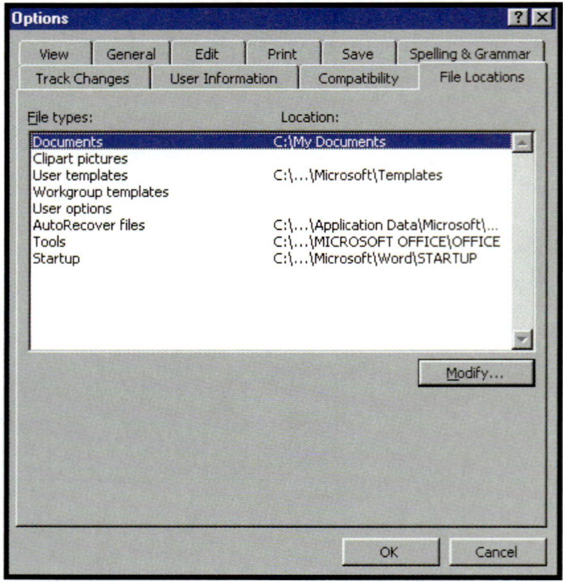

FIGURE GS.21

File Locations options tell Word where to look for documents.

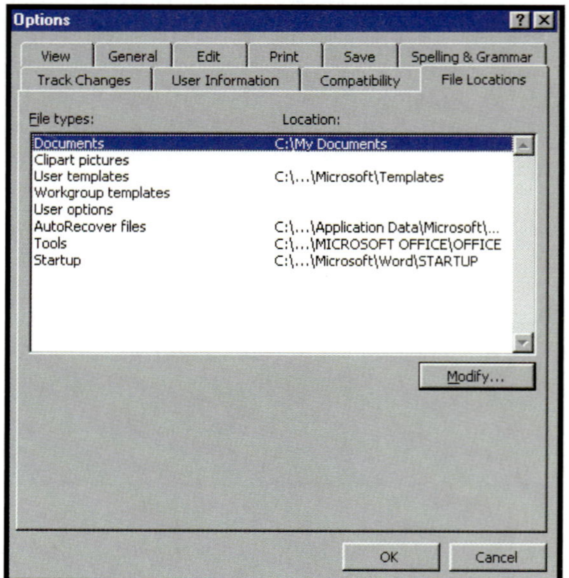

documents should be a folder with your name. Click **Documents** and then click the **Modify** button if you want Word to default to looking for documents in your folder. If others use the computer, your instructor may not want you to do this. You can also create a new folder by clicking the **Modify** command button and the **Create New** **Folder** button in the **Modify Location** dialog box.

12. To carry out the changes you made and close the dialog box, click the **OK** button.

Getting Help with Word

There are several different ways you can use Word's Help system to get information about working with any of the Word features or dialog boxes.

The Office Assistant

The **Office Assistant** can answer questions and provide tips on easier or quicker ways of accomplishing tasks. When you click on the Office Assistant, a balloon appears. The Office Assistant displays suggested help for tasks you are performing and sometimes a yellow light bulb to let you know there is a tip for using features or shortcuts effectively (see Figure GS.22). Click the yellow light bulb to see a tip.

By default, the Clippit Office Assistant is turned on when you begin to use Word. You can turn off the Office Assistant by clicking the Options button in the Assistant's balloon and removing the check mark from the box next to Use the Office Assistant on the Options tab (see Figure GS.23). You can use the Show Office Assistant command on the Help menu to return the Office Assistant to the screen.

NOTE:

We will turn the Office Assistant off for the exercises in this book so you will have one fewer of us competing for your attention. When you are working in Word on your own, however, the Office Assistant can be very useful.

You can display the Gallery tab (see Figure GS.24) in the Office Assistant dialog box. You can then use the <Back and Next> buttons to scroll through the different assistants available for you.

Did You Know?

The Office Assistant is an animated figure and it can be quite funny at times. It moans or stomps off when you turn it off, appears to be checking notes while searching for your topics, and even performs some tricky dance routines while waiting for the system to do something.

FIGURE GS.22
The Office Assistant anticipates when you might want help with tasks or features.

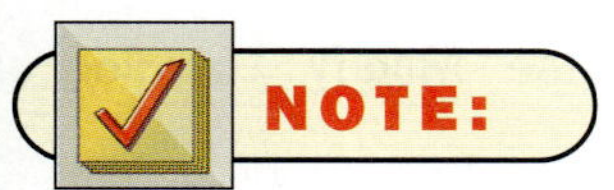

The Office Assistant is shared by Microsoft Office applications. If you change options for the Assistant in one application, you affect the Assistant in other Office applications.

FIGURE GS.23

The Options tab allows users to turn off the Office Assistant feature.

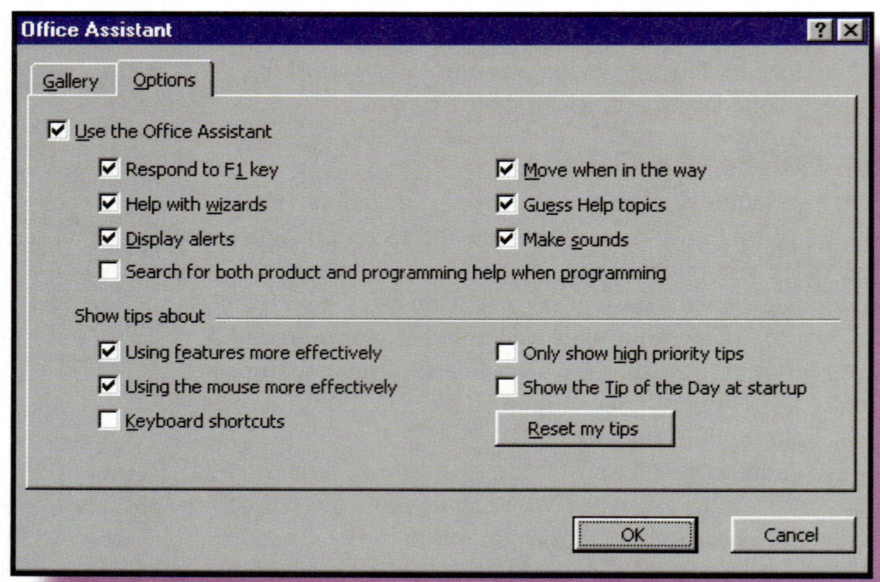

FIGURE GS.24

The Dot is another of the Assistants you can designate.

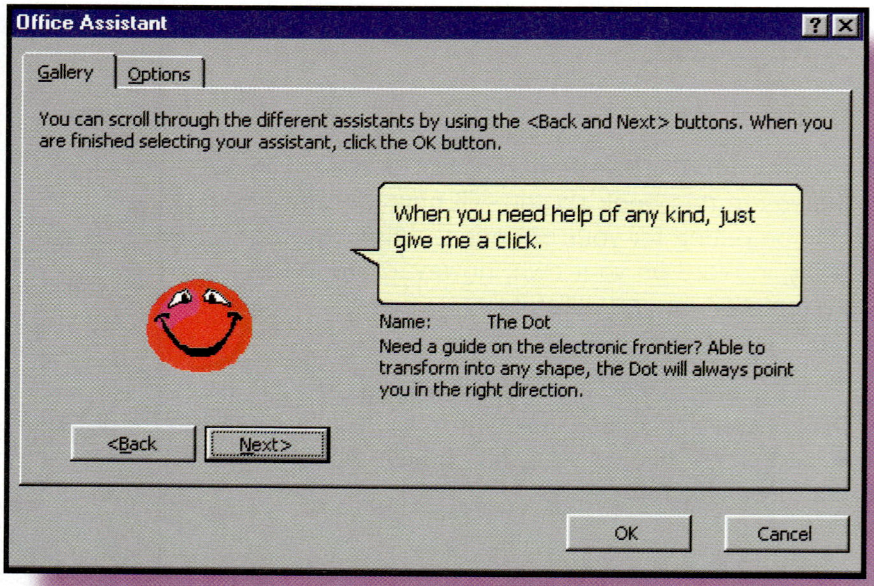

Using Hyperlinks

A **hyperlink** is a shortcut to text or graphics in a document that can be stored on your hard drive, a network server, or the Internet. Many Microsoft Word Help windows have hyperlinks. To follow a hyperlink to its document, point to the hyperlink. When your mouse pointer changes to a hand, click it.

Hyperlinks are underlined; those you have not clicked are blue, and those you have clicked and followed are purple.

Did You Know?

Graphics can also be used for hyperlinks.

The Help Menu

To use Word's interactive Help system, click the Help menu, and then click the Microsoft Word Help command. This command displays the Office Assistant and its balloon. If the Assistant is already displayed, clicking the command displays the balloon. If the Assistant is turned off, Word displays the Microsoft Word Help window (see Figure GS.25).

If the Contents, Answer Wizard, and Index tabs are not displayed, click the Show button (see Figure GS.26) on the Help toolbar.

Use the Contents tab (shown in Figure GS.25) to display topics organized by category. To see a list of topics in a category, click the Expand Indicator button (+) beside the book icon. To see information about a topic, click it.

NOTE:

To determine when you want the Office Assistant to appear, click the Options button, and then the Options tab in the Office Assistant dialog box. You can also use a shortcut menu to select the kinds of tasks with which you want the Office Assistant to help.

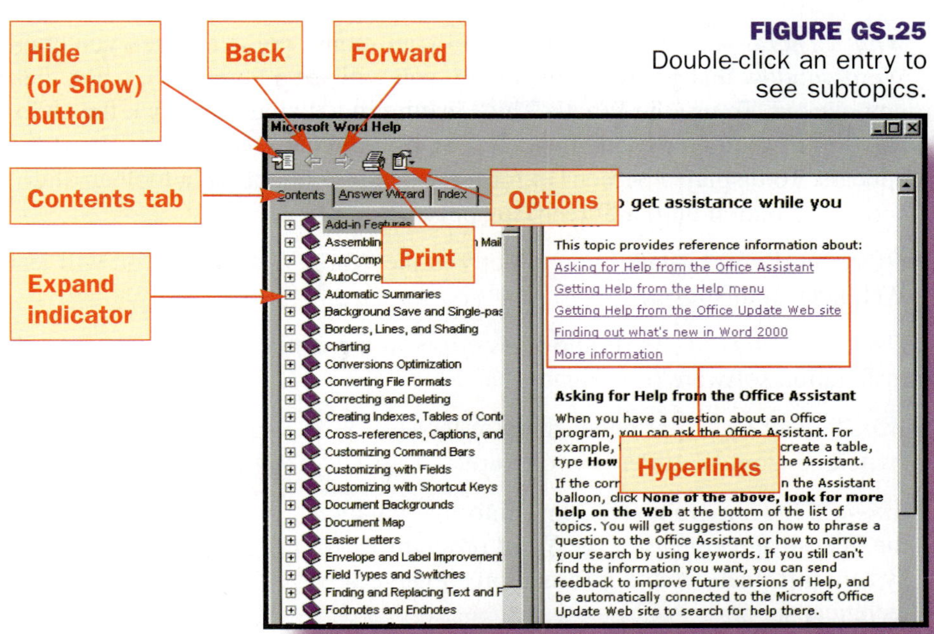

FIGURE GS.25
Double-click an entry to see subtopics.

Click the Show button to display the Contents, Answer Wizard, and Index tabs.

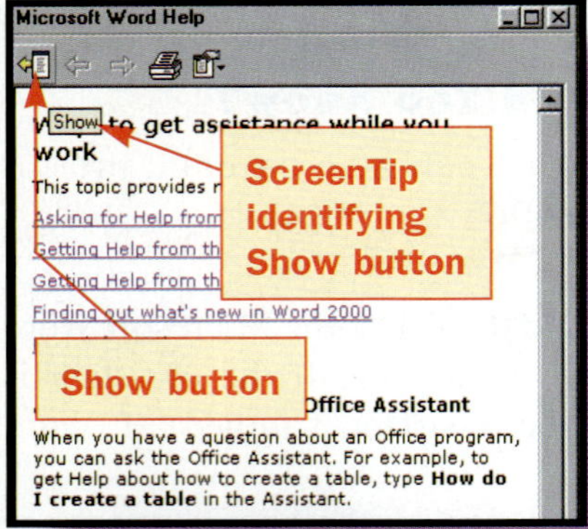

The Index tab is displayed.

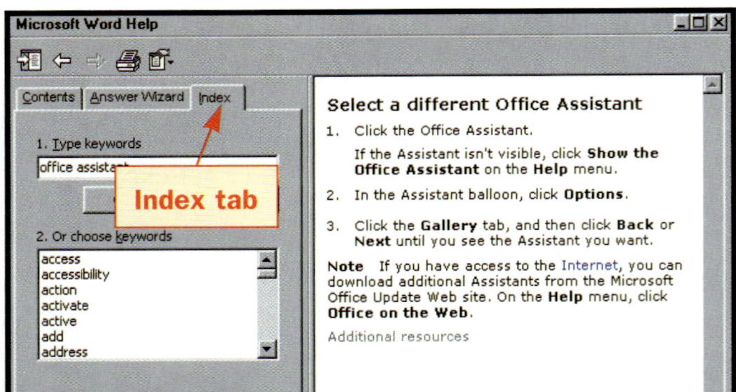

Use the Index tab (see Figure GS.27) to enter a topic you want to find or to scroll through the list of entries. To display information about an entry, click the entry and then click the Search button. Then click a topic in the bottom box to display information about it in the right pane.

Use the Answer Wizard tab to pose a question.

A list of other commands on the Help menu follows.

- *Show or Hide the Office Assistant*—displays or removes the Office Assistant from the window. This menu command *does not* turn the Office Assistant off. You must use the Options button in the balloon.

- *What's This?*—adds a question mark to your mouse pointer. When you click something in the Word window that you want help with, you will see a ScreenTip, a box that explains the item you clicked. To use the What's This? feature in a dialog box, click the Help button at the top right of the dialog box, and then click an option you would like explained. A ScreenTip appears. To display a ScreenTip for the name of a button on a toolbar, slide the mouse pointer across the button until a ScreenTip appears.

- *Office on the Web*—takes you directly to the World Wide Web. You will learn more about the Web later in this lesson.

- *Detect and Repair*—finds and fixes errors in the application. You may need your Word installation software (see Figure GS.28).

- *WordPerfect Help*—provides help for those switching from WordPerfect software.

- *About Microsoft Word*—displays information about the license agreement for the Word program, system information, and information about getting technical support.

Did You Know?

If your display shows only the letters A through Z, click the expand indicator to display topics.

Hot Tips

On many Help screens, you can click the Print button to print a copy of the information.

Word displays this dialog box when you use the
Detect and Repair command.

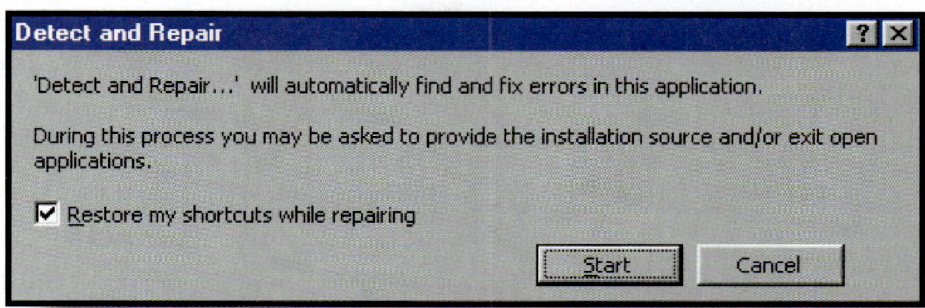

STEP-BY-STEP ▷ GS.5

1. If you do not see the Office Assistant, click the **Help** menu, and then click the **Show the Office Assistant** command.

2. To find out how to get help while you work, click on the Office Assistant, type **How can I get help while I work** in the balloon's text box, and then click the balloon's **Search** button.

3. To display the **Ways to get assistance while you work** topic, click its blue Round Option button. Notice the hyperlinks (shown as underlined text) at the top of the Microsoft Word Help Window.

4. To move to the **Finding out what's new in Word 2000** topic without scrolling down through the other information, point to the hyperlink, and when the hand appears, click the hyperlink. Notice the **new features in Word 2000** hyperlink in the first paragraph.

5. To follow the hyperlink in the first paragraph to information about the new features, click the **new features in Word 2000** hyperlink. Notice that you could follow additional hyperlinks to various new features.

6. To return to the previous page, click the **Back** button on the toolbar at the top of the Microsoft Word Help window.

Hot Tips

Remember to slide your mouse pointer across buttons to see a ScreenTip if you are not sure which button to use.

7. To display the Contents, Answer Wizard, and Index tabs, click the **Show** button on the toolbar at the top of the Microsoft Word Help window.

8. To display the Help topics in table of contents format, click the **Contents** tab.

9. To display subtopics on the Getting Help topic, click the **Expand** indicator (+) to the left of Data Spelling topic.

10. To get help with the subtopic **getting help without the Office Assistant,** click that subtopic. Notice the hyperlinks in the pane to the right, and click the **turn off the Office Assistant** hyperlink.

(continued on next page)

11. To print the Help topic, click the **Print** button on the toolbar at the top of the Microsoft Word Help window.

12. To display the Index tab, click the **Index** tab.

13. To enter a keyword to be used for a search, click in the Type keywords box, type **help,** and click the **Search** button. Notice the list of topics at the bottom of the pane, and click the topic **Ways to get assistance while you work.**

14. To close the Microsoft Word Help window, click its **Close** button.

15. To find out what the button that looks like scissors represents, click the **Help** menu. Click the **What's This?** command. Notice the question mark attached to the mouse pointer. Click the **scissors** button, and read the information in the ScreenTip.

16. To remove the ScreenTip, click anywhere in blank space.

Using the Internet and the World Wide Web

Word 2000 has many features you can use to take advantage of the Internet and the World Wide Web. The **Internet** is a global network of computers that use a common language to communicate. The **World Wide Web** provides a graphical, easy-to-use interface for looking at documents on the Internet.

You must have a modem and an Internet service provider (ISP) to connect to the internet.

Simply put, the Web is like a library on the Internet. Web sites are like books in the library, and their pages are like specific pages in a book. The starting page for a Web site—the equivalent of a table of contents—is called a **home page.**

Each page on the Web has an address called a **Universal Resource Locator (URL).** The home page address for Microsoft, for instance, is http://www.microsoft.com

You can click hyperlinks to jump from one page to another. Hyperlinks have Web addresses embedded in them. You can easily identify a hyperlink because its text is displayed in a different color from the rest of the text on the site. Hyperlinks may also be underlined or have borders around them so they stand out. Graphics can also be used for hyperlinks. You will usually be asked to click on a graphic to move to another Web page.

When you use hyperlinks to access different Web pages, you are *surfing the Web.*

When you finish working on the Internet through an ISP, be sure to close the application and disconnect from the service provider. Remember you are paying service provider charges and may also be paying long-distance telephone charges. You may also prevent others from accessing the Internet if you leave your connection open when you are not using it.

In the next exercise, you will use the Office on the Web command on the Help menu to see how easily you can access and move around on the Web. You will continue learning about and working on the Web throughout this book.

SCANS

1. To use the Office on the Web command and to learn some Web fundamentals, click the **Help** menu, and click the **Office on the Web** command. If necessary, enter a member ID and password to connect to the Internet.

2. To familiarize yourself with the Web site, click some hyperlinks describing items of interest.

3. To print a page, click the **Print** button on the Web toolbar.

4. To exit from the Web, click the **Close** button. If you see a dialog box asking whether you want to disconnect, respond that you do.

Managing Documents and Files

Before you can effectively work with Word, you must know how to create, open, save, and close documents.

Creating Documents

You have already seen that when you start Word, you see a new document window on the screen. The new document is the equivalent of a blank piece of paper where you can begin typing your text.

The first document of any Word session is called Document1. Each new document you open during a session will have a new, consecutive number. You can have as many documents open at one time as the memory in your system allows. That means you can work with more than one document at a time. Each open document will have a button on the taskbar so you can easily move from one document to another.

To create a new document during a Word session, you can either click the New button on the Standard toolbar or open the File menu and choose the New command.

New button

Open button

Opening Existing Documents

Use the Open button or the Open command on the File menu to display the Open dialog box (see Figure GS.29). You can use the Open dialog box to find and open and to manage existing documents on your hard drive, on a floppy drive, on a network drive to which you are connected, on your company's intranet, or on the Internet.

You can use the Open dialog box to find and manage your files. The Places bar (see Figure GS.29) displays the folders and locations you use most often.

Did You Know?

You can click the Files of type drop-down button to display a list of many file types—other than Word documents—you can open. Be sure to click that drop-down button if you want to open a WordPerfect document or a MacIntosh file.

You can use the Open dialog box to find, manage, and open files.

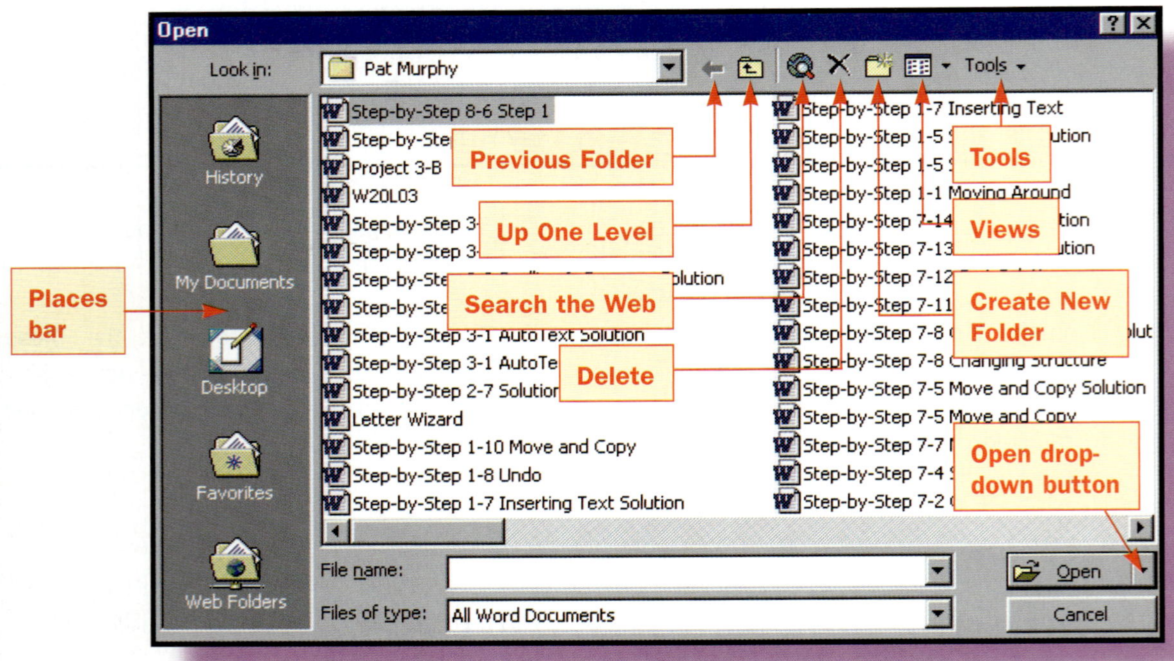

NOTE:

The names of the last four documents opened appear at the bottom of the File menu.

History button displays the last 20 to 50 Word documents or folders with which you've worked.

My Documents button displays all files and folders in the folder named My Documents, which is the default folder for storing Word files.

Desktop button displays files and folders stored on the Windows desktop.

Favorites button contains any shortcuts to Word files you use frequently. When you use a shortcut, the actual file remains in its original location, but you can open it quickly without having to remember where its located.

Web Folders button displays shortcuts to files and folders located on Web servers. You must have access to a Web server to use this feature. See your system administrator to see if there is a Web server to which you can connect.

Concept Builders

Windows identifies the hard disk drives and floppy disk drives by letters. Most hard disk drives are assigned C or D. Floppy disk drives are A and B. A path tells you where a file is located. For instance, the path C:\My Documents\Pat Murphy\First tells you the document called First is on the C drive in a folder named Pat Murphy that is in the My Documents folder.

IMPORTANT:

You can see the contents of Web folders in your browser. A browser is software such as Internet Explorer or Netscape that lets you work with Web files.

You can see the purpose of toolbar buttons and other boxes at the top of the Open dialog box.

OPEN DIALOG BOX TOOLBAR

NAME	WHAT IT DOES
Look In text box	Contains the name of the folder at which Word is currently looking
Previous Folder button	Displays the name of the folder that was previously in the Look in box
Up One Level button	Moves you one folder level higher in the folder hierarchy
Search the Web button	Displays the sign-in dialog box or connects you to the World Wide Web
Delete button	Deletes the selected file by sending it to the Recycle Bin
Create New Folder button	Creates a subfolder in the current folder
Views button	Drop-down button lets you display the names of files in large icon style; with additional information such as date last saved and file size; properties such as title and author for the selected file; or a preview of of the selected file.
Tools button	Contains a list of additional commands that can be used for procedures such as printing or finding files

The drop-down button next to the Open button in the Open dialog box lets you open a file for

- All Uses
- Read-Only (no changes can be saved)
- Open as Copy
- Open in Browser

Did You Know?

Deleted files stay in the Recycle Bin until you empty it. To empty the Recycle Bin, double-click its icon on the desktop, open the File menu and choose Empty Recycle Bin.

Open a copy of a file when you want to keep the original file intact. Revise the copy.

Saving Documents

To save a document for the first time, use the Save button on the Standard toolbar or the Save or Save As command on the File menu. The Save As dialog box appears (see Figure GS.30).

The Save As dialog box is where you make decisions about how you want Word to save a document.

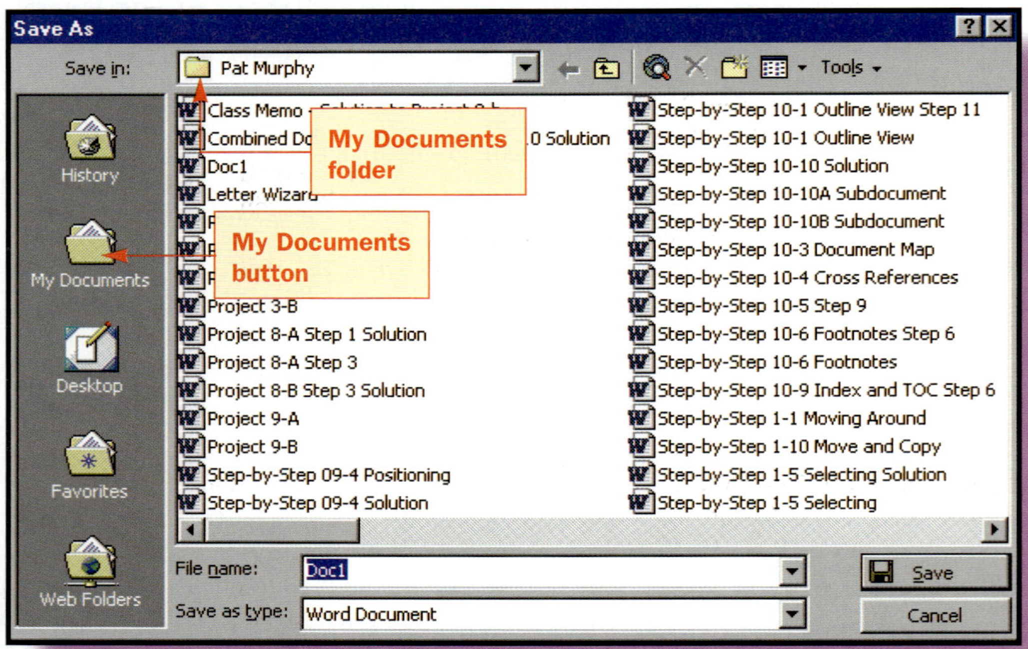

To save a document, display the name of the folder in which you want to place the document in the Save In box. Then, type a file name in the File Name box. Once you have saved the file, you can use the Save button or the Save command on the File menu to update it after you make changes.

The Save As Type box lets you save a document in another format—as a template, as a WordPerfect document, as a MacIntosh file to name just a few options.

The Tools button displays a drop-down list (see Figure GS. 31) that lets you save multiple versions of a document within the same document, set how often the AutoRecover feature saves files, and tell Word whether or not fast saves are allowed.

Closing Documents

To close a document, you can click its Close Window button or choose the Exit command on the File menu. Word prompts you to save your work if you made any changes since you last saved.

It is wise to close documents as soon as you finish using them because they use memory when they are open. Think of it as keeping the desktop neat.

Hot Tips

The Create Folder button lets you create a new folder while working in Word. Display the drive or folder in which you want to place the new folder in the Save in box before clicking the New Folder button.

You can see the Tools drop-down list in the Save As dialog box.

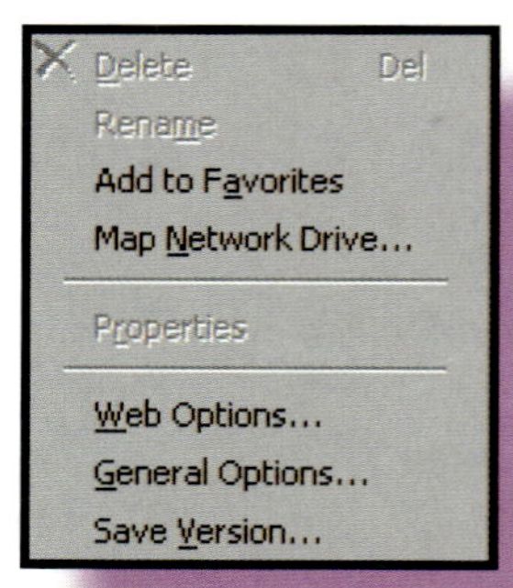

Working with Multiple Documents

The Window menu lists all open Word documents (Figure GS.32). A check mark signals the **active document**—the document on top that you can currently work on. Click the document name on the Window menu to make that document active, or click the document button on the taskbar.

You can use the Arrange All command to display all of your open documents (see Figure GS.33). The document with the colored title bar is the active document. Any commands you select or text you enter will affect the active document. If you want to return to a window that displays only the active document, click on that document's Maximize button.

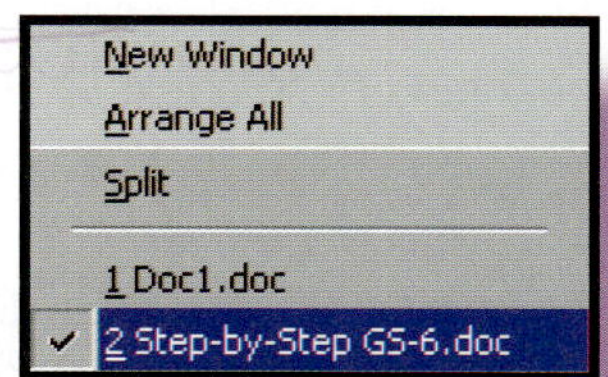

FIGURE GS.32
The Window menu shows open documents.

NOTE:

If your instructor followed the instructions for this book, the folder with your name should be a subfolder of the My Documents folder.

FIGURE GS.33
Use the Arrange All command on the Window menu to display all open documents.

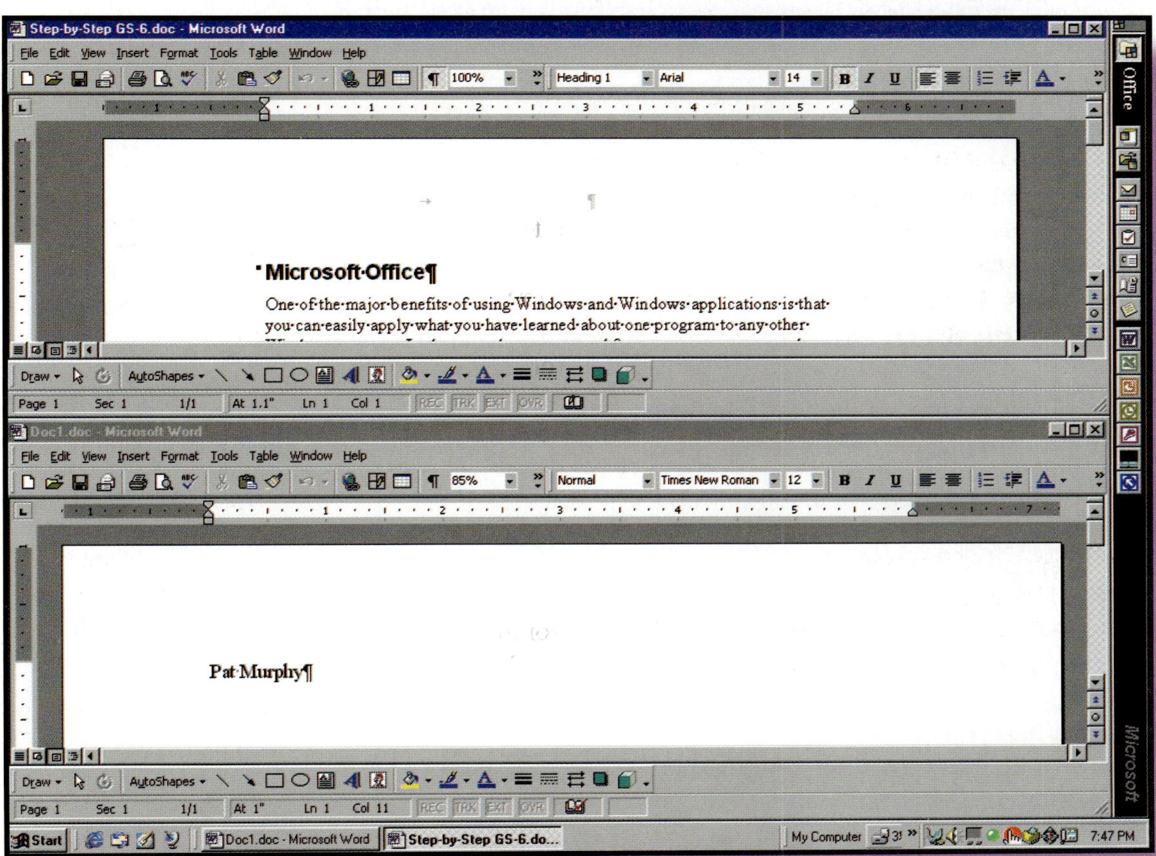

2 5

1. To enter some text in the document on your screen, type your name.

2. To display the Open dialog box, click the **Open** button on the Standard toolbar.

3. To display a list of the files that will be used in exercises in this book, be sure the folder containing the files is the one displayed in the Look In box. If the correct folder is not displayed, click the **My Documents** button on the **Places** bar. Then double-click the folder with your name.

4. To see the sizes and types of files and when they were last modified, click the **Tools** drop-down button in the Open dialog box, and click the **Details** command.

5. To see a preview of the file named **Step-by-Step GS-7 Multiple,** click that file name, click the **Views** button, and then click the **Preview** command in the Open dialog box.

6. To see as much of the list as possible, click the **Views** button in the Open dialog box and click the **List** command.

7. To display contents of the Favorites folder, click the **Favorites** button on the **Places** bar in the Open dialog box.

8. To return to the folder containing the files used in this book, click the **Back** button on the toolbar in the Open dialog box.

9. To open the **Step-by-Step GS-7 Multiple** file, double-click it.

10. To display the original document Word created when you started the program, click the **Window** menu and click **Document1.**

11. To see both documents on the screen, click the **Window** menu and click the **Arrange All** command.

12. To make the inactive document active, click in blank space in the inactive document (the one without the colored title bar).

13. To see the properties information for the active file, click the **File** menu, click the **expand** button, and click the **Properties** button. Click each of the tabs to see the kind of information available. Click the **Cancel** button.

14. To maximize your original document, be sure the document is active, and click its **Maximize** button.

15. To save the original document, click its **Close Window** button, click the **Yes** button when asked if you want to save changes, type your initials and First, be sure the Look in box contains the name of your folder containing files for this book, and click the Save button at the bottom right of the dialog box.

16. To close Word and the **Step-by-Step GS-7 Multiple** file without saving any changes, click Word's **Close** button, and click the **No** button when asked if you want to save changes.

Summary

You have now learned how to start Word, how to customize the application to work with this book, how to work with the Word window, how to use Word's Help system, how to access the World Wide Web, and how to open documents, to close documents, to work with multiple documents, and to exit from Word.

Try the exercises on the following pages to test how well you remember what you learned. Don't be afraid to go back and look up the answers because that will help to reinforce what you learned.

GETTING STARTED REVIEW QUESTIONS

TRUE / FALSE

Circle the T if the statement is true. Circle the F if it is false.

T **(F)** 1. You can open only three documents at a time.

T **(F)** 2. You should leave documents open when you know you will not use them again during the Word session.

(T) **F** 3. It is faster to use menu commands than to use toolbar buttons.

T **(F)** 4. The shortcut keys for many commands are listed on the menus.

(T) F 5. Word opens with the settings used in the previous session.

(T) F 6. There is a Help button in every dialog box.

(T) F 7. You need a modem and a service provider to access the World Wide Web.

(T) F 8. The Office Assistant lets you type specific questions about tasks or features.

T **(F)** 9. More than one document can be active at a time on your screen.

(T) F 10. You can print most of the Help windows that you access with the Search command.

COMPLETION

Complete the following sentences by writing the correct word or words in the blanks provided.

1. You click the _____*Close*_____ button to close an application or a document.

2. You can use the _____*Maximize*_____ button to make your document fill the screen.

3. You can open the _____*files Window*_____ menu to see a list of files that are open.

4. You can open the ___*View File*___ menu to see a list of the last four files used in Word.

5. You can use the ___*Title Folder*___ *arrange all* command on the Window menu to display all of your open documents.

6. The part of a window that shows a document's name is the ___*Title Bar*___

7. You can use the ___*Title Bar*___ *Task Bar* at the bottom of the screen to switch from one open application to another.

8. Use the Look in box in the ___*Text box*___ *Open Dialog Box* dialog box to specify where to find a file. *File of Type*

9. Use the ___*View Button*___ drop-down button in the Open dialog box to display a WordPerfect file.

10. To close a dialog box without selecting any of its options, click ___*(Exit) cancel*___

GETTING STARTED PROJECTS

PROJECT GS-A

Use the list below to identify each of the features of the Word screen shown in Figure GS.34. Write the letter of the feature next to the number that identifies it on the figure.

F 1.　　**a.** Close button

E 2.　　**b.** Scroll bars

H 3.　　**c.** Standard toolbar

A 4.　　**d.** Office Shortcut bar

D 5.　　**e.** Minimize button

P 6.　　**f.** Title bar

L 7.　　**g.** Status bar

M 8.　　**h.** Maximize/Restore button

I 9.　　**i.** Taskbar

G 10.　　**j.** Document window

J 11.　　**k.** Menu bar

K 12.　　**l.** Scroll box

C 13.　　**m.** Office Assistant

N 14.　　**n.** Formatting toolbar

O 15.　　**o.** I-beam pointer

Q 16.　　**p.** Scroll arrows

R 17.　　**q.** Insertion point

B 18.　　**r.** Rulers

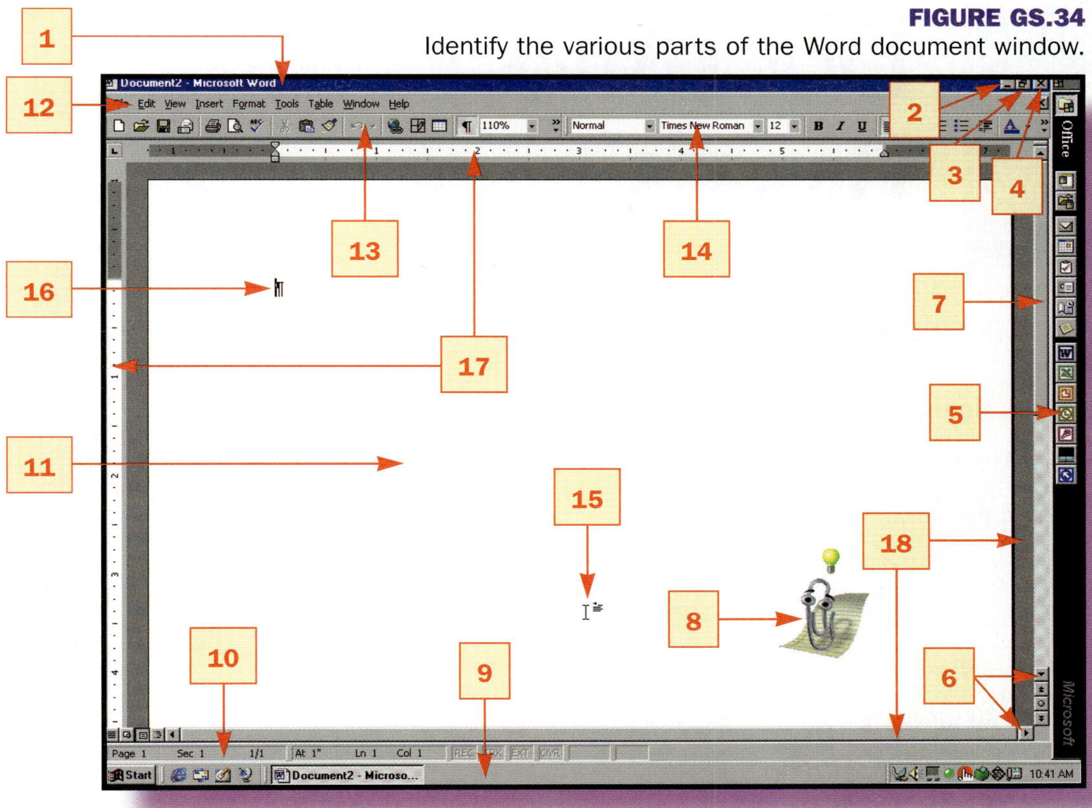

FIGURE GS.34
Identify the various parts of the Word document window.

PROJECT GS-B

Find out what support options are available from Microsoft online. Use Word's Help menu and the Office on the Web command. When you reach the Web site, find out what kinds of Help are available. Remember to disconnect when you finish.

Extra Challenges

Use Help to get information about closing a document. Print the Help window. If you are not sure about how to proceed, return to the Help section, and check how you searched for a topic during the lesson.

CRITICAL THINKING ACTIVITY

Find as much information as you can about the AutoRecover feature and how it will help you in the event of a power failure or system failure.

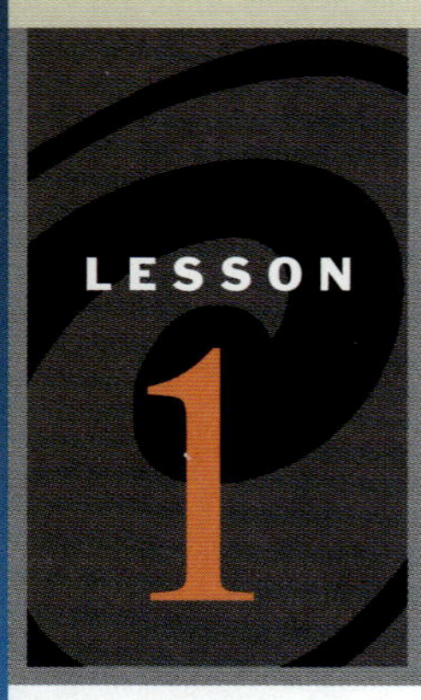

1

DOCUMENT BASICS

OBJECTIVES

When you complete this lesson, you will be able to:

- Move around within a Word document.
- Enter text.
- Select text.
- Insert text.
- Delete text.
- Use Undo, Redo, and Repeat.
- Use the Show/Hide ¶ Button.
- Move, copy, and paste text.

Estimated Time: 1½ hours

Introduction

In this lesson you will learn a good many Word basics. If you have been using other Windows applications, you may already be familiar with the basics. In any event, you will soon be comfortable with many Word procedures.

Moving around the Word Document

Before you can work with an existing document, you have to know how to move your insertion point from place to place within the document. The **insertion point** is the blinking vertical bar that signals where any text or non-printing character you type will appear.

You can move the insertion point

- with the mouse
- with the arrow keys (↑ ↓ → ←) and other keys on the keyboard
- with menu commands
- with a hyperlink

Hot Tips

If you are new to using the mouse, it may take you a few days to get used to clicking the I-beam where you want the insertion point.

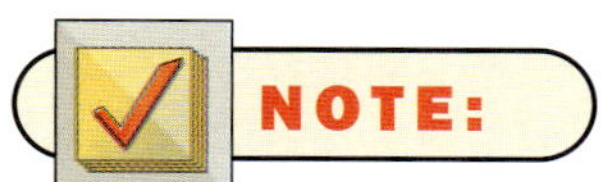

Word documents need to be copied to your hard drive. Microsoft recommends you not work with files on a floppy drive.

Moving with the Mouse

The mouse pointer looks like an **I-beam** (the letter I) when you slide it over text. The easiest way to move the insertion point in existing text is to position the I-beam pointer where you want to work and click. If you move the mouse pointer beyond the text area, it becomes a selection arrow pointer. If you click the I-beam in the right margin, the insertion point moves to the text closest to where you clicked. When you click the pointer in the left margin, you select (highlight) a line of text (see Figure 1.1). You will learn more about that later in this lesson.

You will learn more about Word's Click and Type feature a little later in the lesson.

FIGURE 1.1
The selection arrow pointer appears when you move the I-beam into the left margin.

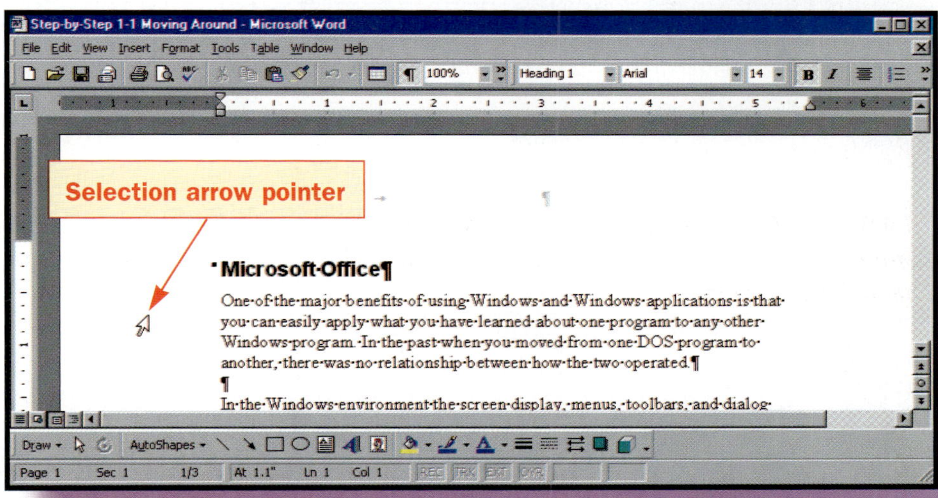

S TEP-BY-STEP ▷ 1.1

1. To open a document, click the **Open** button on the standard toolbar, be sure your folder is displayed in the Look In box, and double- click the file named **Step-by-Step 1-1 Move** listed in the box below the Look In box.

(continued on next page)

2. To place the insertion point before **In the past** on the third line of the first paragraph, click the I-beam before the **I** in **In the past.**

3. To place the insertion point before **In the Windows** at the beginning of the second paragraph, click the I-beam before the **I** in **In the Windows.** Be sure you see the I-beam when you click.

4. To see how the insertion point returns to the closest text or nonprinting character when you click in white space, click the I-beam in white space to the right of the text at the middle of the screen.

5. Continue clicking the I-beam until you are comfortable positioning the insertion point.

If you want to move to a position not displayed in the document window, use the scroll buttons or bars (see Figure 1.2). To enter text in the new area, you must click the I-beam to place the insertion point where you want to make the change.

Scroll bars and scroll arrows let you move through a document quickly.

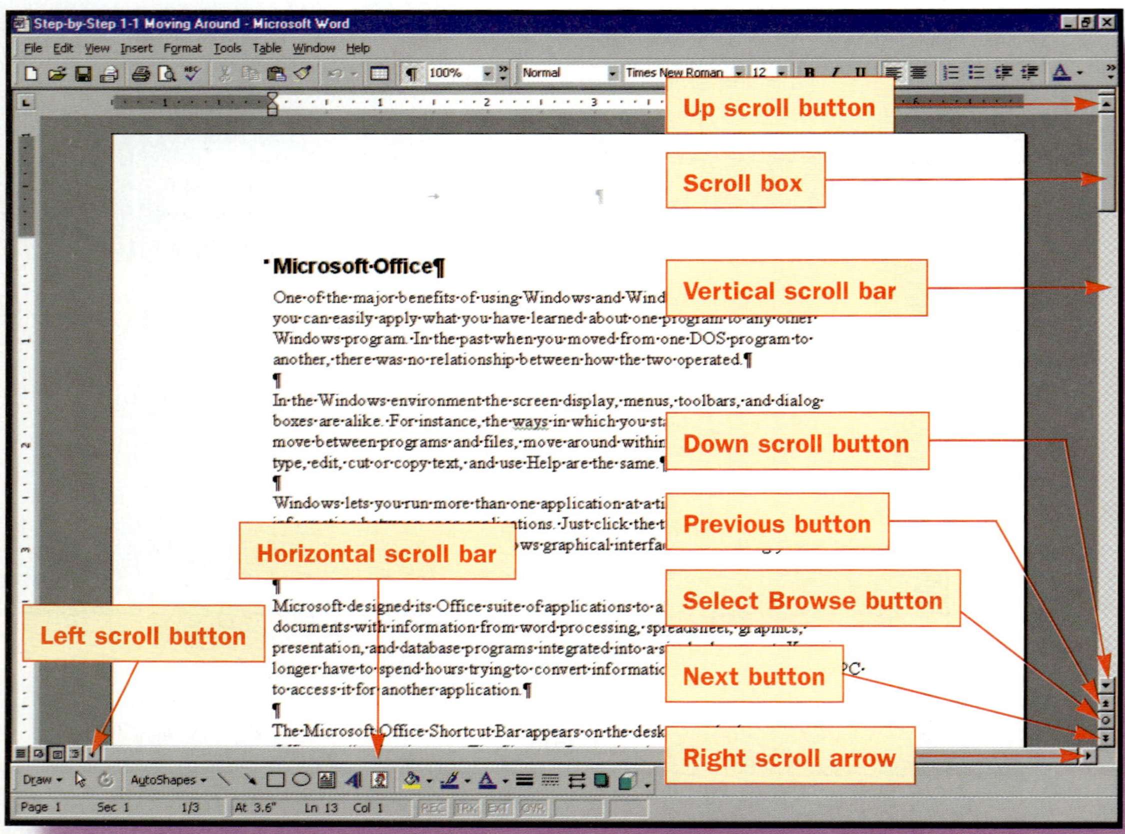

You can use the Select Browse Object feature to display a pop-up palette (see Figure 1.3) that lets you quickly move to the next or previous field, endnote, footnote, comment, section, page, edit, heading, graphic, or table. You will learn about these features throughout this book. There are also buttons on the pop-up palette that let you display the Go To or Find dialog box.

Table 1.1 contains directions for using the scroll bars and the Select Browse Object feature.

FIGURE 1.3
The Select Browse Object pop-up palette lets you move
quickly to a number of objects in a document.

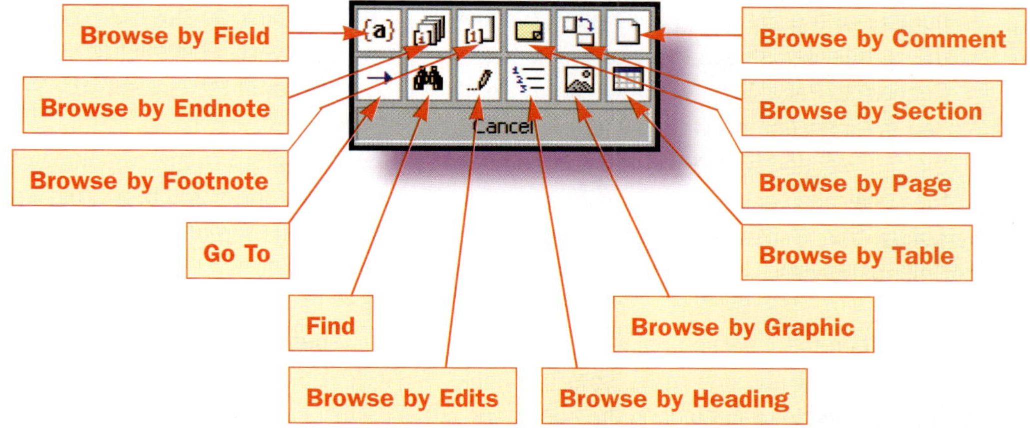

TABLE 1.1

USING SCROLL BARS	
DO THIS	**TO**
Click the up or down scroll button	Scroll up or down one line
Click above or below the scroll box in the vertical bar	Scroll up or down one screen
Drag the scroll box (page numbers display in a ScreenTip)	Move to a new location
Hold the Shift key and click the left scroll button	Move into left margin beyond text
Click the left or right scroll button	Scroll left or right
Click the Select Browse Object button	See a palette of items you can search for in the document
Click Previous or Next button	Move to the previous or next browse object (the browse object is the last item selected in the Select Browse Object palette)

STEP-BY-STEP 1.2

1. To move to the end of the document using the mouse, point to the **down** scroll button, and click and hold the mouse button until you scroll to the end of the document. You should see a dimmed file name and a page number at the bottom of each page. Notice the status bar shows you are on Page 3, Section 1, Page 3 of 3. Notice you do not see the insertion point because it is still in the first section where you left it. Because the insertion point is not showing, the status bar is blank in the At, Line, and Column spaces.

2. To position the insertion point at the end of the document and enter text, scroll up until you see the last paragraph in the document, click the I-beam at the end of the last paragraph, and press the **Enter** key.

3. To enter text, type your name.

4. To move to page 2, drag the scroll box in the Vertical scroll bar until you see **Page: 2 Excel** in the ScreenTip.

5. To return to the beginning of the document, drag the scroll box in the Vertical scroll bar to the top of the scroll bar.

6. To position the insertion point at the beginning of the document, click the I-beam before **Microsoft Office.**

Moving with Keystrokes

Table 1.2 on page 35 contains some of the keystrokes you can use to move the insertion point.

STEP-BY-STEP 1.3

1. To move the insertion point to the end of the document, hold the **Ctrl** key and press the **End** key. Press the ↑ key once.

2. To move the insertion point up one screen, press the **Page Up** key.

3. To move the insertion point down one screen, press the **Page Down** key.

4. To return the insertion point to the beginning of the document, hold the **Ctrl** key and press the **Home** key.

5. Take a few minutes to practice using the keys to move through the document.

Moving with Commands

You can use the Go To command on the expanded Edit menu to display the Go To tab in the Find and Replace dialog box (see Figure 1.4) to move to various locations in your document. You can also double-click the page number on the status bar or the Go To button on the Select Browse Object pop-up palette.

TABLE 1.2

USING KEYSTROKES TO MOVE AROUND

PRESS KEY(S)	TO MOVE
←	One character to the left
→	One character to the right
↑	One line up
↓	One line down
Ctrl + ←	One word to the left
Ctrl + →	One word to the right
End	To the end of a line
Home	To the beginning of a line
Page Up	Up one screen
Page Down	Down one screen
Ctrl + Page Down	To the top of the next page
Ctrl + Page Up	To the top of the previous page
Ctrl + End	To the end of the document
Ctrl + Home	To the beginning of the document

FIGURE 1.4

The Go To tab in the Find and Replace dialog box lets you move to a specific location in your document.

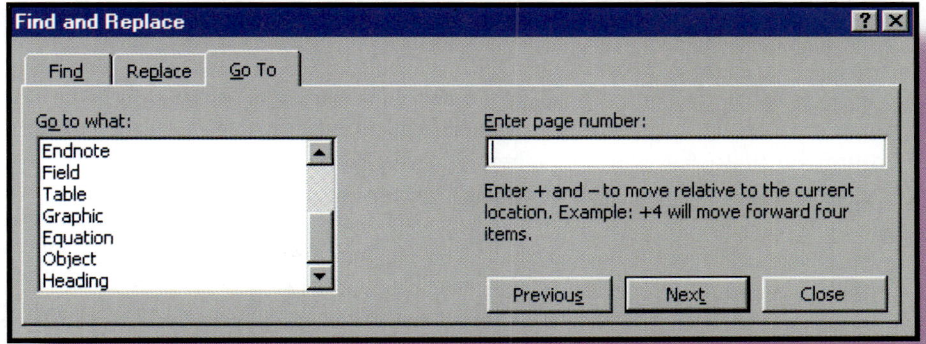

You can use the Go To command or Go To button to move to a page, section, line, bookmark, comment, footnote, endnote, field, table, graphic, equation, object, or heading. (You will learn about many of these items in later lessons.) You can use plus sign (+) and minus sign (–) or the Next and Previous buttons to move relative to the current location.

When you use the Find command, you can use the More button to ask Word to match case, find whole words only, use wildcards, look for phonetic matches, and find all word forms. You can also find special marks or formatting.

You can also use the Find command on the Edit menu (see Figure 1.5) or the Find button on the Select Browse Object pop-up palette to move to a position in your document. For example, if you know you want to do some editing near the words **relational database** somewhere in your document, you can use the Find command to get there quickly and easily without scrolling and watching the display. Display the Find tab, if necessary; type the text you want to find in the Find What text box; and click the Find Next button to move to the first instance of the word or phrase you typed.

FIGURE 1.5

The Find command on the Edit menu can help you move to a position in the document.

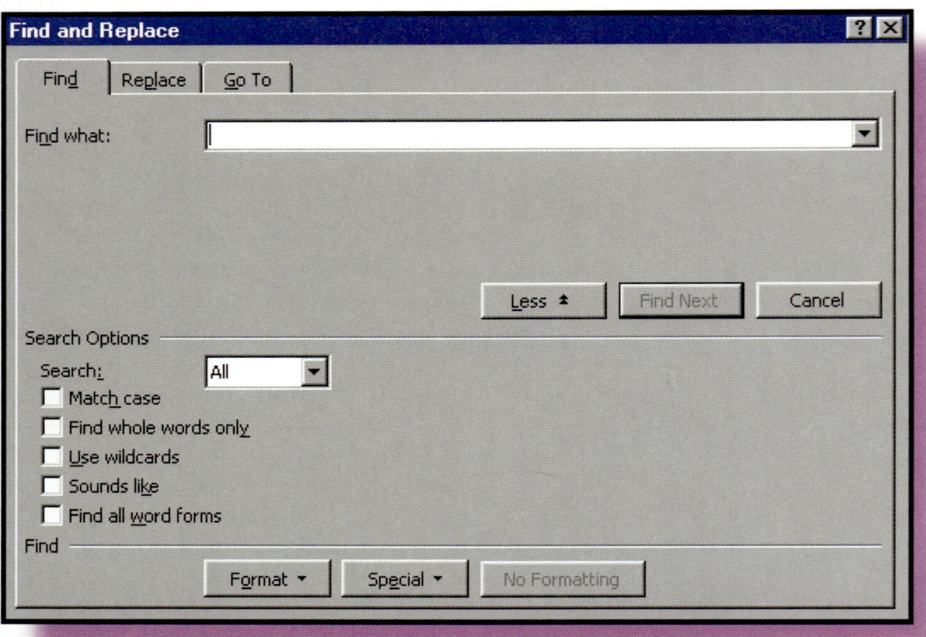

You can also use the Bookmark command on the expanded Insert menu to move around a document efficiently. For example, place a **bookmark,** or marker, at a position in your document that you often return to for editing. Whenever you have to reach that position, simply use the Bookmark command or the Go To command.

You create the bookmark by choosing the Bookmark command and displaying the Bookmark dialog box (see Figure 1.6).

If a dialog box covers a part of your document that you want to see, simply drag the dialog box by its title bar to another position on the screen.

You can use the Bookmark dialog box to sort the list of bookmarks by name or by location in the document or use the Add, Delete, Go To buttons to add, delete, or go to a bookmark.

IMPORTANT:

If anything in your document is selected when you use the Find command, Word will search only within the selection. Word will prompt if the text was not found within the selection and ask whether to check the rest of the document.

Moving with a Hyperlink

You can move to another Word document, to another Windows file, or to a Web page by clicking a hyperlink in your document. You can return to your original document by clicking its application on the taskbar or its document name on the Window menu. You will learn about adding hyperlinks to your documents in Lesson 2.

FIGURE 1.6
The Bookmark dialog box lets you mark a position in your document so you can move to it quickly.

STEP-BY-STEP 1.4

1. To display the Go To tab in the Find and Replace dialog box, click the **Edit** menu and click the **Go To** command.

2. To set the top of page 3 as a bookmark so you can access it quickly, click **Page** in the Go To What box; type **3** in the Enter Page Number box; click the **Go To** button, and click the **Close** button in the dialog box.

3. To display the Go To tab again, click the **Edit** menu and click the **Go To** command.

4. To move back two pages, type **–2,** click the **Go To** button, and click the **Close** button in the dialog box.

5. To use the Find command to move to the words **relational database,** click the **Edit** menu, click the **Find** command, type **relational database,** and click the **Find Next** button. You now see the first occurrence of the text you entered, and the text is selected.

6. To cancel the selection, click in the document to activate it, and press the → key. Notice Word still displays the Find and Replace dialog box, but its title bar has no color.

7. To activate the Find and Replace dialog box, click in the dialog box.

8. To find the next occurrence of the words **relational database,** click the **Find Next** button. Then click the **Cancel** button to close the dialog box.

(continued on next page)

9. To insert a bookmark at the second occurrence of **relational database,** click the **Insert** menu, click the **Bookmark** command, type **relational** to name the Bookmark, and click the **Add** button to add the bookmark to the list box.

10. To return the insertion point to the beginning of the document, hold the **Ctrl** key and press the **Home** key.

11. To move to the bookmark you created, click the **Insert** menu, click the **Bookmark** command, and click the **Go To** button because **relational** is already selected.

12. To close the Bookmark dialog box, click its **Close** button.

13. To use a hyperlink to move to another document, scroll through the document until you see the hyperlink in the section

Concept Builders

Remember, the Select Browse Object pop-up palette and the Go To, Find, and Bookmark buttons can make it much easier to move through and edit your documents.

entitled **Word.** (It is a different color and underlined.) Point to the hyperlink with your mouse, and when you see the hand icon, click the **hyperlink** to jump to the document to which the text is linked. Word opens the document.

14. To return to the original document, click its button on the taskbar.

15. To close both open documents, click their **Close** buttons and click the **No** buttons when you are asked to save changes.

Entering Text

To insert text, position the insertion point where you want to insert text, and type the text.

If Word displays a wavy red or green line under text, it means Word has detected a possible spelling or grammatical error. Word checks spelling and grammar as you type. You will learn how to check the underlined text in Lesson 3.

To position the insertion point with the mouse so you can enter text, you click once, either at the beginning of the document or within existing text. You can also take advantage of Word's Click and Type feature. Double-click in a blank area, and Click and Type pointer appears. When you type, formatting for the position where you double-clicked is automatically applied to your new text. You can see the Click and Type pointer with left alignment formatting in Figure 1.7. You will learn more about alignment in Lesson 4.

Did You Know?

When you enter text, you press the Enter key only at the ends of paragraphs. Word automatically wraps text to the next line within a paragraph. When you finish a paragraph, press the Enter key to signal you want to move to a new line.

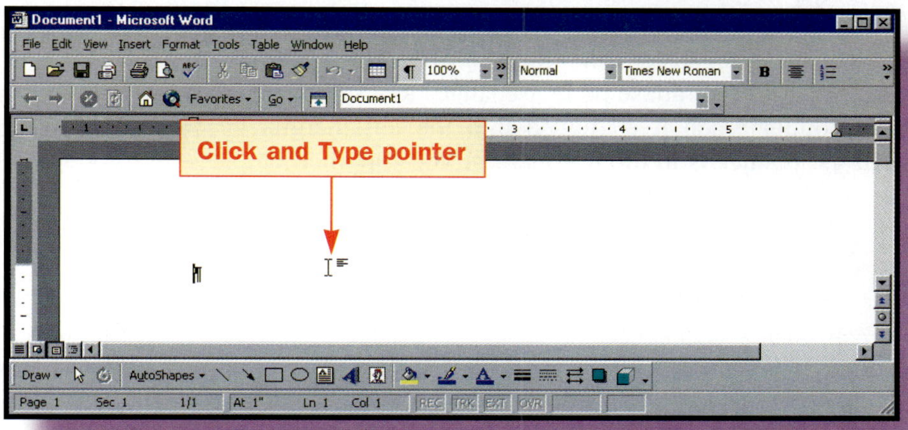

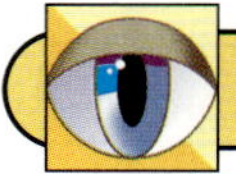

IMPORTANT:

You must be in Print Layout View or Web Layout view to use the Click and Type feature. You cannot use Click and Type in multiple columns, bulleted and numbered lists, next to floating objects, to the left or right of indents, or to the left or right of pictures that allow top and bottom text wrapping.

Selecting Text

In Word and other Windows applications, you select and then do. That means before you can format text or move or delete text or graphics, you must select the area you want to change.

Remember also that (unless you change the setting in the Options command on the Tools menu) whenever something is selected in your document, the first character you type replaces the entire selection. This feature can sometimes cause problems when you first work with Word. Because it is really much faster to work, however, you should not change the setting unless you find it impossible to adjust to it.

You can cancel a selection by pressing an arrow key or clicking outside the selection.

Did You Know?

In older programs, selecting is sometimes called highlighting or blocking.

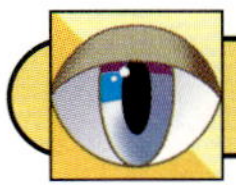

IMPORTANT:

Clicking outside a selection cancels it. Be sure you do not click a part of the window that will change your display. Click on white space on the right side of the document.

Selecting with the Mouse

You will probably do most of your selecting with the mouse once you are comfortable with it. Table 1.3 describes how to select with the mouse. You saw in Figure 1.1 how the mouse pointer changes to a selection arrow pointer when it is moved into the left margin. When the pointer is in the left margin, you can click or drag to select various amounts of text.

You can select text as a vertical block. You can use this feature to select the first letter in each line of a list. The feature is not available within a table.

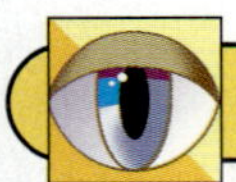

IMPORTANT:

When you click in the middle of a word and drag into a second word, Word automatically selects both words and the spaces after them.

TABLE 1.3

SELECTING WITH THE MOUSE	
TO SELECT	**DO THIS**
Any item or amount of text	Drag across the text you want to select, or double-click the Extend Selection mode (EXT) button on the status bar, and then use keystrokes in Table 1.2 to select text
Word	Double-click the word
Line of text	Click in the left margin to the left of the line (your mouse pointer will take the upward-right pointing shape)
Multiple lines of text	Drag in the left margin to the left of the lines
Sentence	Hold the Ctrl key and click anywhere in sentence
Paragraph	Double-click in left margin by paragraph, or triple-click in paragraph
Entire document	Triple-click in left margin
Vertical block of text	Hold the Alt key and drag vertically over text

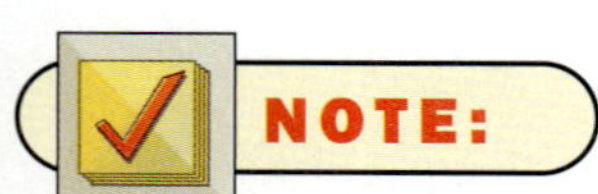

NOTE:

You can also select by clicking the I-Beam at the beginning of the selection, then holding the Shift key and clicking at the end of the selection.

S TEP-BY-STEP ▷ 1.5

1. Open the file named **Step-by-Step 1-5 Select.**

2. To select the title **Microsoft Office,** drag across **Microsoft Office.**

3. To cancel the selection, click on white space on the right side of the document window.

4. To select the line with the title **Microsoft Office,** click the **selection arrow** pointer in the **left margin** to the left of the line.

5. To cancel the selection, click in blank space at the right side of the document window.

6. To select the first four-line paragraph, click and drag in the **left margin** to the left of the paragraph.

7. To select the paragraph beginning **In the Windows,** triple-click anywhere in the

paragraph. You may have to try triple-clicking a few times before you are successful.

8. To select the word **Microsoft** in the heading line, double-click it.

9. To move to the end of the document, hold the **Ctrl** key and press the **End** key. Scroll so you can see a couple of inches of blank space at the bottom of the text.

10. To type and center the word **End** about an inch below the text, point to the middle of the page about one inch below the text (notice the Click and Type pointer), double-click the Click and Type pointer, and type **-End-.**

11. Practice using the mouse to select text until you feel very comfortable about selecting.

Selecting with the Keyboard

Table 1.4 on page 42 describes the keystrokes you use to select text and graphics with the keyboard.

Hot Tips

You also can select the entire document with the Select All command on the Edit menu.

S TEP-BY-STEP ▷ 1.6

1. To move to the beginning of the document, hold the **Ctrl** key and press the **Home** key.

2. To select the title **Microsoft Office,** click the I-Beam before the **M,** hold the **Shift** key, and click at the end of **Office.**

3. To select the word to the right of the insertion point, hold the **Ctrl** and **Shift** keys and press the → key.

4. To select to the end of the line, hold the **Shift** key and press the **End** key.

5. To cancel the selection, press an **arrow** key.

6. To return to the beginning of the document, hold the **Ctrl** key and press the **Home** key.

(continued on next page)

7. To get comfortable using keystrokes to select text, practice using any of the keystrokes shown in Table 1.4 that you think you might use to select text.

8. To save the document, click the **Save** button on the Standard toolbar.

9. To close the document, click its **Close** button.

TABLE 1.4

KEYBOARD COMMANDS

TO SELECT	PRESS KEYS
One character to the right	Shift + →
One character to the left	Shift + ←
To the end of a word	Ctrl + Shift + →
To the beginning of a word	Ctrl + Shift + ←
To the end of a line	Shift + End
To the beginning of a line	Shift + Home
To the end of a paragraph	Ctrl + Shift + ↓
To the beginning of a paragraph	Ctrl + Shift + ↑
To the end of a document	Ctrl + Shift + End
To the beginning of a document	Ctrl + Shift + Home
To include the entire document	Ctrl + A

Inserting Text

Word's default setting for entering text is called **insert mode.** That means Word enters text you type at the insertion point—to the left of anything that may be there already.

In **overtype mode,** text you type overwrites text that already exists in the document until you reach the end of the current paragraph. Even if you are accustomed to using overtype mode, you should leave Word's setting as is because it is faster and easier to work in insert mode. You can double-click the OVR button on the status bar to toggle overtype mode on or off. The OVR button is dimmed when overtype mode is turned off.

Use the Office on the Web command on the Help menu to find and look over frequently asked questions about Word 2000.

STEP-BY-STEP ▷ 1.7

1. Open the file **Step-by-Step 1-7 Insert**.

2. To move to the end of the first line and enter some text, press the **End** key, press the **Spacebar**, and type **Suite**.

3. To switch to overtype mode, double-click the **OVR** button on the status bar. Notice that the OVR button is no longer dimmed.

4. To display the Find and Replace dialog box, click the **Edit** menu and then click the **Find** command. In the Find What box, type **An added benefit.** Click the **Find Next** button.

5. To close the Find and Replace dialog box, click the **Cancel** button.

6. To use overtype mode to insert text, type **Any Windows application can share data with any other Windows application with the greatest of ease.** Notice that the first character you enter replaces the selection. Then each character overstrikes a character.

7. To turn off overtype mode and dim OVR, double-click the **OVR** button on the status bar.

8. To save and close the document, click its Close button and click **Yes** when asked to save changes.

Deleting Text

Several ways of deleting text in Word are listed below:

- Press the Delete key to delete a character after (to the right of) the insertion point.

- Press the Backspace key to delete a character just before (to the left of) the insertion point.

- Select text; then click the Cut button on the Standard toolbar or the Cut command on the Edit menu, or press the Backspace key or the Delete key.

Using Undo, Redo, and Repeat

You can undo many, but not all, of the actions you take in Word with the Undo command on the Edit menu or with the Undo button on the Standard toolbar. The Undo command on the Edit menu lets you undo your most recent action. Clicking the Undo button on the Standard toolbar undoes the last action. Clicking a second time undoes the prior action, and so on. If you click the drop-down button to the right of the Undo button, you see a list of actions you can undo.

It is important to undo a mistake immediately, because the drop-down list can be confusing. For example, if you undo the third item on the list, the first two are undone as well. You may not remember what those actions were or see what happens when they are undone.

You can use the Redo button on the More Buttons drop-down palette on the Standard toolbar when you have used the Undo command and would like to redo the action last undone. When you can't redo an action, the button is dimmed.

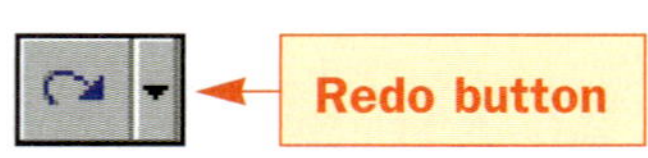

You can use the Repeat command on the Edit menu to repeat your last action. If you cannot repeat the action, the command changes to Can't Repeat.

S TEP-BY-STEP 1.8

1. Open **Step-by-Step 1-8 Undo.** To select the first sentence in the paragraph beginning **One of the major benefits,** including the space after the sentence, drag across it.

2. To delete the sentence, press the **Delete** key. Notice the selected sentence is gone.

3. To undo the delete, click the the left side of the **Undo** button on the Standard toolbar. To cancel the selection, press the ← key.

4. To delete the blank line between the first and second paragraphs of text, position the insertion point at the beginning of the second text paragraph, and press the **Backspace** key. To delete the blank line before the paragraph beginning with the word **Windows,** click before the **W,** click the

Edit menu, click the **expand** button, and click **Repeat Typing.**

5. To see the list of actions you can undo, click the **drop-down button** to the right of the **Undo** button on the Standard toolbar. Notice it lists just two actions—**Typing.**

6. To undo one deletion, click the top **Typing.**

7. To redo the undo action, click the **More Buttons** button on the Standard toolbar, slide the pointer over the **Redo** button until you see the ScreenTip, and then click the *left* side of the **Redo** button.

8. To restore the deletion again, click the *left* side of the **Undo** button.

Using Show/Hide ¶

You can use the Show/Hide ¶ button, which looks like a paragraph mark, on the More Buttons button on the Standard toolbar to show or hide paragraph marks, spaces, tabs, and other nonprinting symbols. It is often wise to have the nonprinting symbols displayed when editing text.

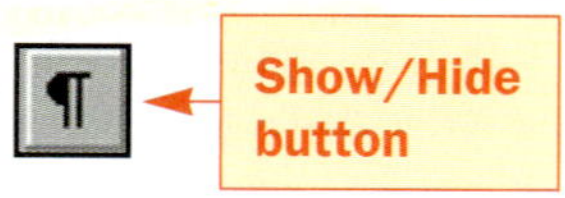

4 4

Word defines a **paragraph** as any amount of text or graphics with a paragraph mark after it.

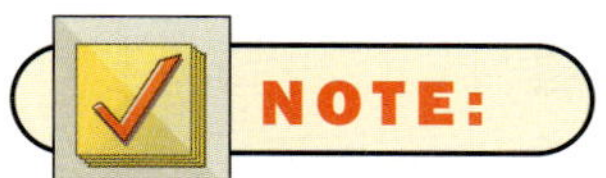

NOTE:

The preceding Using Show/Hide ¶ heading is considered a paragraph because the person who typed it pressed the Enter key after typing those words.

STEP-BY-STEP ▷ 1.9

1. To display nonprinting symbols (if they are not already displayed), click the **Show/Hide ¶** button.

2. To move the insertion point to the beginning of the document, hold the **Ctrl** key and press the **Home** key.

3. To move the insertion point to the end of the first line of the document before the paragraph mark, press the **End** key.

4. To delete the paragraph mark, press the **Delete** key. Notice the heading and the paragraph are now run together in one paragraph, and the format of the entire paragraph is the heading's format.

5. To return the paragraph mark to its position, click the left side of the **Undo** button.

6. To close the file without saving changes, click its **Close** button, and click the **No** button when asked to save changes.

Moving and Copying Text

Word offers two different clipboards you can use to move or copy text. A **clipboard** is an area of memory that temporarily stores cut or copied selections. In addition, you can use the drag-and-drop feature to move or copy a selection.

Using the Windows Clipboard to Move or Copy

When you move a selection, you remove (cut) the selection from one position and paste the selection in another position.

When you copy a selection, you duplicate the selection so you can paste the selection into another position.

Word offers several ways that use the Windows Clipboard to copy or move data:

- You can use the Cut, Copy, Paste, Paste Special, Paste Hyperlink, and Paste Append commands on the expanded Edit menu to move or copy data from one location to another.

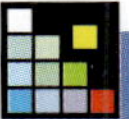

Concept Builders

The Paste Special command paste links or embeds Windows clipboard contents in the format you specify. Paste Hyperlink inserts the contents of the Windows clipboard as a hyperlink and is only available if the cut or copied selection is from another application.

- You can use the Cut, Copy, and Paste buttons on the Standard toolbar to move and copy data.

- You can use the shortcut menu to move or copy data.

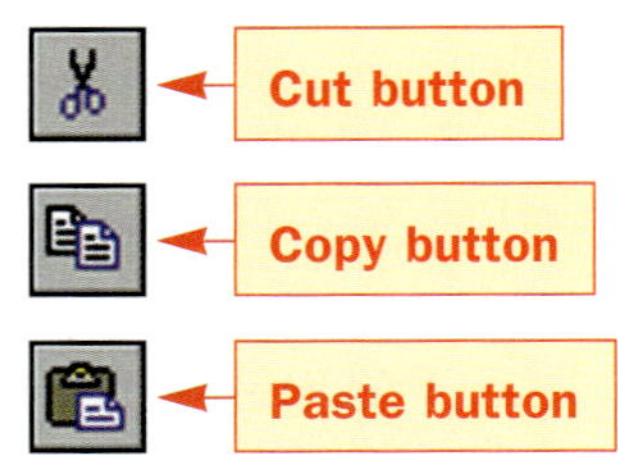

When you cut or copy a selection in any Windows application with the Cut or Copy command or using toolbar buttons, Windows stores a copy of the selection in an area of memory called the Windows Clipboard. Windows stores the cut or copied selection in the Windows Clipboard until you cut or copy another selection from Word or another Windows application or until you close Windows.

You can use the Paste button or the Paste command to place the contents of the Windows Clipboard in any Word document or in documents in other Windows applications.

Using the Office Clipboard to Move or Copy

You must use the Toolbars command on the View menu to turn on the Clipboard toolbar to use the Office Clipboard (see Figure 1.8). The Office Clipboard can hold up to 12 cut or copied items instead of the single item the Windows Clipboard holds. You can copy items from any program that has copy-and-cut functionality. However, you cannot paste items from the Office Clipboard into documents created by applications other than those in the Microsoft Office suite of applications.

Each time you cut or copy an item using commands or buttons, it is added to the Office Clipboard. To see up to the first 50 characters of each item as a ScreenTip, slide the mouse pointer over the item in the Office Clipboard until its ScreenTip appears.

To paste an individual item, position the insertion point where you want to paste the item, and then click the item on the Office Clipboard toolbar.

When you want to paste all items in the Office Clipboard, use its Paste All button.

Use the Clear Clipboard button to clear the entire Office Clipboard contents.

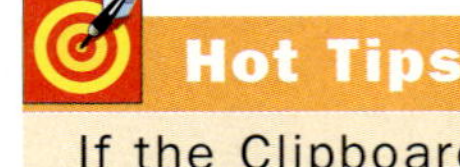

If the Clipboard is docked (attached) to another toolbar, click the Item's drop-down button to see the items on the clipboard. Then slide the mouse pointer over each item to see its first 50 characters.

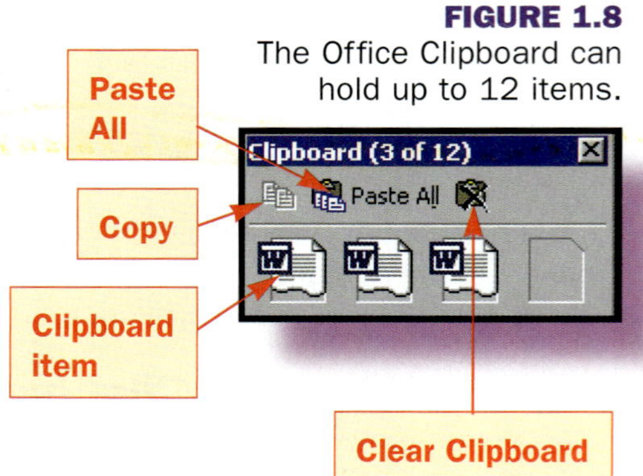

FIGURE 1.8
The Office Clipboard can hold up to 12 items.

The Office Clipboard toolbar must be displayed to be sure it is storing your cut or copied selections.

Using Drag-and-Drop Editing

You can also use the **drag-and-drop feature** to move or copy a selection to a new location.

To move a selection, position the mouse pointer on the selected item, press and hold the mouse button until you see the drag-and-drop pointer, drag the dotted insertion point to its new position, and drop it.

When you move or copy a selection using the drag-and-drop method, the selection is not stored in either the Windows or the Office Clipboard.

To copy a selection, hold the Ctrl key while you drag and drop the selection. When you copy a selection, you will see a plus sign (+) with the drag-and-drop pointer.

NOTE:

When copying or moving a paragraph, include the paragraph mark at the end of the paragraph in your selection so you do not have to go back to adjust line spacing.

Hot Tips

Try pasting text between Word documents without including either a section break or the final paragraph mark. The text takes on the section formatting of the text into which you paste it.

STEP-BY-STEP 1.10

1. Open **Step-by-Step 1-10 Copy.**

2. To select the paragraph beginning **In the Windows environment,** triple-click anywhere in the paragraph.

3. To move the selection, point to it, click and hold down the mouse button until you see the drag-and-drop pointer. Drag the dotted insertion point to the beginning of the previous paragraph, and release the dotted insertion point when it is just before the **O** in **One.**

4. To cancel the selection, press the → key. Notice that the line spacing between paragraphs needs to be adjusted.

5. To insert a blank line between the two paragraphs, press the **Enter** key.

6. To remove the extra line space left behind, press the ↓ key four times, and press the **Delete** key.

7. To display the Office Clipboard if it's not already on the screen, click the **View** menu, click the **Toolbars** command, and click **Clipboard.**

8. To copy the **Microsoft Office** heading, triple-click the heading, click the **Edit** menu, and click **Copy.**

9. To use the Paste Special command to paste the heading without formatting, hold the **Ctrl** key and press the **End** key, and press the **Enter** key twice. Click the **Edit** menu, click the **expand** button, click **Paste Special,** click **Unformatted Text,** and click **OK.** Notice the original heading format is missing.

10. To select the paragraph beginning **One of the major benefits,** including the blank line after the paragraph, drag in the selection bar until the four lines and the blank line are selected.

11. To remove the paragraph from its current position and put it in the Windows Clipboard, click the **Cut** button on the Standard toolbar. Notice the paragraph disappears from the document.

12. To remove the third paragraph beginning **Microsoft designed,** drag in the **left margin** until the paragraph and the blank line are selected and click the **Cut** button.

(continued on next page)

4 7

13. To paste a paragraph, position the insertion point before the first letter of the preceding paragraph, which begins **In the Windows,** slide your mouse pointer over each of the items displayed on the Clipboard toolbar until you see the ScreenTip **One of the many benefits of using Windows and...,** and then click the item.

14. To create a new document to practice pasting between documents, click the **New** button.

15. To display both open documents, click the **Window** menu, and then click the **Arrange**

All command on its expanded menu. Notice the insertion point is in the document you just created.

16. To enter the Office Clipboard contents in the new document, click the **Paste All** button on the Office Clipboard toolbar. You could have clicked on the individual item buttons to paste the items in a different order.

17. To close the documents with the Close All command, hold the **Shift** key, click the **File** menu, and click the **No** button each time you are asked to save changes.

Summary

You have learned a good many Word basics, including how to move around within documents, to save documents, to select text, to insert and delete text, to use Undo and Redo, to work with the Cut, Copy, and Paste commands and buttons, to use the Windows Clipboard and the Office Clipboard, and to move and copy using the drag-and-drop feature.

Try the exercises on the following pages to test how well you remember what you learned. Don't be afraid to go back and look up procedures. You won't be able to remember everything you did. Using Help or looking back through this book will reinforce what you learned.

LESSON 1 REVIEW QUESTIONS

TRUE / FALSE

Circle the T if the statement is true. Circle the F if it is false.

T (F) **1.** You should try to work from files on the A drive when using Word.

T (F) **2.** The easiest way to move through a long document to find an area that needs editing is to scroll line by line.

(T) F **3.** If you click the mouse in the left margin, you select the line.

T (F) **4.** Typing Replaces Selection means each character you type replaces the selection and replaces the characters one character at a time as you type.

T F 5. You will probably do most of your selecting with the mouse.

T F 6. The Office Clipboard can hold 12 items.

T F 7. An easy way to find every occurrence of the word *mountain* in a document is to use a bookmark.

T **F** 8. The opposite of overtype mode is insert mode.

T F 9. Word's drag-and-drop editing lets you quickly move selected text to a new location.

T **F** 10. When you copy text, it is stored in the Clipboard.

COMPLETION

Complete the following sentences by writing the correct word or words in the blanks provided.

1. You can cancel a selection by pressing a(n) _arrow_ key.

2. When you click to close a menu, you should be careful to click in _white_ space.

3. You can hold _ctrl_ and press _Home_ to move to the beginning of a document.

4. You can _Double_-click on a word to select it.

5. You can click _three_ times on a paragraph to select it.

6. When you delete something by mistake, click the _undo_ button immediately.

7. The _Bookmark_ command lets you mark specific locations in a document so that you can move quickly to them.

8. When you use the Cut button or the Copy button on the Standard toolbar, a copy of the cut or copied text is placed in the _memory_.

9. When you cut or copy a whole paragraph, select all of the text and the _paragraph mark_

10. It is wise to use the _Show/Hide More Buttons_ button to display nonprinting marks when editing.

LESSON 1 PROJECT

PROJECT 1A

To practice what you've learned in this lesson, complete the following project:

1. Open **Project 1-A** and make the following revisions.

2. In the first paragraph:

   a. Insert the word **Microsoft** before the first occurrence of the word **Windows.**

   b. Delete **and Windows.**

   c. Delete the words **that** and **easily** in the first paragraph.

   d. Change the words **any other** to **another.**

   e. Move the second sentence to the beginning of the paragraph.

3. In the second paragraph:

   a. Delete the words **For instance** in the second sentence, and capitalize **the.**

   b. Delete the comma after the word **cut.**

4. In the fourth paragraph:

   a. Delete **of applications** in the first sentence.

   b. Change the words **integrated into** to **used in.**

Find, read, and print the Help screens for the selecting with keystrokes.

5. In the fifth paragraph:

   a. Move the first sentence to the end of the paragraph.

   b. Change **The toolbar** to **The Shortcut Bar.**

   c. Delete the word **very** before **easy** in what is now the first sentence.

6. Save the document as Revise Document.

7. Select the entire document one paragraph at a time, and use the Copy command to put it on the Clipboard.

8. Close the document, but do not shut down the computer until you finish the Critical Thinking Activity for this lesson.

CRITICAL THINKING ACTIVITY

Create a new document. Paste the contents of the Office Clipboard (from Project 1A) one item at a time in an order of your choosing in the new document. Save the document as **Critical Thinking Activity 1,** and close it.

CREATING, PRINTING, AND SENDING A DOCUMENT

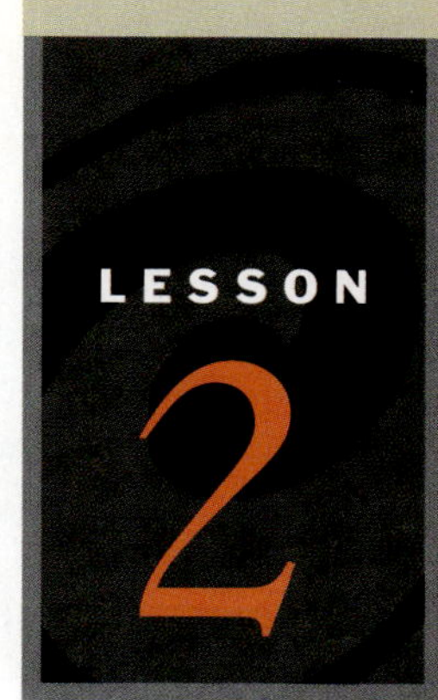

OBJECTIVES

When you complete this lesson, you will be able to:

- Use templates and wizards.
- Use the Print Preview feature.
- Print a document.
- Create and print an envelope.
- Use Word's Web tools.
- Send documents electronically.

Estimated Time: 1½ hours

Introduction

Now that you are familiar with Word basics, you are ready to create your own documents. In this lesson you will learn about using Word wizards and Word templates to create memos. You will preview a document before you print it and then create and print an envelope. In addition, you will learn about Word's Web tools and how to route and send documents electronically.

Using Templates and Wizards to Create New Documents

You can work more efficiently by basing many of your new documents (such as memos, letters, fax cover sheets, and reports) on templates that Word provides. A **template** is a master copy for a certain type of document.

Templates contain the settings for margins, the page size and orientation, and any text or graphics that are standard for the type of document. Instead of having to create a layout each time you want to create a memo, for instance, you can use one of the memo templates.

Wizards take you step-by-step through creating the type of document you choose and let you make more decisions about the format of the document than you can when using a template.

In an earlier lesson you used the New button on the Standard toolbar to create a new document. When you use the New button, the new document automatically uses Word's Blank Document template. The blank template is a general-purpose template for any document. Unless you choose another template in the New dialog box, Word uses the Blank Document when you create a new document. Even the Blank Document template contains default settings for margins, page size and orientation, and text styles.

Word has many other templates you can use to create various kinds of documents. To use one of these templates, you must use the New command on the File menu. The New dialog box contains tabs for the different types of templates you can use (see Figure 2.1).

Word displays a preview of a template when you select it.

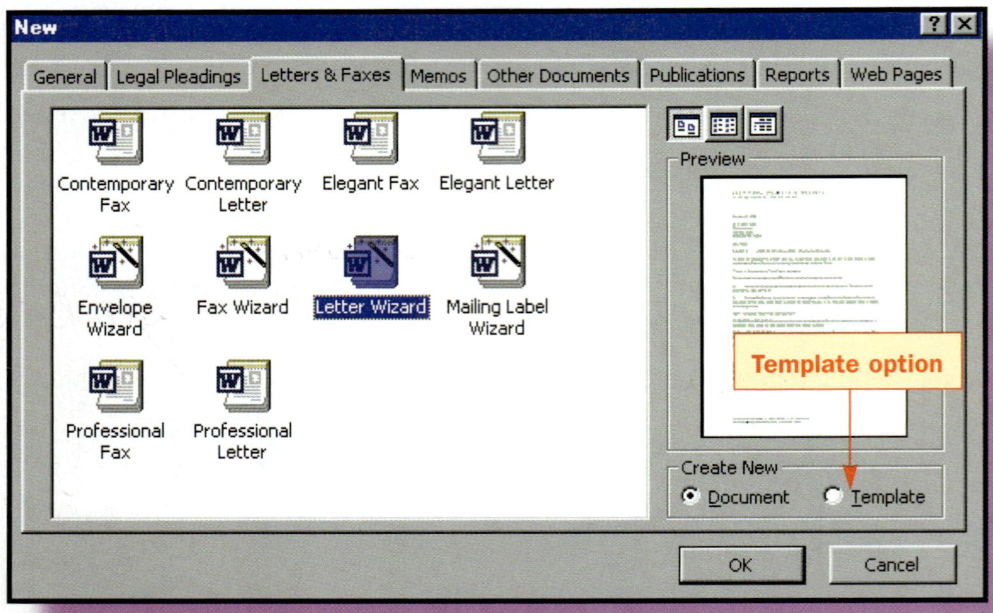

The New dialog box lets you preview what each template (except the Blank Document) looks like. Create New Document is automatically selected at the bottom right of the dialog box. You can select the Template option to create a template rather than a document. You might want, for instance, to create a template based on one Microsoft has already provided.

If you choose a wizard in the New dialog box, Word displays a series of dialog boxes that walk you through creation of the document.

Using the Letter Wizard

Word's Letter Wizard can help you quickly create a letter by asking you to supply information and then formatting the letter for you. After you create a letter with the Letter Wizard, the wizard stores the information so that you can use it again simply by clicking items on a list.

When you select the Letter Wizard, Word displays a dialog box that asks whether you want to send one letter or send a letter to a list of recipients (see Figure 2.2).

When you choose to send one letter, Word displays the Letter Wizard dialog box shown in Figure 2.3. The dialog box contains four tabs. On the Letter Format tab (step 1), you can choose whether to display a date and a header and footer on your letter. You choose a page design and a letter style for the letter. You can also indicate whether you will be printing the letter on letterhead and, if so, you can allow space for the letterhead.

Step 2 of the Letter Wizard, the Recipient Info tab, is where you enter the name and address of the person who will receive the letter (see Figure 2.4). If your system is set up to use any of Microsoft's e-mail services, such as Exchange or Outlook, you can select the name and address from an existing Address Book by clicking the Address Book button. You can also select one of four salutation options for your letter.

Step 3 of the Letter Wizard, the Other Elements tab, is where you can include such elements as a reference line, mailing instructions, an attention line, a subject line, and courtesy copies (see Figure 2.5).

Step 4 of the Letter Wizard, the Sender Info tab, is where you insert the name and return address of the person sending the letter or select these items from an Address Book (see Figure 2.6). You can choose to omit the return address from the letter and specify exactly what information should be used in the letter's closing.

When you complete this dialog box, your letter appears as a new document with the information you entered already in place (see Figure 2.7).

Your letter is now formatted and contains the basic information about sender and recipient. You still need to type the body of the letter. You do so by selecting the placeholder copy that tells you where to insert your text and then typing your text.

If you want to change your letter, you do not have to run the Letter Wizard again. Choose the Letter Wizard command on the expanded Tools menu to see the Letter Wizard dialog box with the same four tabs. Any change you make in the dialog box will appear in your letter.

FIGURE 2.2

You can use the Letter Wizard for a letter to one recipient or to a list of recipients.

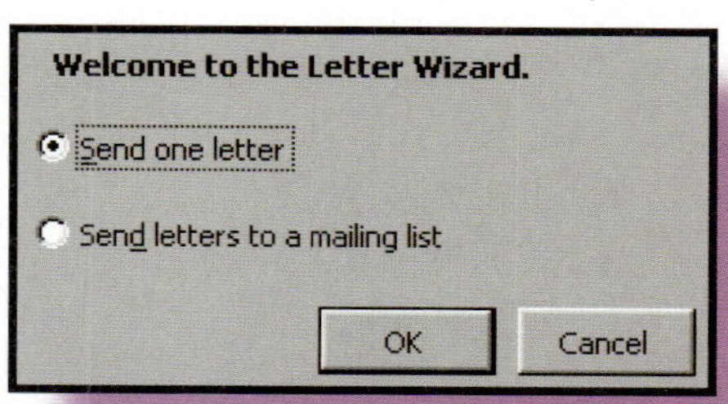

FIGURE 2.3

Step 1 contains settings for the letter's format.

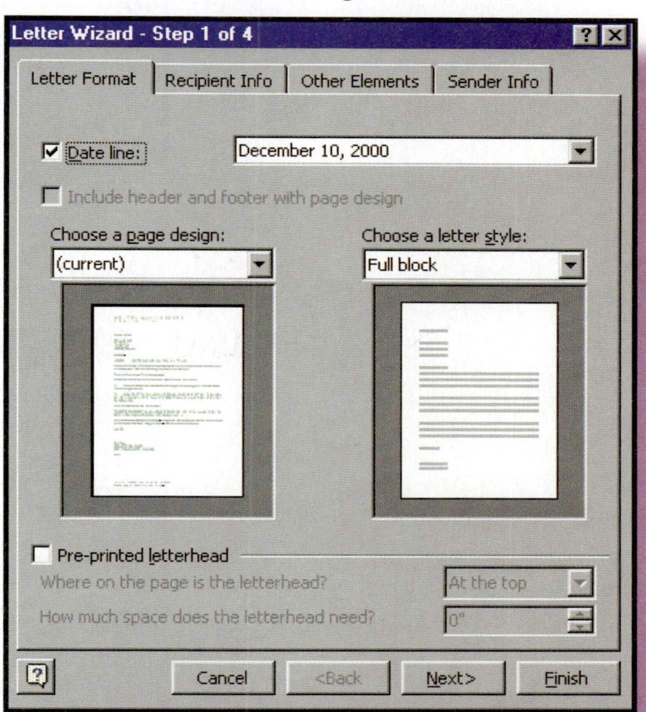

Step 2 contains the recipient information.

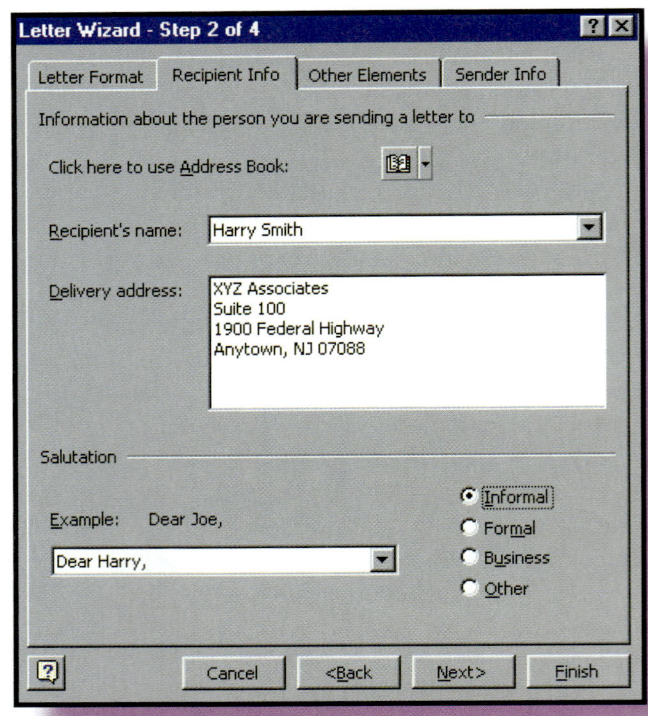

Step 3 contains other elements you can add to a letter.

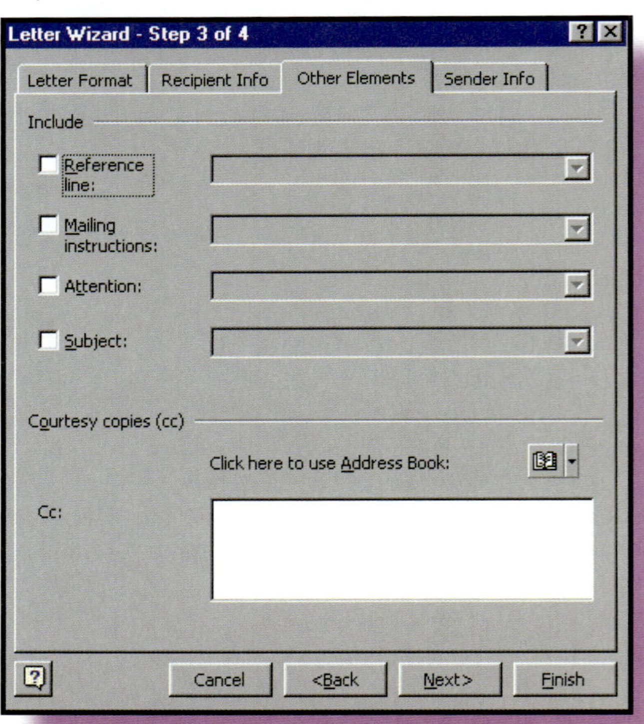

FIGURE 2.6

Step 4 contains sender information.

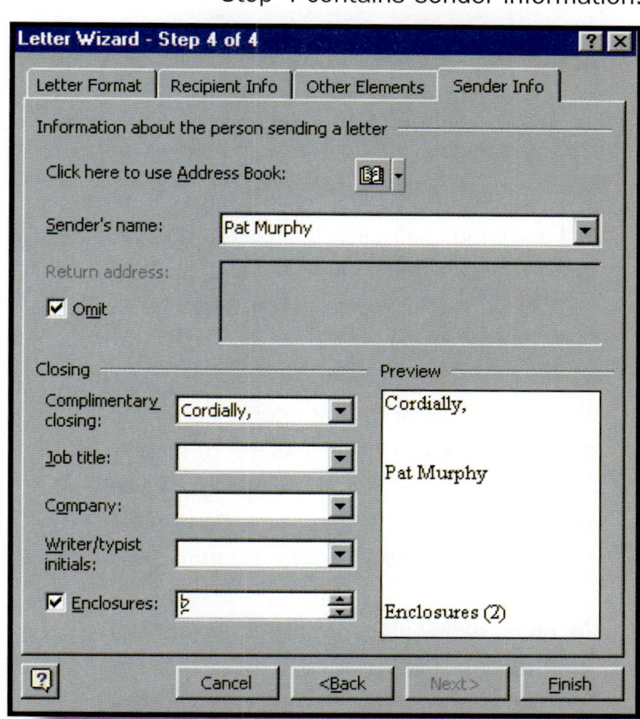

FIGURE 2.7

The letter is now ready for you to type the body text.

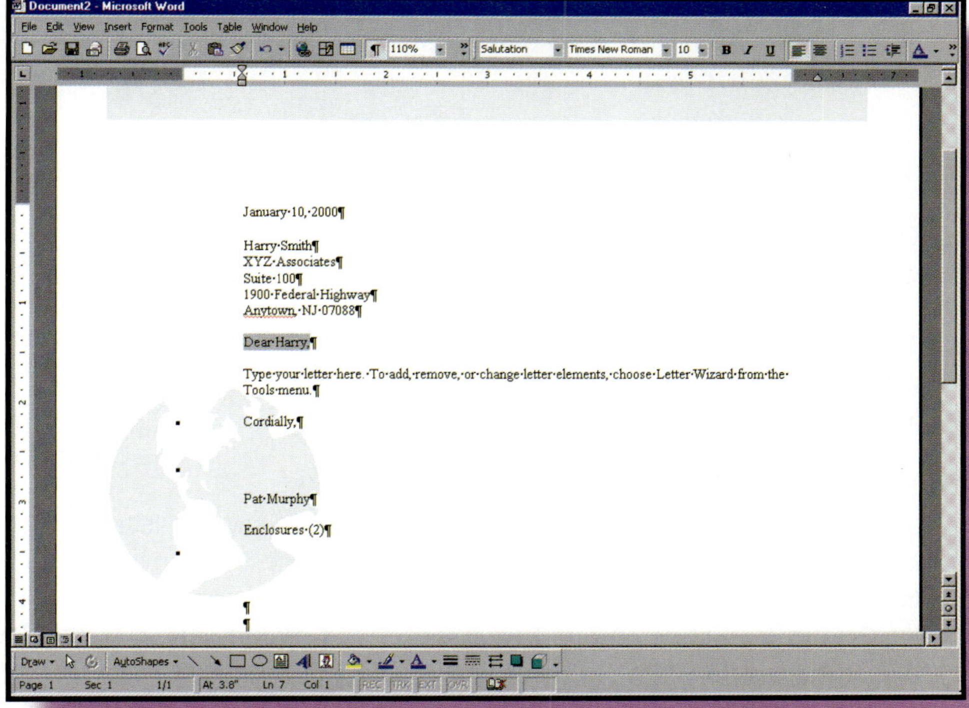

1. To open the New dialog box, click the **File** menu and click the **New** command.

2. To start the Letter Wizard, click the **Letters & Faxes** tab, and click the **Letter Wizard.** Word displays a sample letter and a dialog box. Click the **Send One Letter** button, and click the **OK** button.

3. To enter the letter format information, click the **Date Line** box, if necessary, to display the current date. Click the **Choose a Page Design** drop-down button, click **Contemporary Letter**, and click the **Next** button.

4. To enter recipient information, type **Harry Smith** in the Recipient's Name box, press the **Tab** key, and type the delivery address shown below. Press the **Enter** key at the end of each line.

```
XYZ Associates
Suite 100
1900 Federal Highway
Anytown, NJ 07088
```

5. Change the salutation to the Informal option, and click the **Next** button.

6. To skip the Step 3 dialog box because you will not use any of those options in this letter, click the **Next** button.

7. To enter the sender information, select the sender's name in the box if any, type your name, press the **Tab** key, and type your home address. Be sure there is a check in the **Omit In The Return Address** box, click the **Complimentary Closing** drop-down

button, and click **Cordially.** Be sure there is a check in the **Enclosures** box, and set the number in the spin box to **2.**

8. To display the letter, click the **Finish** button.

9. To enter the body of the letter, select the text in the paragraph that begins **Type your letter here,** and type the paragraphs shown below, pressing the **Enter** key only once between paragraphs. Don't worry about any wavy green lines that appear under words or sentences. If any wavy red lines appear under your words, check to make sure that you've spelled them correctly.

```
Thank you for contacting me
about your computer needs. I
am glad to hear the computer
systems you purchased from us
last year are doing so well
for you! I will be glad to drop
by to see your new offices.

We can discuss the network
upgrade you will need to put
more systems online. I enclose
some literature on the newest
NetFare product. We have had
excellent results with this
product and I think you will
like its affordability.

I will call you early next week
to set up a time when we can
meet to look over the literature
and your requirements.
```

10. To save the letter, click the **Save** button on the Standard toolbar, be sure your folder is displayed in the **Save in** box, type **Letter Wizard,** and click the **Save** button in the dialog box.

Using Print Preview

Use the Print Preview button on the Standard toolbar or the Print Preview command on the File menu to preview entire pages of your document before printing. You can zoom in and out to see different magnifications of your document and even edit the document in this view.

Word displays the current page of your document when you click the Print Preview button or command. If you or another user has not changed the default setting, you should see a one-page display like the one in Figure 2.8.

Did You Know?

You save time and paper when you use Print Preview because you reduce the number of times you print a document before getting exactly the look you want.

FIGURE 2.8

Use Print Preview to see your document before printing.

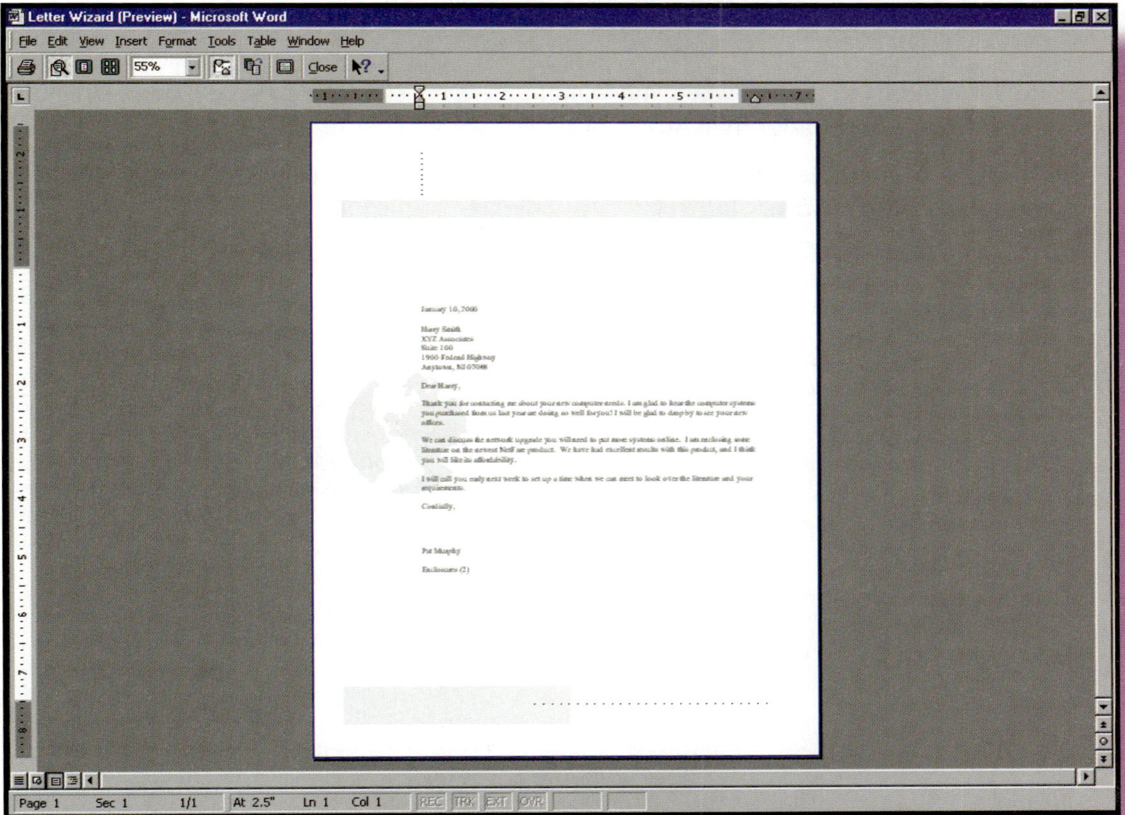

The Print Preview toolbar at the top of the Print Preview screen has many useful tools you can use to work with your document while preparing it for printing (see Figure 2.9).

■ Use the Print button to print the document with default settings.

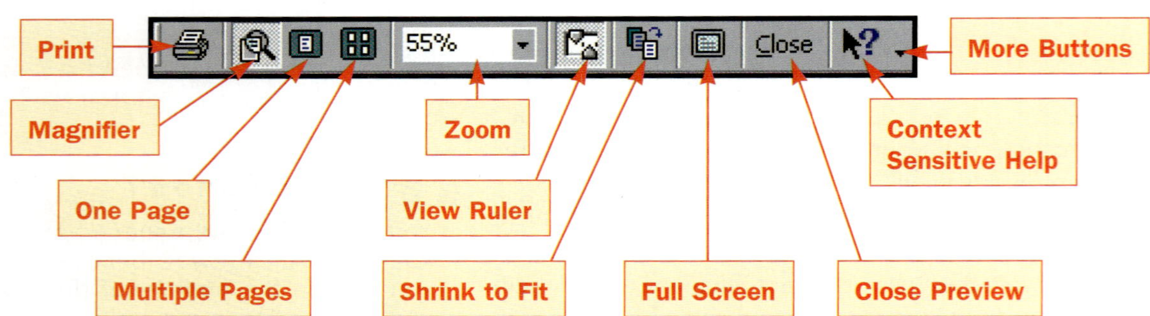

FIGURE 2.9
The Print Preview toolbar has useful tools.

- Use the Magnifier button to zoom in on an area of your document. Notice the Magnifier button is automatically selected (its button looks pushed in).

- Use the One Page button if more than one page is displayed and you would prefer to see just one page at a time.

- Use the Multiple Pages button when you want to see more than one page at a time. Drag over the grid and click the bottom right box to designate the number of pages.

- Use the Zoom box to select a greater or lesser magnification. You can enter a figure or choose one from the drop-down list.

- Use the View Ruler button to display the ruler to change the page layout.

- Use the Shrink to Fit button to make a document with a short paragraph on a page by itself fit on the previous page.

- Use the Full Screen button to display just the page and the toolbar.

You can zoom in on an area of your document by moving the magnifier to the area you want to see and clicking. To return to the original magnification, click again.

You have access to some menu commands while you are in the Print Preview screen. For instance, you can save your document while using Print Preview.

Hot Tips

If you want to edit a document (and do not see the I-beam), click the Magnifier button to turn magnification off. When you see the I-beam, you are in edit mode and can position the insertion point in your document.

STEP-BY-STEP 2.2

1. To preview your document, click the **Print Preview** button on the Standard toolbar.

2. To zoom in on the area at the top left of the page, point to the location, and click with the magnifying pointer.

3. To turn off the magnifying pointer and see the I-beam on the screen, click the **Magnifier** button.

4. To center the letter attractively on the page, click the I-beam just before the date,

and press the **Enter** key twice to move the text down.

5. To leave edit mode, click the **Magnifier** button.

6. To zoom back to the original display, click the **magnifying pointer** on the letter.

7. To hide all but the Print Preview toolbar, click the **Full Screen** button.

8. To return to the original display, click the **Close Full Screen** button.

9. To return to print layout view, click the **Close** button on the Print Preview toolbar.

10. To save the document, click the **Save** button on the Standard toolbar.

Using the Print Command

You can use the Print command on the File menu to access the Print dialog box (see Figure 2.10). You can use the Print button on the standard toolbar to print a document with default settings without opening the Print dialog box.

FIGURE 2.10
The Print dialog box provides various printing options.

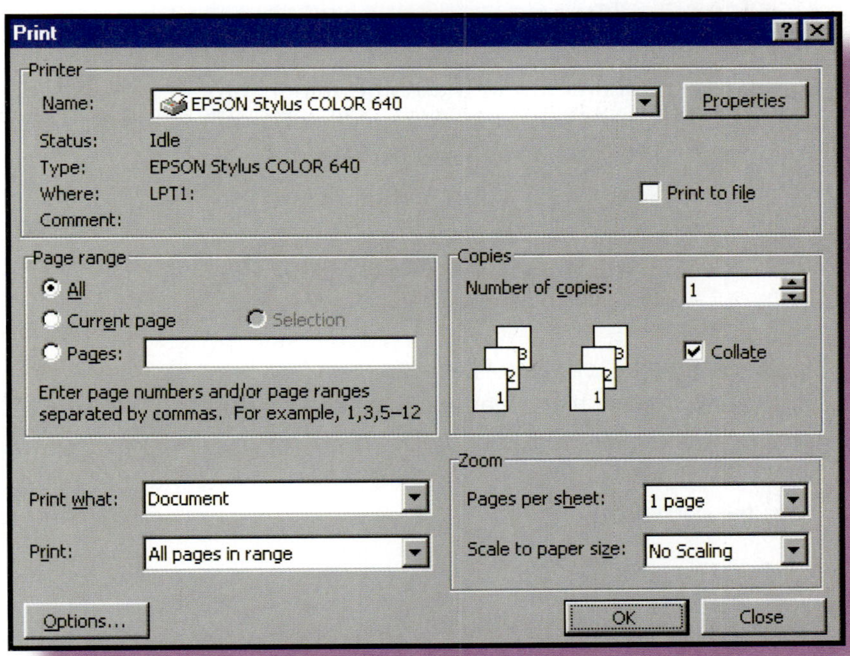

In the Print dialog box, you can do the following:

■ Choose the printer you want to use.

■ Print to a file if you need to print a document from a computer that does not have Microsoft Word.

- Print either all or specified parts of the document. Type **1-10** to print pages 1 through 10. Type **1,10** to print pages 1 and 10. Type **5-** to print pages 5 through the end of the document.

- Specify the number of copies to print.

- Collate copies of documents.

- Print the document, Document Properties, Comments, or other information you will learn about in later lessons.

- Print all pages in a range, or print only odd or even pages in the range.

- Use the Options button to display a dialog box that lets you make other decisions about how your document will be printed. The Reverse print order option is very useful if you find your printer prints long documents with the first page at the bottom of the pile.

- Print one page per sheet through 16 pages per sheet and scale to various paper sizes.

The Properties button displays options pertaining to your selected printer.

When Word is printing your document, you will see a printer icon at the right side of the taskbar. Double-click the icon to display the dialog box in which you can see the print jobs in the queue or cancel the print job. To cancel the print job, select the document, open the Document menu, and choose Cancel Printing.

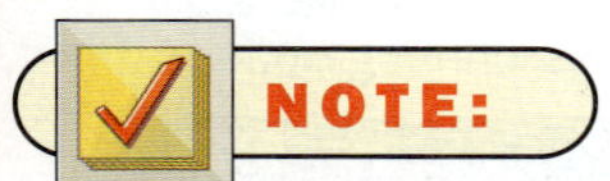

NOTE:

To print several documents in the same folder without opening them yourself, click the Open button, hold the Ctrl key and click the name of each document, click the Commands & Settings button, and click Print.

S TEP-BY-STEP 2.3

1. To print your letter, click the **File** menu and click **Print.** Notice the options you have available in the Print dialog box. Click **OK.**

2. Save the document.

If you use an electronic personal address book, you can use the Address Book button to enter either a delivery or a return address.

Creating an Envelope

Word makes creating and printing envelopes easy. You use the Envelopes and Labels command on the Tools menu to open the Envelopes and Labels dialog box (see Figure 2.11).

You can save time by selecting a name and address before choosing the command.

The Add to Document button lets you add the envelope to the beginning of the document so you can print the two together.

FIGURE 2.11

The Envelopes and Labels dialog box lets you create envelopes easily.

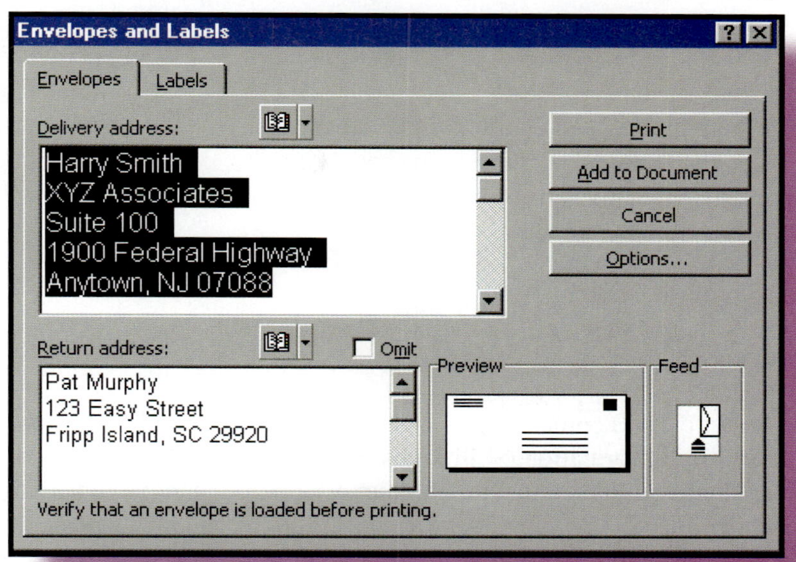

Use the Options button to change the envelope size, add bar codes for the Postal Service, and change the position of and fonts for the addresses. You will learn more about fonts in a later lesson.

Word includes an Envelope Wizard in the New dialog box to help you create envelopes.

Display the Label tab to enter an address for printing on either a single label or on an entire sheet of labels. You will learn more about labels in Lesson 8.

Hot Tips

Unless you expect to mail this letter to the addressee again, there does not seem to be a need to save the envelope with the document.

STEP-BY-STEP ▷ 2.4

1. To insert Harry Smith's name and address in the envelope, select his name and address.

2. To display the Envelopes and Labels dialog box, click the **Tools** menu, and click the **Envelopes and Labels** command. Click the **Envelopes** tab. Notice Harry's name and address from the letter are already in place.

3. To display the **Labels** tab, click it.

4. To return to the **Envelopes** tab, click it.

5. To use a return address, click in the Return Address box, and type your name and address.

6. To see that you can change the envelope size, add bar codes for the Postal Service, and change fonts for and positions of the delivery and return addresses, click the **Options** button.

7. To return to the Envelopes and Labels dialog box, click the **Cancel** button.

(continued on next page)

6 1

8. To see if you have to insert an envelope in your printer before you click the Print button, read and follow the directions on the bottom line of the dialog box. Notice also the instructions on how you are to feed the envelope.

9. To print the envelope, click the **Print** button. If you changed the return address, you will be prompted to save the new address. Click the **No** button.

Using Web Tools

Word 2000 comes with a wide variety of tools and features that can help you connect to the Internet, find information of all kinds, and even insert hyperlinks directly in your documents so the reader can jump to another file on your system, to a site on your intranet, or to the Internet.

The reader must have access to the hyperlink addresses you insert in documents, or the hyperlinks will be useless. You should not, for instance, put a hyperlink to a document on your drive to which the reader does not have access.

Using the Web Toolbar

You can use the Toolbars command on the View menu to display or to turn off the Web toolbar (see Figure 2.12).

The Web toolbar contains the following buttons to help you easily negotiate the Web:

■ Use the Back and Forward buttons to move back to a previous site or forward to the following site.

■ Use the Stop Current Jump button to cancel a jump. The button is especially useful if it seems to be taking a very long time to display a page.

FIGURE 2.12
The Web toolbar helps you move around and work with the World Wide Web.

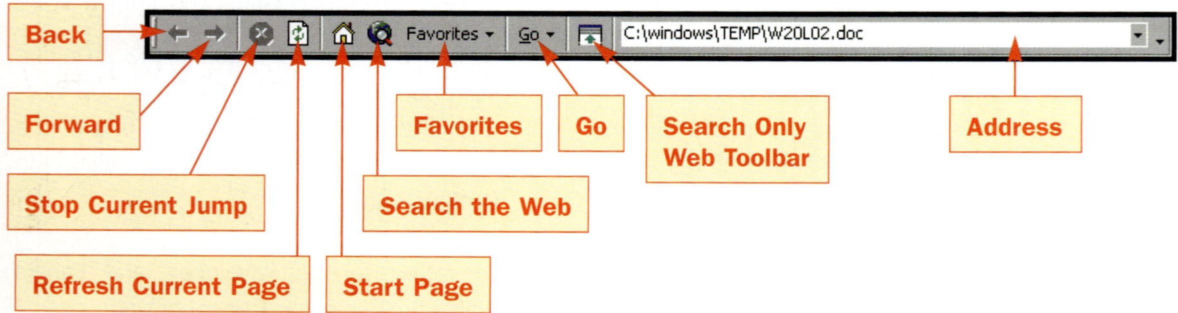

- Use the Refresh Current Page button to update the current page by reloading it.

- Use the Start Page button to go to a starting page of your choosing. Use the Set Start Page command on the Go button drop-down list to designate a start page.

- Use the Search the Web button to access the World Wide Web. From there you can use one of the search engines to find information about a subject of your choosing.

- Use the Favorites button to return to a site you have added to your favorites list or to enter a site as a favorite.

- Use the Go drop-down list to access some of the Web toolbar commands as well as to set the start pages for the Web itself and for searching the Web.

- Use the Show Only Web Toolbar button to turn off the other Word toolbars and display only the Web toolbar.

- Use the Address box to enter a URL to go directly to a Web site or page of your choosing or to a page on your intranet or a document on your system.

> **INTERNET** Different search engines search Web sites differently so you need to be aware how the engines available from your Internet service provider work.

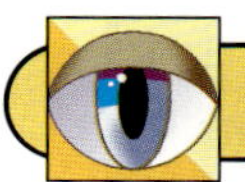

IMPORTANT:

Most Internet service providers (ISPs) have software that will disconnect you after a particular period of inactivity.

S TEP-BY-STEP ▷ 2.5

1. To display the Web toolbar if it is not already on your screen, click the **View** menu, click **Toolbars,** and click **Web.**

2. To display the Microsoft Office home page, click the **Address** box on the Web toolbar, type **http://www.microsoft.com,** press the **Enter** key, sign in, and connect to your Internet service provider, if necessary. Read some of Microsoft's latest news.

3. To return to your Word document, click the **Microsoft Word** document button on the taskbar. If you are asked to disconnect, click the **No** button.

4. To access the Web for a search, click the **Search the Web** button on the Web toolbar, select the **Find a Web Page** option. Type **Microsoft Office 2000** in the **Find a Web Page** box, click a search engine, and then click a hyperlink to see one of the category matches the search engine displays.

5. To return to the Word document, click the **Microsoft Word** document button on the taskbar.

Using the Highlight Button

The Highlight button on the More Buttons button on the Formatting toolbar lets you mark text so it is highlighted and stands out from the surrounding text. This feature is particularly useful for when someone is reviewing a document online. The recipient can easily see important passages when they are highlighted. The default color for highlighting is yellow, but you can change the color by clicking the drop-down button to the right of the Highlight button and choosing another color.

To add highlighting, select the text to be highlighted, and click the Highlight button. You can also click the Highlight button, drag the highlight pointer over the text to be highlighted, and click the Highlight button again or press the Esc key to turn off the highlighting.

To remove highlighting that's been added to text, select the highlighted text, click the Highlight button drop-down button, and click None.

Creating Hyperlinks

You have already learned that hyperlinks are underlined or bordered words or graphics that have Web or other document addresses embedded in them. You can use hyperlinks to add additional or supporting information to Word documents that can be read online. The hyperlink destination (link) can be to another location in the same document, to a file on your hard drive, to a file on a company intranet, or to a Web page on the Internet. You can even use hyperlinks to jump to multimedia files, such as videos and sounds.

When you click a hyperlink, Word automatically displays the Web toolbar. You can use its Back button to return to the original location in the Word document.

IMPORTANT:

You must have access to the hyperlink's destination to access it. For instance, to access a destination on the Internet, you must have a modem and an Internet service provider.

To insert a hyperlink in a document, select the position, text, or object you want to display as the hyperlink. Then use either the Insert Hyperlink button on the Standard toolbar or the Hyperlink command on the Insert menu to display the Insert Hyperlink dialog box (see Figure 2.13).

To enter the path for the file or the URL (address) for the Web site you want to jump to, use the Browse For button or select from the list of files. Then enter any subaddress (Word bookmark, Excel range, Access database object, or PowerPoint slide number) you want to specify.

You can also insert a hyperlink by simply typing a URL in your document. Word recognizes it as a hyperlink and formats it automatically.

To delete a hyperlink, right-click the hyperlink, click Hyperlink on the shortcut menu, and click Remove Hyperlink.

Type or select an address for a hyperlink in this dialog box.

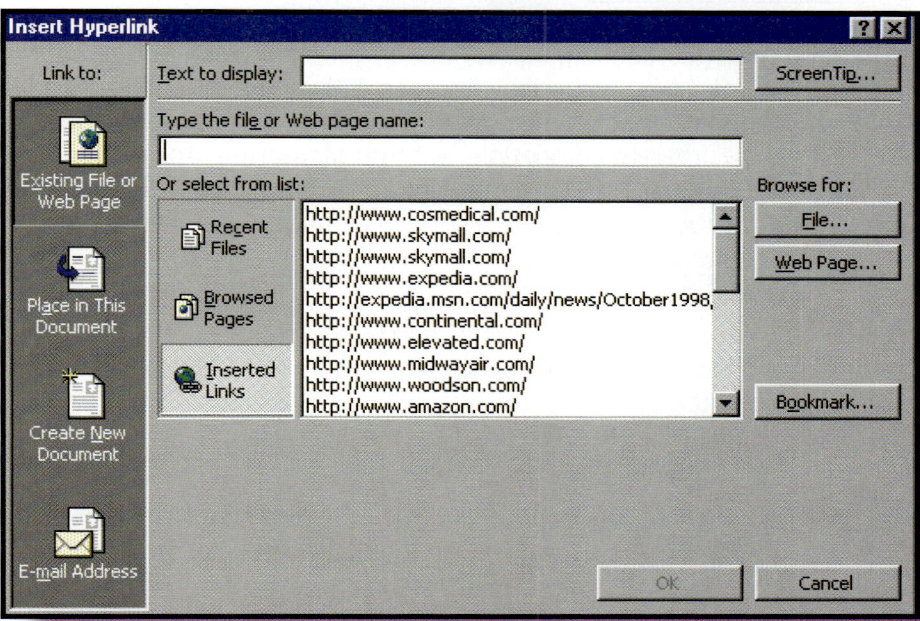

STEP-BY-STEP ▷ 2.6

1. To add highlighting to the second sentence in the first paragraph in the body of the letter, hold the **Ctrl** key and click anywhere in the sentence, click the **More Buttons** button on the Formatting toolbar and then click the **Highlight** button.

2. To insert a sentence containing a hyperlink, position the I-beam at the end of the first paragraph in the body of the letter and type **In the meantime you can visit http://www.microsoft.com to get more information about Microsoft.** Notice Word recognizes the address as a URL and adds hyperlink formatting.

Sending Documents Electronically

You can use the commands on the File menu's Send To submenu to send an e-mail message in the "universal" HTML format. A message can include animated graphics, multimedia objects, and anything else you can put on a Web page.

Did You Know?

HTML is an acronym for Hypertext Markup Language—the universal language or file format used on the Web.

To send an e-mail message in HTML format from Word, you need Word 2000 and either Outlook 2000 or Outlook Express 5.0 or later. To send an e-mail or route a document as an attachment in Word format, you need Word 2000 *and* either a 32-bit e-mail program compatible with the Messaging Application Programming Interface (MAPI) *or* a 16-bit e-mail program compatible with Vendor Independent Messaging (VIM).

To view an e-mail message or document sent in HTML format, the recipient needs a Web browser or e-mail program that can read documents in HTML format.

To view a document sent as an attachment in Word format, recipients need Word 97 or later.

You can use the commands on the File menu's Send To submenu to deliver documents electronically (see Figure 2.14).

When you use the Mail Recipient or Routing Recipient commands, your document is the e-mail message (see Figure 2.15). Your document is sent in HTML format, and the recipient does not need to have Word installed to view your message.

When you use the Mail Recipient (as Attachment) command, your document is sent as a Word document and an icon is displayed in the title bar (see Figure 2.16). The recipient simply double-clicks the document icon to open it. The recipient needs Word 97 or later installed.

FIGURE 2.14

Notice the commands on the Send To submenu.

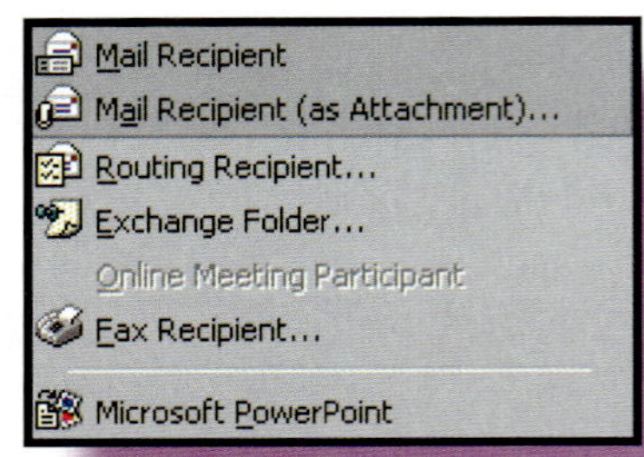

FIGURE 2.15

Your document is the message.

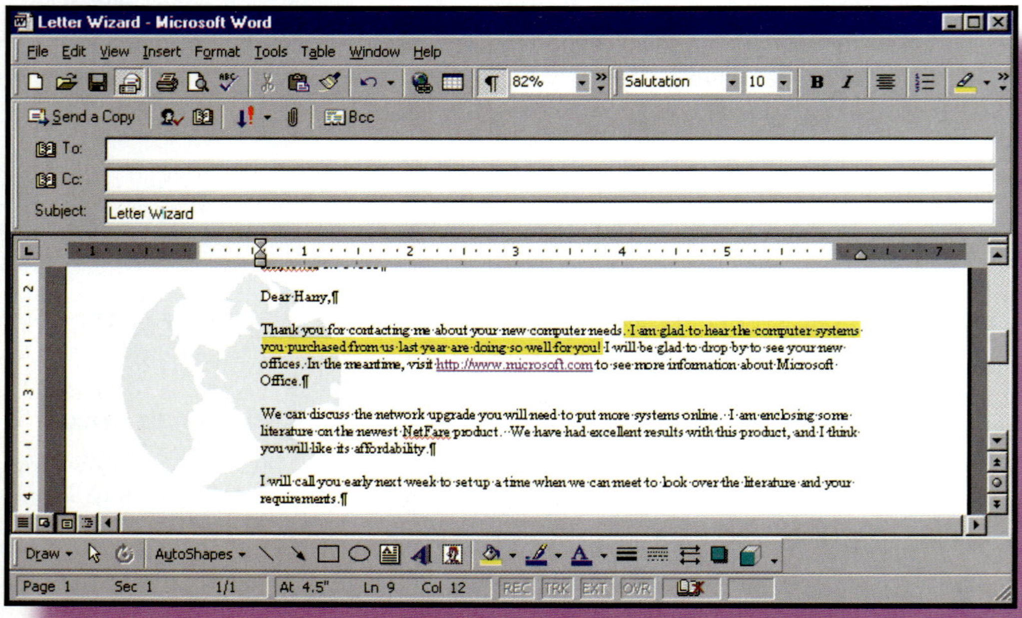

FIGURE 2.16
Your document appears as an icon in the message.

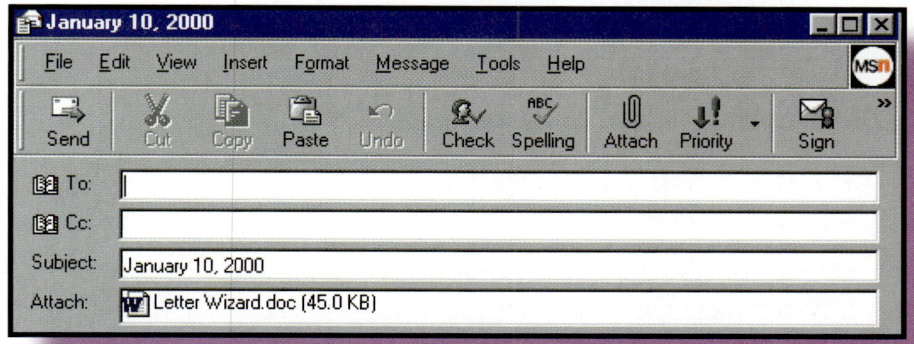

You can use the following commands on the Send To submenu:

- Use the Mail Recipient or the Mail Recipient (as Attachment) command to send a document to an individual or group of individuals. The document is sent at the same time. You enter the recipients' e-mail addresses, the subject, additional documents, and a message. Microsoft recommends you use this option when you want to distribute a document quickly to a specific list of people.

- Use the Routing Recipient command to send a document to a group of recipients, each of whom will receive the document in the order you specify. When a person finishes reviewing and adding comments to the document and clicks the Send To command, the Next Routing Recipient appears on the submenu. When the last person finishes with the document, the document is returned to you. You will learn more about reviewers' comments in Lesson 6.

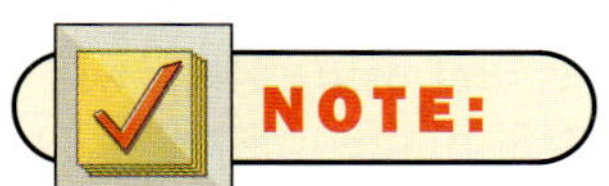 **NOTE:**

If you are saving different versions of the document within the document itself, save a separate file containing the version of the file you send to others for review.

- Use the Exchange Folder command to post a document to a Microsoft Exchange public folder so others can access the document over the network. You might use this command when you have a document, such as a company manual, that needs to be available to many network users.

- Use the Online Meeting Participant command if you are the host of an online meeting. You will learn more about online meetings later in this book.

- Use the Fax Recipient command to send the open document via fax. A Word wizard walks you through the steps necessary for sending the fax. Be sure you enter any numbers necessary to access an outside line or to make a long distance call when you enter fax numbers.

 **Did You Know?**

Click the e-mail button on the Standard toolbar if you decide not to use the e-mail options after choosing the command.

■ Use the Microsoft PowerPoint command when you want to send the document as a PowerPoint presentation.

1. To send the open letter as an e-mail message, click the **File** menu, click the **Send To** command, and click the **Mail Recipient** command.

2. To send the letter to yourself via e-mail, type your e-mail address in the To box, and click the **Send a Copy** button. You may have to reconnect to your Internet service provider.

3. To save and close the Word document, click the **Save** button, and then click the document's **Close** button. Word saves the e-mail information, and you can access it by clicking the **e-mail** button on the Standard toolbar whenever the document is open.

4. To check on how an e-mail message works, wait until the mail has been sent and received. Then open the message.

5. Close your mail application, disconnect from your ISP if necessary, and return to Word.

Summary

You have now learned how to use a Word template to create a document, how to use the Print Preview feature, how to print documents and envelopes, how to use Word's Web tools, and how to send documents electronically.

Try the exercises on the following pages to test how well you remember what you have learned. Once again, remember that going back through parts of the first three lessons and using Help will reinforce learning. Good luck!

LESSON 2 REVIEW QUESTIONS

TRUE / FALSE

Circle the T if the statement is true. Circle the F if it is false.

T F   1. You can use the New button to create a document using a template.

T F   2. The Blank Document is the only template you can use with the New button.

T F   3. You can edit a Word template to suit your needs.

T F   4. You cannot edit your document in Print Preview.

T F   **5.** A wizard takes you step-by-step through creating a document.

T **F**   **6.** You cannot use any menu commands while in Print Preview.

T F   **7.** You have more options available when you use a wizard than you do when you use a template.

T F   **8.** You can cancel printing.

T F   **9.** You must have a compatible system to send documents electronically.

T F   **10.** You can type a Web URL and Word will automatically format it as a hyperlink.

COMPLETION

Complete the following sentences by writing the correct word or words in the blanks provided.

1. The Envelopes and Labels command on the _Tools_ menu makes creating envelopes and labels easy.

2. You can use the _Shrink to fit_ button in Print Preview to squeeze a little extra text onto a page.

3. You can use the _Multiple Page_ button when you want to see more than one page in Print Preview.

4. You must use the _New_ command on the File menu to create a document with a wizard or template.

5. The _blank_ template is a general-purpose template for any document.

6. When in Print Preview, you can use the _Magnifier_ button to enlarge an area of the document.

7. To view only a single page when you are in Print Preview, click the _One Page_ button.

8. A(n) _Wizard_ gives you step-by-step instructions for creating a particular type of document.

9. The _Options_ button lets you change envelope size, add bar codes, or select new fonts for the envelope text.

10. You can use the _Routing Recipient_ / _Send To_ command to specify that a document should be electronically routed to a list of people.

PROJECT 2A

To practice what you've learned in this lesson, complete the following project:

1. Use Word's Memo Wizard to send a memo to yourself, from you, using the subject Learning Word, and with a copy to your instructor.

2. Write a short paragraph about how you feel about learning Word.

3. Save as Memo Wizard, print, and close the document.

4. Send your instructor a copy via e-mail. If that is not possible in your environment, print a copy for the instructor.

Extra Challenges

Search Help for information on hyperlinks, and print copies of any information you find. Then discuss with your classmates the information you found.

PROJECT 2B

To practice what you've learned in this lesson, complete the following project:

1. Use Word's Search the Web button on the Web toolbar to access a search engine. Search for information on a topic of interest to you. Copy the URL for the page that most interests you.

2. Use the Letter Wizard to prepare a letter to a friend who has an e-mail address and who shares your interests. In the body of the letter, describe how you found the information on your topic of interest. Insert a hyperlink in the letter so your friend can also access the Web site. Save and print the letter.

CRITICAL THINKING ACTIVITY

Edit the Contemporary Letter template to make a template with stationery for your personal use. Replace the company name at the top of the template with your initials. After you have inserted your personal information, choose the Save As command on the File menu. On the Save As Type drop-down list, select Document Template. Now you can use this template whenever you want to write a letter.

WORKING WITH BASIC WRITING TOOLS

Introduction

You have learned to create and print documents and to do some basic text editing. Now you will work with some of the Word features that make proofreading and protecting documents easier. You will check spelling, correct grammatical errors, and find synonyms. You will also use the AutoCorrect and AutoText features and insert symbols. In addition, you will learn to put a password on a document to ensure that others cannot open a confidential file.

Automating Text Entry

Word includes a number of features to help you with your writing. The AutoText and AutoCorrect features not only save time but also ensure consistency and accuracy throughout documents.

Using AutoText

You can use the AutoText command on the Insert menu to display the AutoText submenu. You can choose to store or access text and graphics you use often (see Figure 3.1). In addition to AutoText entries you add, Word includes a number of AutoText entries that you can insert in your documents.

You can insert an existing AutoText entry in your document by selecting it on the submenus Word displays when you choose the AutoText command (see Figure 3.2).

You can add, delete, or insert AutoText entries in the
AutoCorrect dialog box.

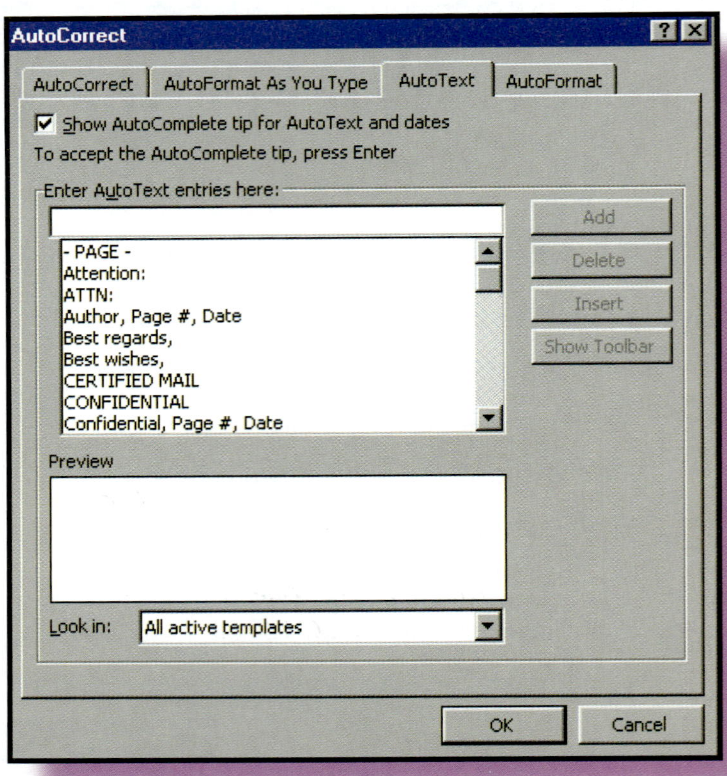

Notice the number of letter Closings displayed
on the closing submenu.

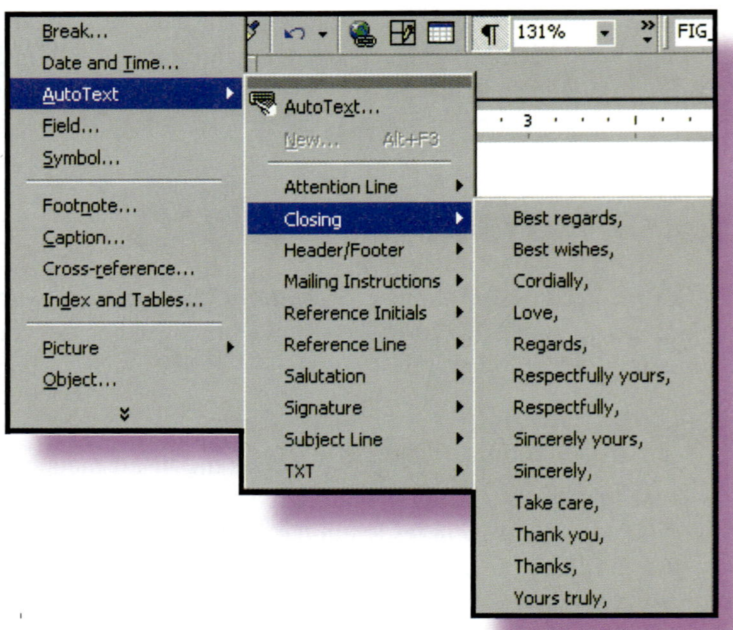

7 2

You can also create and store your own AutoText entries. If you store a paragraph mark with your AutoText entry, the text will take on the formatting in that paragraph mark. Otherwise, it will take the formatting of the paragraph into which you insert it. To store an entry, type the entry, select the entire entry, choose AutoText on the Insert menu, and choose New on the submenu. You can use the selected text as a name for the entry or you can type a new name.

To edit a long AutoText entry, insert the AutoText entry in a document, make the changes, select the entry, and choose the New command on the AutoText submenu. Give the entry the same name as the original entry.

To delete an AutoText entry, select it on the AutoText tab, and use the Delete command button.

Word makes the AutoText entries available to all documents by storing them in all active templates, including the Normal template when you create the entry, unless you change the information in the Look In box. If you want to limit the entry to certain documents, be sure to specify a template at the time you create the AutoText entry.

A feature called AutoComplete is associated with AutoText. AutoComplete lets Word complete some common words or phrases as well as AutoText entries. For example, if you type **sept,** Word will display a ScreenTip above the letters suggesting the word **September.** Press the Enter key to accept the AutoComplete item or continue typing to ignore it.

FIGURE 3.3

Notice the ScreenTip for December.

Did You Know?

As you type the first few characters in your name, a ScreenTip for your entire name appears. Press the Enter key to use the AutoText entry or continue typing if you want to enter something different from your name.

STEP-BY-STEP ▷ 3.1

1. Open **Step-by-Step 3-1 AutoT.**

2. To add space above the inside address, press the **Enter** key ten times.

3. To see how AutoComplete works with months of the year, position the insertion point at the paragraph mark four blank lines above the inside address, and type **Dece.** When the ScreenTip appears, press the **Enter** key, type a space, and then type **13, 2000.**

4. To add the entire closing for the letter beginning with the word **Sincerely** as an AutoText item, drag in the left margin until all six lines are selected, click the **Insert** menu, click **AutoText** on the expanded menu, and click **New** on the submenu.

5. To give the closing a name that will be easy to remember, type **Mary's Closing** and click **OK.**

6. To create a new document, click the **New** button.

7. To enter the AutoText entry, click the **Insert** menu, click the **AutoText** command, click **Normal** on the submenu, and click **Mary's Closing** on the second submenu.

(continued on next page)

8. To insert another AutoText entry, press the **Enter** key, type **Cord,** notice the ScreenTip, and press the **Enter** key.

9. To close the new document without saving changes, click its **Close** button and click **No** when asked to save changes.

10. To delete **Mary's Closing** as an AutoText entry, click the **Insert** menu, click **AutoText,**

click **AutoText** on the submenu, scroll through the list of entries and click **Mary's Closing,** click the **Delete** button, and click the **OK** button.

11. To close **Step-by-Step 3-1 AutoT** without saving changes, click its **Close** button, and click the **No** button when asked to save changes.

Using AutoCorrect

The AutoCorrect command on the Tools menu automatically corrects many common typing errors, such as typing **the** for **the.** As you can see in the AutoCorrect tab in Figure 3.4, AutoCorrect replaces typed characters with symbols and corrects common capitalization errors. Because the feature is so much faster to use than AutoText, you might want to consider using it for text you often type.

FIGURE 3.4
AutoCorrect automatically corrects frequently misspelled words and offers other spelling and capitalization options.

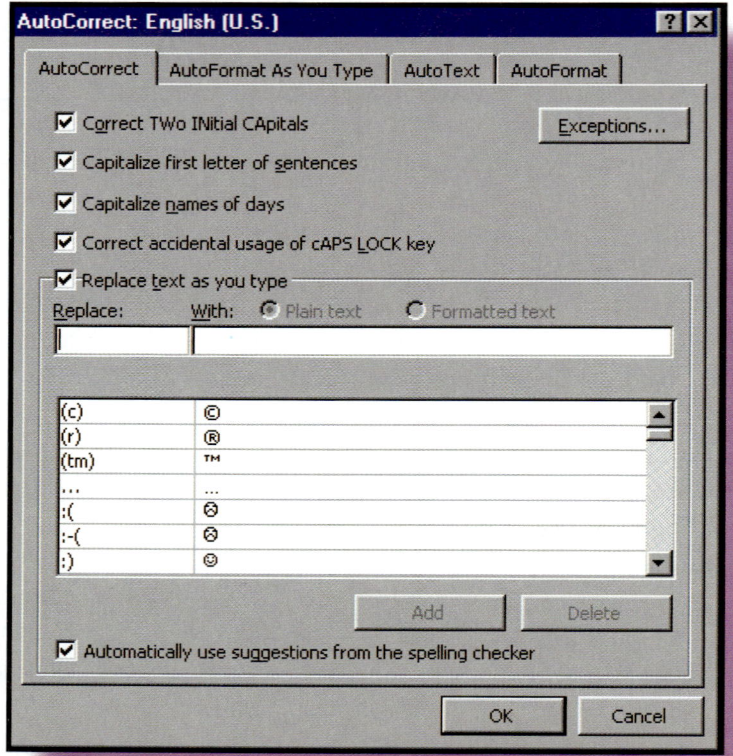

You could, for instance, create an entry in AutoCorrect that replaces your initials with your name. Then, every time you type the initials followed by a space, Word automatically enters your full name. If you type your initials followed by 's, Word forms the possessive of your name.

NOTE:

If your initials are also a common word or abbreviation, don't use this shortcut.

Hot Tips

If I were to have my initials, which are p.m., replaced by Pat Murphy, I could very likely see things like 4 Pat Murphy instead of 4 p.m. in documents. If your initials might cause a similar problem, you could use any letters. I would use pz because it is not likely those letters would cause any problems.

Use the Exceptions button and check Automatically Add Words To List option to store items you don't want corrected. You can also press the Backspace key to remove an entire correction and retype the word to add your correction to the exceptions list. You can turn off AutoCorrect features by removing check marks from their option boxes.

Word can automatically correct two initial caps, capitalize names of days, and correct accidental usage of Caps Lock.

The list at the bottom of the dialog box contains the characters and words that Word changes automatically. You can add words that you commonly misspell to have Word correct your spelling as you type.

Did You Know?

If you find you often type the same word incorrectly, you can add the word to the AutoCorrect list.

You can opt to replace the text you type with plain or formatted text. Most times you will probably want to replace the text with plain text, so it uses the formatting of the text around it.

To delete an AutoCorrect entry, click it on the AutoCorrect dialog box list and press the Delete key.

S TEP-BY-STEP ▷ 3.2

1. To create a new document, click the **New** button.

2. To display the AutoCorrect dialog box, click the **Tools** menu, and then click the **AutoCorrect** command.

3. To set your options to match those shown in Figure 3.4, be sure the AutoCorrect tab is displayed and click any option box that does not have a check mark.

4. To see some of the words that AutoCorrect changes, scroll through the list.

5. To add an entry to the list so AutoCorrect will replace your entry (your initials) with your complete name, type your initials in the **Replace** box, click the insertion point in the With box, type your full name, click the **Add** button, and then click the **Close** button.

(continued on next page)

6. To see AutoCorrect enter your full name, type the initials you entered followed by a space. Notice Word entered your name.

7. To remove the AutoCorrect entry, click the **Tools** menu, click the **AutoCorrect** com-mand, type your initials in the Replace box to display the area where your name is positioned, click your entry, click the **Delete** button, and click the **OK** button.

8. Close the document without saving.

Checking Spelling and Grammar

You can check both spelling and grammar by selecting the Spelling and Grammar command on the Tools menu or using the Spelling and Grammar button on the Standard toolbar. You already set the option for Word to check spelling and grammar as you type.

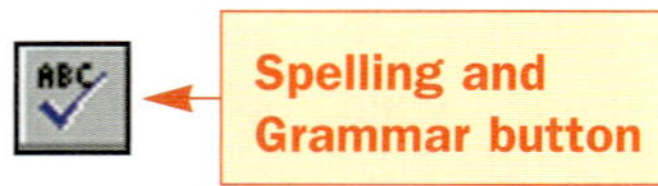

Word compares the words you type to those in its dictionary and to its rules of grammar. Word marks words that may be misspelled with a wavy red line. If Word detects a grammatical construction that does not conform to rules of grammar, it adds a wavy green underline to the word or words.

You can correct spelling and grammatical errors in two ways:

- Choose the Spelling and Grammar command on the Tools menu, or use the Spelling and Grammar button on the Standard toolbar to display the dialog box shown in Figure 3.5.

- Right-click on the underlined word or words to see a shortcut menu listing suggested corrections.

Word's main dictionary contains most common words, including country names, names of many U.S. cities, some company names, and many personal names. You probably use words that are not in Word's main dictionary. You can add those words to a custom dictionary so Word does not flag them each time.

FIGURE 3.5
The Spelling and Grammar feature checks your document for spelling errors.

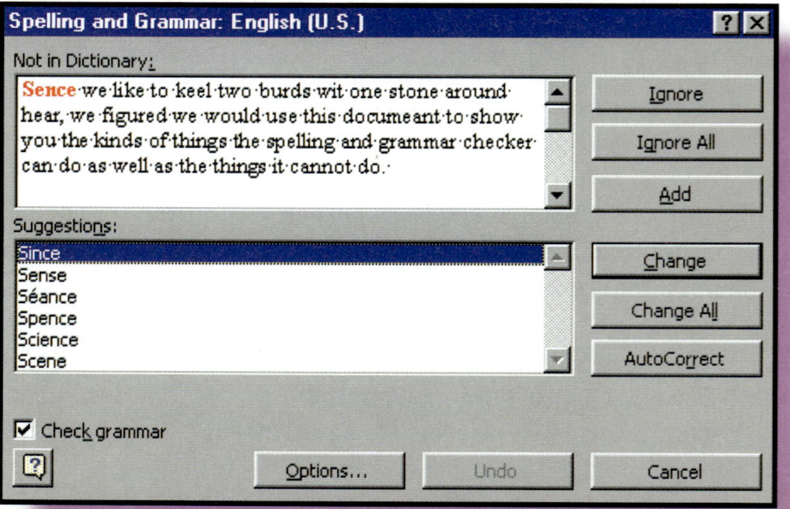

A word that is not in the dictionary appears in red type in the Not in Dictionary text box, which also displays the portion of the text where the word is located. A possible grammatical error appears in green type in the text box. Suggestions for corrections appear in the Suggestions box.

Use the Change button to replace an error or the Change All button to replace all instances of the same error. You also can choose to ignore the word or phrase or ignore all occurrences of the word or phrase.

When you use the Spelling and Grammar command or button, Word checks the entire document from the insertion point forward, and then works from the beginning of the document to the insertion point. To check only a portion of your document, select the area before starting the check.

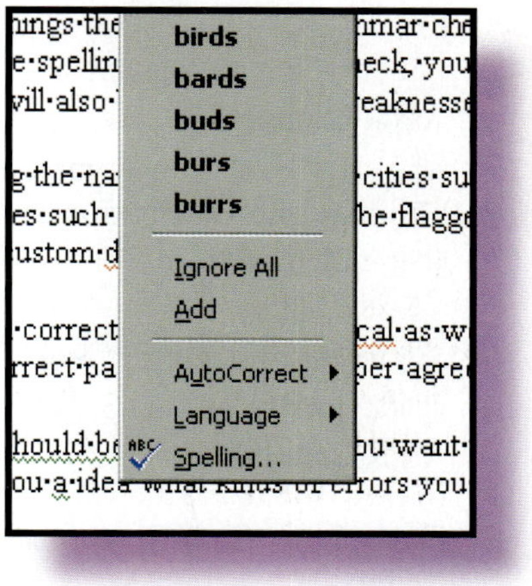

IMPORTANT:

Remember the Spelling and Grammar feature does not eliminate the need to proofread a document. If a word that you misspelled is another English word, the spelling feature will not notice it. Likewise, the grammar feature is not foolproof. While it finds many common errors, the Spelling and Grammar feature does not always understand the context of the text and may suggest inappropriate corrections. Be sure to look at suggestions carefully before you decide to accept them.

If you choose Add, Word adds the word to your custom dictionary.

If you use the Options button in the Spelling and Grammar dialog box and check the box in the Grammar section asking Word to show readability statistics, Word displays readability statistics when it finishes checking grammar. You can use these statistics to determine how easily a reader can understand your document.

You can change the writing style for a document in the Options dialog box on the Spelling & Grammar tab so Word checks different kinds of grammatical elements.

Concept Builders

If you are using Microsoft Office, any word you add to a custom dictionary in any of the Office programs is available for all programs.

FIGURE 3.6

You can see red and green lines and a shortcut menu.

Teamwork

If you are working on a network, you can share with other users a dictionary with words commonly used in your organization.

S TEP-BY-STEP 3.3

1. Open **Step-by-Step 3-3 Spell.** Notice the many wavy red and green underlines.

2. To begin checking spelling and grammar, click the **Spelling and Grammar** button on the Standard toolbar.

(continued on next page)

3. To correct the word **Sence** with Word's first selection, click the **Change** button.

4. To correct the word **burds,** click the word **birds** in the Suggestions box, and click **Change.** Notice Word did not select the words **keel, wit,** or **hear** as being misspelled. Those words are in the dictionary.

5. To enter the correct spelling for **documeant,** click **Change.**

6. To enter the correct spelling for **strenghts,** click **Change.**

7. To enter the correct spelling for **awase,** click **aware** in the Suggestions box, and click **Change**.

8. To correct the incorrect form of the word **its,** click **Change.**

9. To have Word ignore all occurrences of the proper name **Janowitcz** in this document, click **Ignore All.** (If Word does not display **Janowitcz** as being misspelled, someone has already used this exercise on your computer.)

10. To enter the correct spelling for **dictionery,** click **Change.**

11. To enter the correct spelling for **sicological,** select **sicological,** type **psychological,** and click **Change.**

12. To delete the repetition of the word **as,** click the **Delete** button in the Spelling dialog box.

13. To correct the passive voice shown in green, click **Change.**

14. To accept the suggested **an** instead of the **a,** click **Change.**

15. To respond to the prompt that the spelling and grammar check is complete, click **OK.**

16. To use a shortcut menu to correct a spelling error, type an extra **g** at the end of the word **Spelling,** and press the **Spacebar.** When the wavy red line appears, right-click the word, and click the correct word at the top of the shortcut menu.

17. To change **keel** to **kill, wit** to **with,** and **hear** to **here** in the first paragraph of text, select each incorrect word, and type the correct one.

18. Print the document. Save and close the document.

Using Language Features

Word includes a number of features on the expanded Tools menu to help you work with language: the Set Language, Thesaurus, Hyphenation, and Word Count commands.

Using the Thesaurus

You can use the Thesaurus to replace a word or phrase with a synonym, a antonym, or a related word. Select the word for which you want to find a synonym or antonym, and choose the Language command on the Tools menu. Then select Thesaurus on the submenu to display the Thesaurus dialog box (see Figure 3.7).

You can use the Replace button to replace the selected word with the selection in the Replace With Synonym list. Use the Look Up button to look up a selected word in the Replace With Synonym box; select a meaning in the Meanings box to see more replacement options; select an antonym if there is one in the listed suggested replacements and then look up its meaning when you want to see more antonyms.

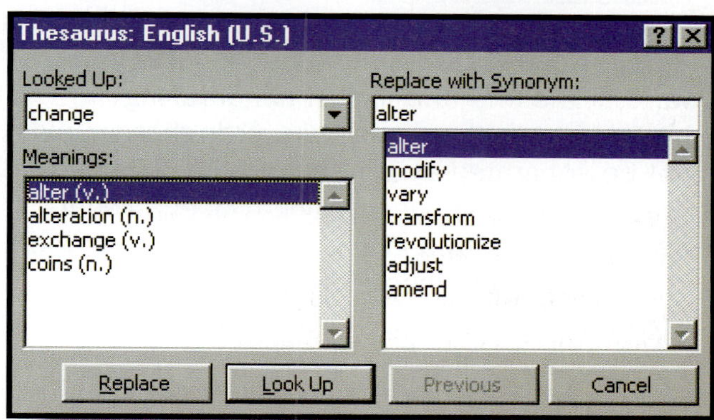

FIGURE 3.7
The Thesaurus dialog box displays synonyms for words.

STEP-BY-STEP ▷ **3.4**

1. Open **Step-by-Step 3-4 Thesaur.**

2. To select the word **change** in the last line of the paragraph, double-click it.

3. To display the Thesaurus dialog box, click the **Tools** menu, click the **Language** command on the expanded menu, and then click **Thesaurus** on the submenu. Notice the different meanings for the word **change.**

4. To use a synonym for the **alter(v.)** meaning, click **modify** in the Replace with Synonym list and click the **Replace** button.

5. Save and close the document.

Using Hyphenation

Hyphenation reduces the ragged appearance of text at the right margin. To put hyphens in your document, open the Tools menu, and use the Hyphenation command on the Language command's submenu.

Word will display the Hyphenation dialog box (see Figure 3.8). It is considered incorrect to hyphenate a capitalized proper noun. You might want to toggle off that option. You also might want to limit the number of consecutive hyphens because more than three hyphens on a page is distracting to the reader.

FIGURE 3.8
Use the Hyphenation dialog box to insert hyphens in a document.

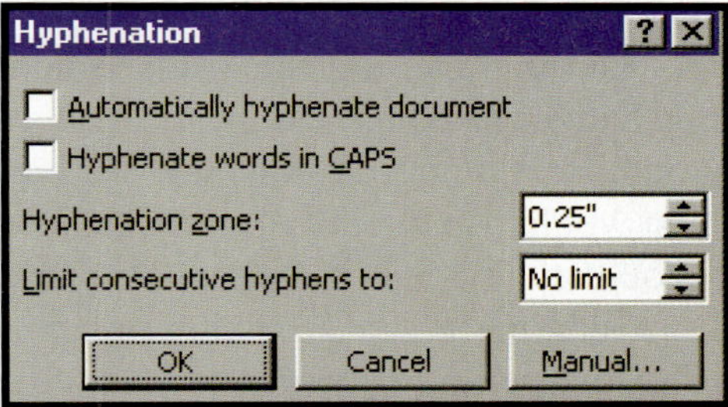

A *soft* hyphen is a hyphen Word inserts in a word at the end of a line. A *nonbreaking* hyphen is one that joins two words that should not be separated at the end of a line by word wrap. To insert a nonbreaking hyphen in your text, hold the Ctrl and Shift keys and press the hyphen key; or click the Symbol command on the Insert menu, click the Special Characters tab, select Nonbreaking Hyphen, and click OK.

Concept Builders

A narrow hyphenation zone reduces the raggedness of the right margin. A wide zone reduces the number of hyphens.

STEP-BY-STEP 3.5

1. Open **Step-by-Step 3-5 Hyphen.**

2. To display the Hyphenation dialog box, click **Tools,** click **Language,** and click **Hyphenation.**

3. To hyphenate the current document, click **Automatically Hyphenate Document,** and click **OK.** Notice Word entered three hyphens.

4. To see how Word breaks a hyphenated last name when you use a regular (soft) hyphen, move to the end of the document, and type the following text: **My friend's married surname is Mary Jones-Smith.** Notice when you use a regular hyphen, the last name separates.

5. To insert a nonbreaking hyphen, select the original hyphen, hold the **Ctrl** and **Shift** keys, and press the **hyphen** (-) key. Notice Word now treats the name as one word and keeps it together.

Working in Other Languages

You can use the editing and proofing tools to check text in other languages. First you must install the language dictionary for each language you want to check. Then you can use the Tools command and then the Set Language command on the Language submenu to mark the text. Figure 3.9 displays the Language dialog box you would use to check text in another language.

You can also select an area of your document and mark it using the language dialog box so it will not be checked for spelling or grammar. This feature is useful when you enter text that is purposely misspelled.

FIGURE 3.9
The Language command lets you check text in another language.

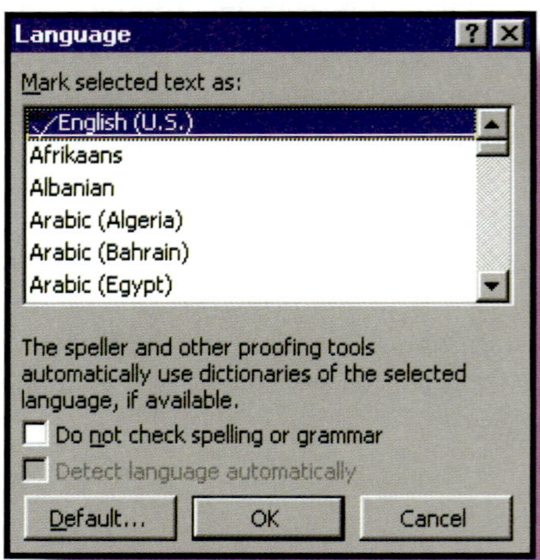

Using Word Count

You can use the Word Count command on the Tools menu to count the number of pages, words, characters (with or without spaces), paragraphs, and lines in a document or in a selection. When you choose this command, Word analyzes the document and displays statistics (see Figure 3.10).

Word Count does not count tabs, line breaks, paragraph marks, page breaks, column breaks, section breaks, headers or footers, or hidden text. You can include footnotes and endnotes. Character count includes letters, numbers, and punctuation marks. Blank lines are counted in the line count but not in the paragraph count.

FIGURE 3.10
The Word Count dialog box displays statistics about the number of pages, words, characters, paragraphs, or lines in a document.

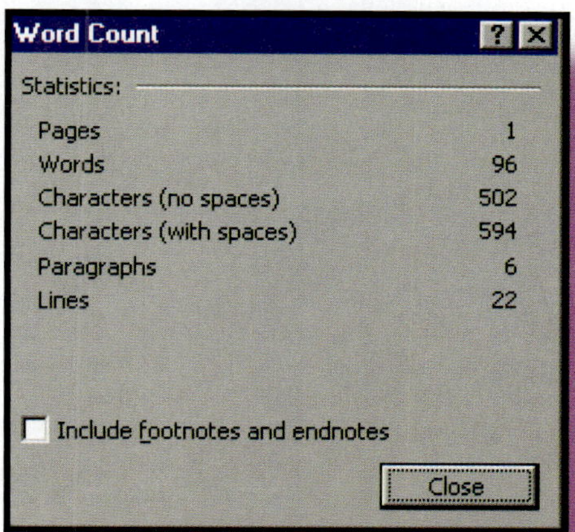

STEP-BY-STEP 3.6

1. To see the count for the pages, words, characters, paragraphs, and lines, click the **Tools** menu, click the **Expand** button, and click **Word Count.**

2. To close the Word Count dialog box, click its **Close** button.

Inserting Symbols

You can use the Symbol command on the Insert menu to insert symbols such as those shown on the Symbols tab in Figure 3.11 or on the Special Characters tab in Figure 3.12.

Hot Tips

You can use the Special Characters tab in the Symbol dialog box to enter printers' em and en dashes.

NOTE:

Word will automatically replace two hyphens with an em dash when you enter them between words.

If you do not see the symbol you need on the Symbols tab, you can select a different font in the Font box and check the symbols in that font. When you click a symbol, Word enlarges that symbol. Click Insert when you find the symbol you need, and Word inserts it at the insertion point.

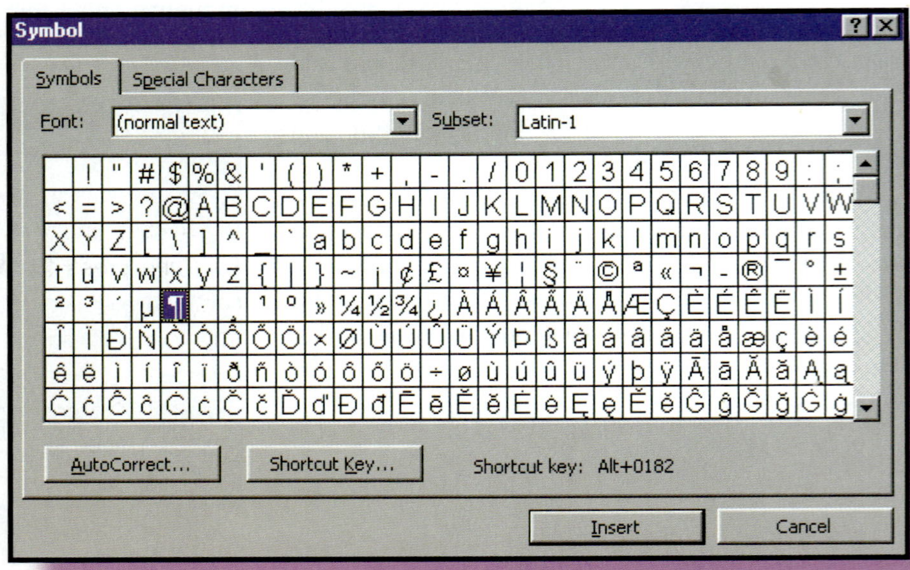

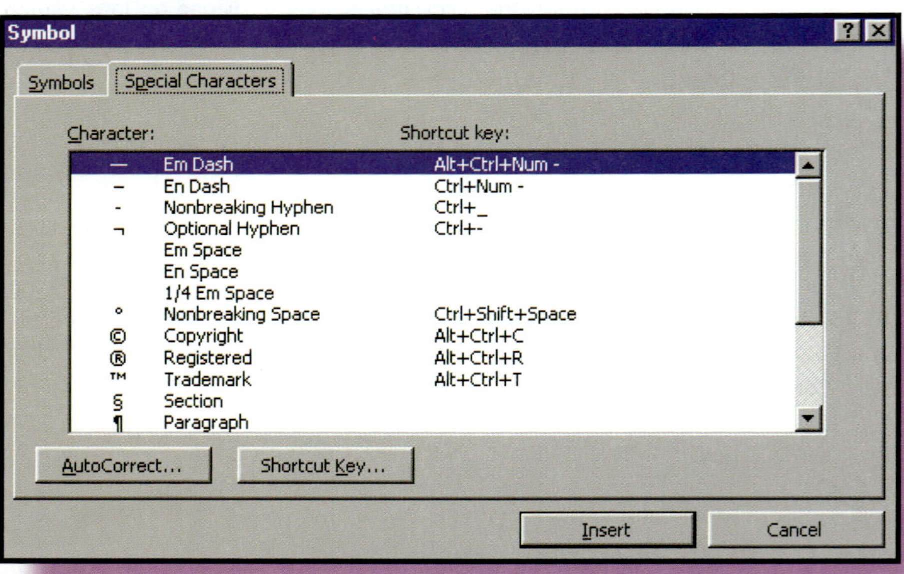

The nonbreaking space is a special character on the Special Characters tab. Word's word-wrap feature will wrap text to the next line whenever it finds a normal space, but there are certain pairs that you do not want Word to separate. For example, you do not want to see

You can type a nonbreaking space by holding the Ctrl and Shift keys and pressing the Spacebar.

the title Ms. on one line and a first or last name on the next. Also, you do not want the month on one line and the day on the next. Use the nonbreaking space as you enter such pairs.

STEP-BY-STEP 3.7

1. Begin a new paragraph, hold the **Ctrl** key and press the **End** key, and then press the **Enter** key twice.

2. To display the Symbol dialog box, click the **Insert** menu and then click **Symbol.** Click the **Symbols** tab if it is not displayed.

3. To enter the copyright symbol, be sure (normal text) is displayed in the Font box, click the © symbol (on the fourth row), click **Insert,** and then click **Close.** Notice the copyright symbol in your document.

4. To use the Special Characters tab in the Symbols dialog box to enter the copyright symbol, click the **Insert** menu, click **Symbol,** click the **Special Characters** tab, scroll through the list to see the various special characters, click **Copyright,** click **Insert,** and click **Close.**

5. To enter a nonbreaking space, type **September,** and then hold the **Ctrl** and **Shift** keys and press the **Spacebar.** Type **19,** a comma, and the current year. To display nonprinting marks if they are not already displayed, click the **Show/Hide ¶** button on the More Buttons button on the Standard toolbar. Notice the mark that signals the nonbreaking space.

7. To browse through the symbols to become familiar with those you can insert in your documents, click the **Insert** menu, and click **Symbol** again.

8. To close the Symbol dialog box when you have seen the fonts and their symbols, click **Cancel.**

Protecting a Document with a Password

When you display the Save As dialog box with the Save As command on the File menu, you can use the General Options command on the Tools button to enter a password for the document (see Figure 3.13). You can add a password that will be required to open the document or a password that will be required to modify the document. You can also use the Read-only

Write down your password, and keep it in a safe place so you can always check it.

recommended box to allow others to open the document and edit or change the contents of the document. They cannot, however, save their changes in the same document. To save changes, they need to use the Save As command to create a new file with a new name for the document.

You need to be very careful when requiring a password to open a document. *If you forget your password, you cannot open your document.* Be sure to choose a password that you will remember weeks or months from now, or write it down.

You can remove a password only after you open the document with the password.

Always check your fingers on the keyboard when entering a password to make sure your fingers are not on the wrong keys. Word displays a Confirm Password dialog box (see Figure 3.14) where you enter your password a second time. Even when entering the password a second time, you have no way of knowing from the screen if you are actually typing what you think you are typing unless you check the position of your fingers on the keyboard.

A password can contain up to 15 characters and can include letters, numbers, symbols, and spaces.

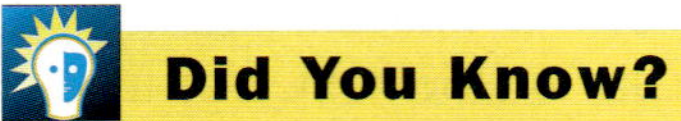

Passwords are case sensitive. **PASSWORD, password,** and **PaSsWoRd** are three different passwords.

FIGURE 3.13
Save options let you enter a password to keep others from opening or modifying your document.

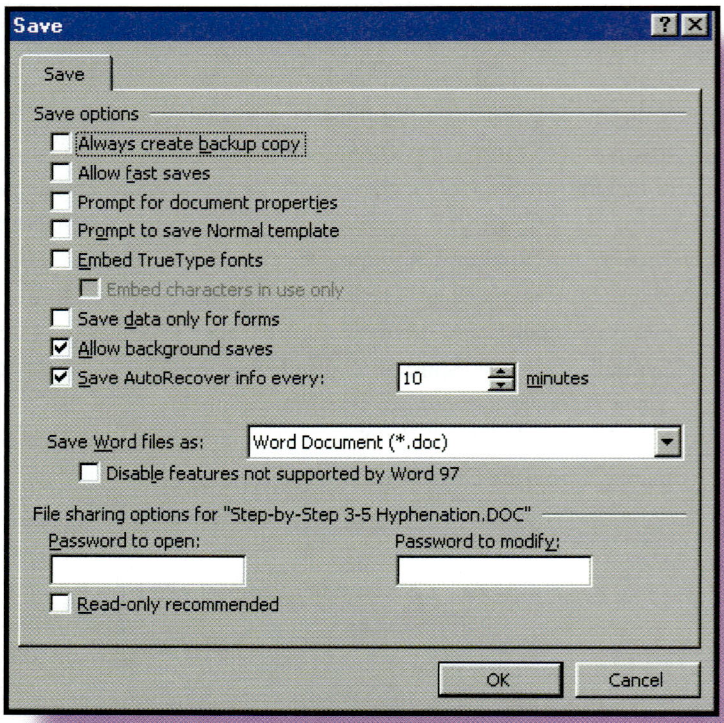

FIGURE 3.14
The Confirm Password dialog box.

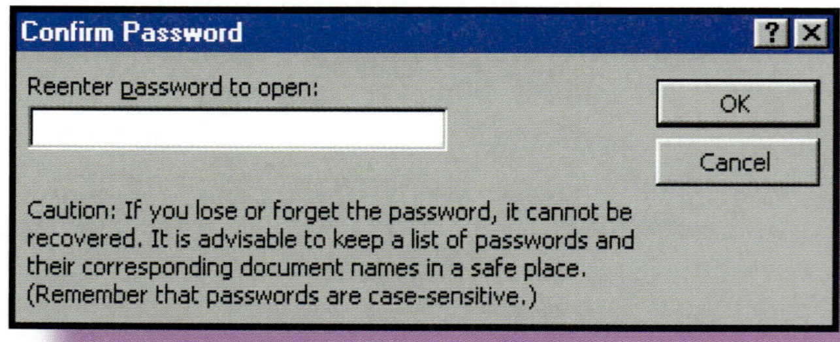

S TEP-BY-STEP ▷ 3.8

1. To save the current document with a new name and password, click the **File** menu, click **Save As**, and type **Hyphenating** in the file name box.

2. To enter a password, click the **Tools** button on the toolbar in the dialog box, click **General Options,** click the **Password To Open** text box, and type **password.** Notice Word inserts an asterisk for each character you type. Click **OK.**

3. To confirm the password, type **password** again and click **OK.**

4. To save and close the document, click **Save** in the Save As dialog box, and click the document's **Close** button.

5. To test the password, click the **File** menu, and click the document named **Hyphenating.** Type **password** in the dialog box, and click **OK.**

6. To remove the password, click **File,** click **Save As,** click the **Tools** button, click **General Options,** select the **asterisks** in the Password to open text box, and press the **Delete** key. Click **OK** in the Save dialog box, and click **Save** in the Save As dialog box.

7. To be sure you removed the password, close the document and then try opening it again. Close the document.

Using AutoFormat

Without knowing much about how to format a document, you can quickly and easily apply formatting with Word's AutoFormat features. The AutoFormat features apply formatting, such as headings, bulleted or numbered lists, borders, numbers, symbols, and fractions, to text in your document.

You can have Word format your document either as you type or after you've finished typing. Word checks each paragraph to see how it's used in the document and then applies an appropriate style.

Word automatically formats Internet, intranet, and e-mail addresses as hyperlinks, applies bold or italic formatting to text you surround with asterisks (*) or underscores (_); and replaces two hyphens (--) with an em dash (—).

NOTE:

You will learn more about applying formatting of your own choosing in later lessons.

To format text as you type, choose the AutoCorrect command on the Tools menu, display the AutoFormat As You Type tab, and choose the options you want in place (see Figure 3.15).

Notice the AutoFormat options available as you type.

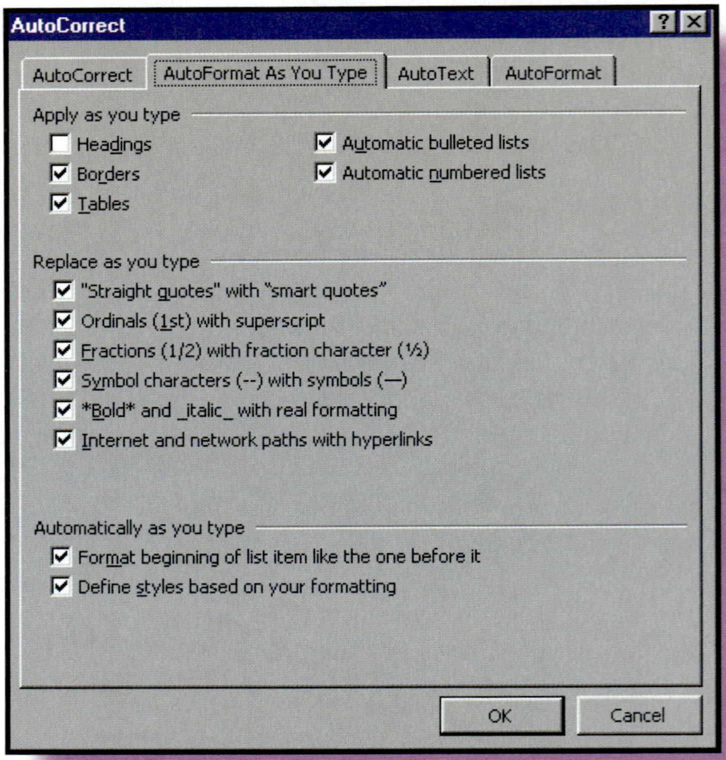

To format an existing document, use the AutoFormat command on the Format menu (see Figure 3.16).

You can choose to format your document as a general document, as a letter, or as an e-mail. Word formats your document in one pass and then lets you review the changes and accept or reject each one (see Figure 3.17).

You can format as a general document, a letter, or an e-mail.

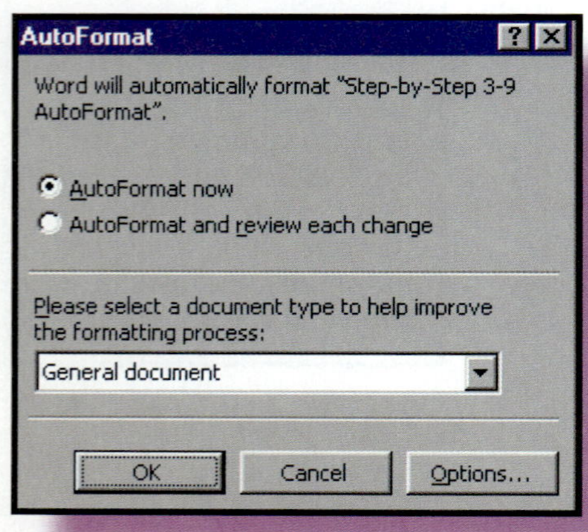

You can choose to accept or reject changes.

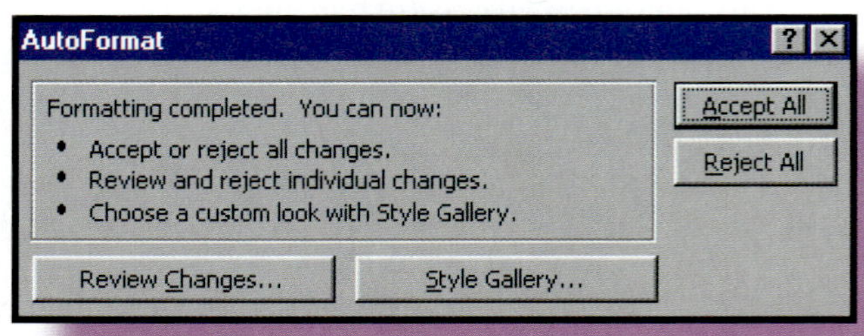

S TEP-BY-STEP ▷ 3.9

1. Open **Step-by-Step 3-9 AutoF.** Notice the asterisks surrounding the word **Windows** in the first paragraph.

2. To display the AutoFormat dialog box, click the **Format** menu and click **AutoFormat.**

3. To format the document as a general document, be sure that option is selected in the drop-down list box, and click **OK.**

4. To accept the changes Word made, click **Accept All.** Notice the headings and the word **Windows.**

5. To save and close the document, click **Close** and click **Yes** when asked whether to save changes.

Summary

You have now learned to use the AutoText and AutoCorrect features; check spelling and grammar; use the Thesaurus; use the Hyphenation, Set Language, and Word Count commands; insert symbols; enter and remove a password; and automatically format your document.

Try the exercises on the following pages to test how well you remember what you learned. Don't be afraid to go back and look up answers or procedures, because that will help to reinforce what you learned.

LESSON 3 REVIEW QUESTIONS

TRUE / FALSE

Circle the T if the statement is true. Circle the F if it is false.

T **F**   1. AutoText stores the entry with the template you specify.

T F   2. The spelling feature checks for double occurrences of a word.

T **F**   3. You need not proofread a document when you use the Spelling and Grammar feature.

T F   4. Hyphenation is automatically used for all documents.

T F   5. The grammar feature checks for sentences using passive voice.

T F   6. Word Count can display Readability Statistics.

T **F**   7. You can check text in more than one language with the dictionary that comes with Word.

T F   8. You can use the nonbreaking space to ensure that words are not separated at the end of a line.

T F 9. A nonbreaking hyphen ensures a hyphenated word is not separated at the end of a line.

T F 10. If you forget your password, Microsoft will help you access your document.

COMPLETION

Complete the following sentences by writing the correct word or words in the blanks provided.

1. The _____*auto correct*_____ feature automatically changes **the** to **the.**

2. The Thesaurus lets you find _____*synonym*_____ and _____*antonym*_____ for a selected word.

3. The _____*Hyphenation*_____ command improves a ragged right text edge.

4. You can use the _____*set lang*_____ command to mark text that you do not want Spelling and Grammar to check.

5. The _____*Word Count*_____ command counts the number of pages, words, characters, paragraphs, and lines in a document.

6. _____*Passwords*_____ are case sensitive.

7. The Symbol command is on the _____*Insert*_____ menu.

8. The _____*Spelling and grammar*_____ feature checks for double occurrences of a word.

9. The _____*grammar*_____ feature checks for agreement errors.

10. _____*Readability statistics*_____ help you determine how easily others can read your document.

LESSON 3 PROJECTS

PROJECT 3A

To practice what you've learned in this lesson, complete the following project:

1. Create a new document.

2. Type the following heading for the new document:

```
EMPLOYEE GUIDELINES
Core Hour Policies
```

3. Type **November** using AutoComplete, and type **15, 2000.** Press the Enter key twice.

88

4. To save time typing the paragraph below, set up an AutoCorrect entry to change the company initials **FW** to the complete company name **Fehrbach-Warner.** Type the following paragraph:

```
Here at FW we support the idea of flextime to give our employees
some freedom to set their own hours. FW understands that many
employees have child-care and carpool responsibilities that make it
difficult to adhere to rigid starting/ending times for the workday.
To participate in FW's flextime policy, however, employees must be
present for the FW core hours of 9:00 to 3:30.
```

5. Turn on hyphenation in the document to correct the ragged right edge. Choose to have Word ignore all instances of **Fehrbach.**

6. Delete the AutoCorrect entry.

7. Print the document. Save the document as **AutoCorrect Document,** and close it.

PROJECT 3B

To practice what you've learned in this lesson, complete the following project:

1. Open **Project 3-B.**

2. Check spelling and grammar in the document. Proofread the document to find other errors and correct them.

3. Use the Word Count command.

4. Print the document.

5. Save and close the document.

Extra Challenges

Use the Help command to find information about how Word calculates Readability Statistics. Read the information, and then print it.

CRITICAL THINKING ACTIVITY

SCANS

You have been asked to provide monthly calendars for two friends to hang by their desks. Use the Calendar Wizard to create calendars for the next two months. Print two copies of the calendars. There is no need to keep a file copy so close without saving changes.

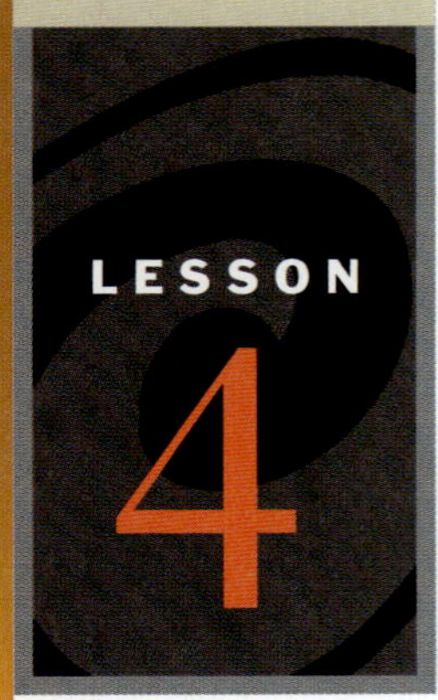

Using Basic Formatting Techniques

OBJECTIVES

When you complete this lesson, you will be able to:

- Change page size and orientation.
- Set margins.
- Control pagination and adjust vertical alignment.
- Apply character and paragraph formatting.
- Use tabs.

⏱ Estimated Time: 1½ hours

Introduction

In this lesson you will learn to use Word's formatting features to change the appearance of text on a page. You will learn how to change page size and orientation, change margins, control pagination, apply character and paragraph formatting, and use tabs.

Changing Page Size and Orientation

One of the first things you might do when you begin working with a new document is format the page.

You can use the Page Setup command on the File menu to change how you set up your document's pages.

You can use the Paper Size tab in the Page Setup dialog box (see Figure 4.1) to choose **orientation,** the direction the page is printed, and page size. You can select either portrait (vertical) or landscape (horizontal) orientation. You can also choose predefined paper or envelope sizes or even define custom sizes.

 **Did You Know?**

The availability of some of the options may depend on your printer's capabilities. Not all printers support landscape orientation.

You can change paper size and orientation for the whole document or for part of the document. If you change the paper size or orientation from the insertion point forward, Word inserts a section break before the insertion point. If you change the paper size or orientation for selected text, Word inserts a section break before and after the selected text. You will learn more about section breaks later in this lesson.

Determine the paper size and orientation in the
Page Setup dialog box.

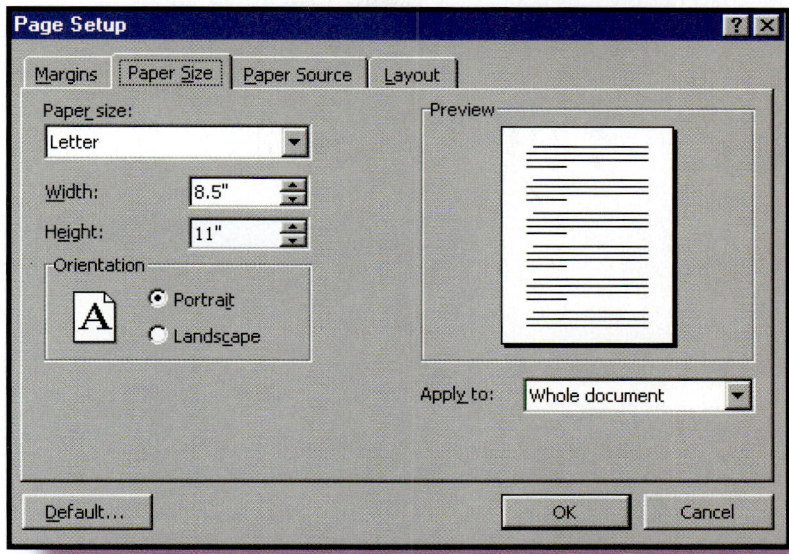

STEP-BY-STEP 4.1

1. Open **Step-by-Step 4-1 Page.**

2. To display the Page Setup dialog box, click the **File** menu and click **Page Setup.**

3. To display paper size options, click the **Paper Size** tab.

4. To see the paper sizes available, click the **drop-down** button in the **Paper size** box. Notice the Custom size item; you may at some time want to use a paper size not shown on the list. Be sure **Letter 8.5" x 11"** is selected.

5. To change to a horizontal orientation, click **Landscape.** Notice the Preview box changed the orientation of the paper.

6. To return to the vertical orientation, click **Portrait.**

7. To see the list in the Apply to box, click the **drop-down** button.

8. To apply the changes to the whole document and close the dialog box, be sure **Whole document** is selected and click **OK.**

Setting Margins

Margins are the white space separating the text on a page from the edges of the paper. There are two different ways to set margins. You can use the Margins tab in the Page Setup dialog box or the Horizontal ruler to set margins.

Concept Builders

Most printers cannot print all the way to the edge of the paper and therefore have rules for minimum margin settings.

Using the Margins Tab

To set margins in the Page Setup dialog box, display the Margins tab (see Figure 4.2). The default margins for a new document are 1 inch at the top and bottom of the page and 1.25 inches at the right and left of the page. You can change the margins in any of the margin boxes.

Use the Margins tab in the Page Setup dialog box to change margins.

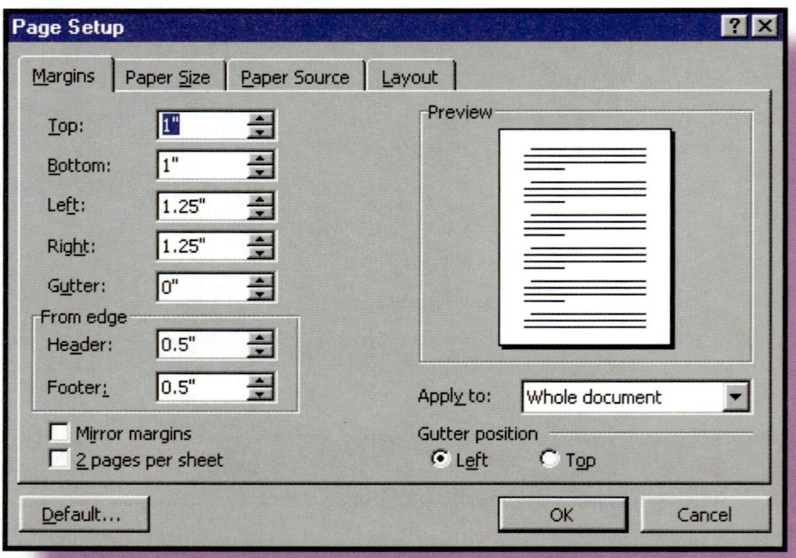

You can change margins for the whole document, from the insertion point forward, or for a selection. Word inserts a section break if you choose from the insertion point forward or for a selection.

Use Mirror margins when you will print on both sides of the paper. When you choose Mirror margins, the Preview box changes to show you facing pages. You can change the gutter measurement to allow extra space for binding between mirrored pages.

Using the Ruler

You can also use the **ruler**—a vertical or horizontal measuring feature—to set margins. Before you can use the ruler to set margins, however, you must be sure you are in Print Layout view.

To change margins, position the pointer on the dividing line between the margin area and text area on the Vertical or Horizontal ruler. The pointer becomes a double-headed arrow, and you may see a ScreenTip identifying the Left or Top Margin. Simply click and drag to increase or decrease the margin width (see Figure 4.3).

You can display the measurements while you change the margins by holding the Alt key while dragging.

Drag the margin boundaries on the ruler to change margin width.

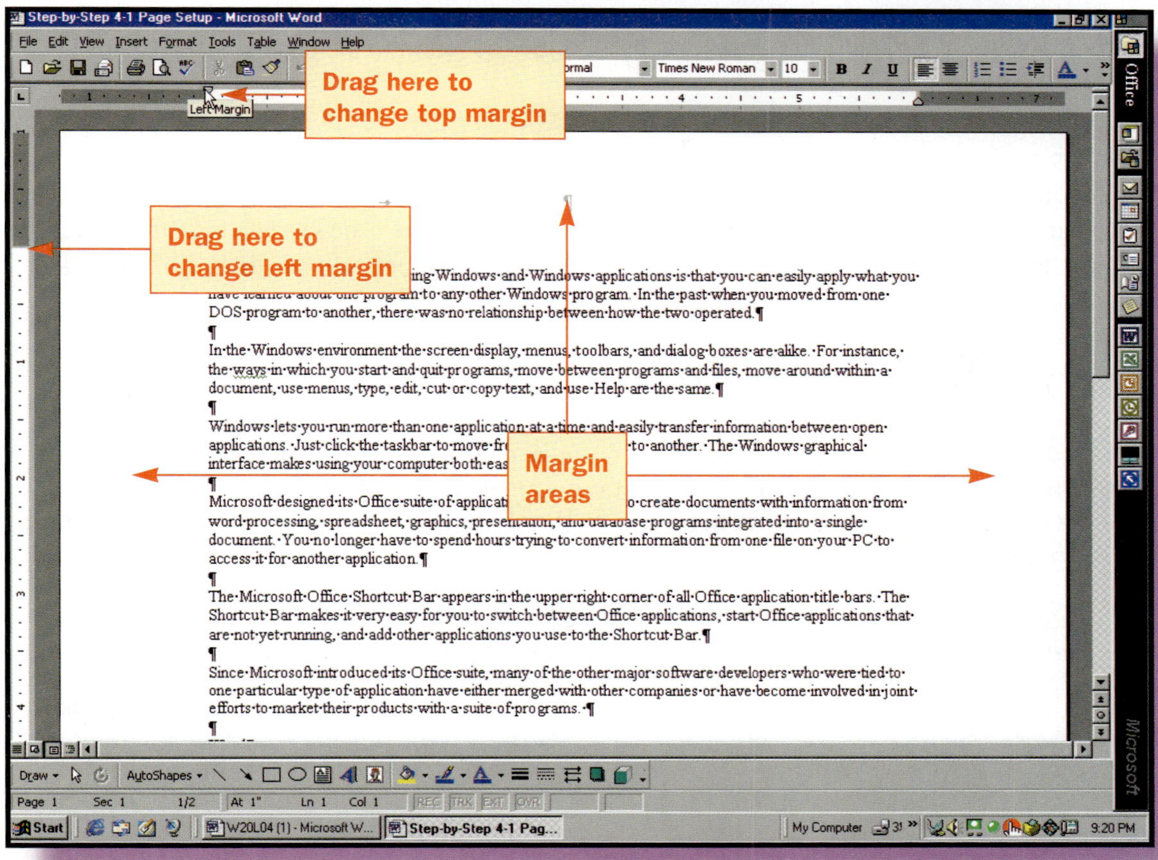

STEP-BY-STEP 4.2

1. To display current margins, click **File,** click **Page Setup,** and click the **Margins** tab.

2. To change the left margin to 1.5 inches, click the **up** button in the spin box until you see **1.5".**

3. To change the right margin to 1 inch, select **1.25",** and then type **1.**

4. To set up facing pages, click **Mirror margins.** Notice the Preview.

5. To see the binding area increase, click the Gutter box **up** button until it displays **.5".** Notice the Preview.

6. To remove the mirror margins and reset the gutter measurement, click **Mirror margins,** use the **down** button to reset the gutter to **0,** and click **OK.**

7. To change to print layout view and display the ruler if it is not displayed, click the **Print Layout View** button at the left of the

(continued on next page)

horizontal scroll bar, click the **View** menu, and click **Ruler.**

8. To increase the top margin to 1.5 inches, hold the **Alt** key and drag the margin boundary on the Vertical ruler until you see the **1.5"** on the top section.

9. To return to the original margin, click **Undo.**

10. To make the left margin 1 inch, hold the **Alt** key and point to the left margin boundary on the Horizontal ruler until the pointer becomes a double-headed arrow. Drag to the left until you see **1"** in the margin area.

Controlling Pagination

Word automatically starts a new page when a page fills. The page breaks Word enters automatically are called **soft page breaks.** As you reformat or edit, Word adjusts soft page breaks. You cannot delete a soft page break. In normal view Word displays a soft page break as a dotted line across the page (see Figure 4.4).

FIGURE 4.4

Word displays a soft page break as a dotted line and a hard page break as a dotted line with the words **Page Break,** and a section break as a double dotted line with the words **Section Break.**

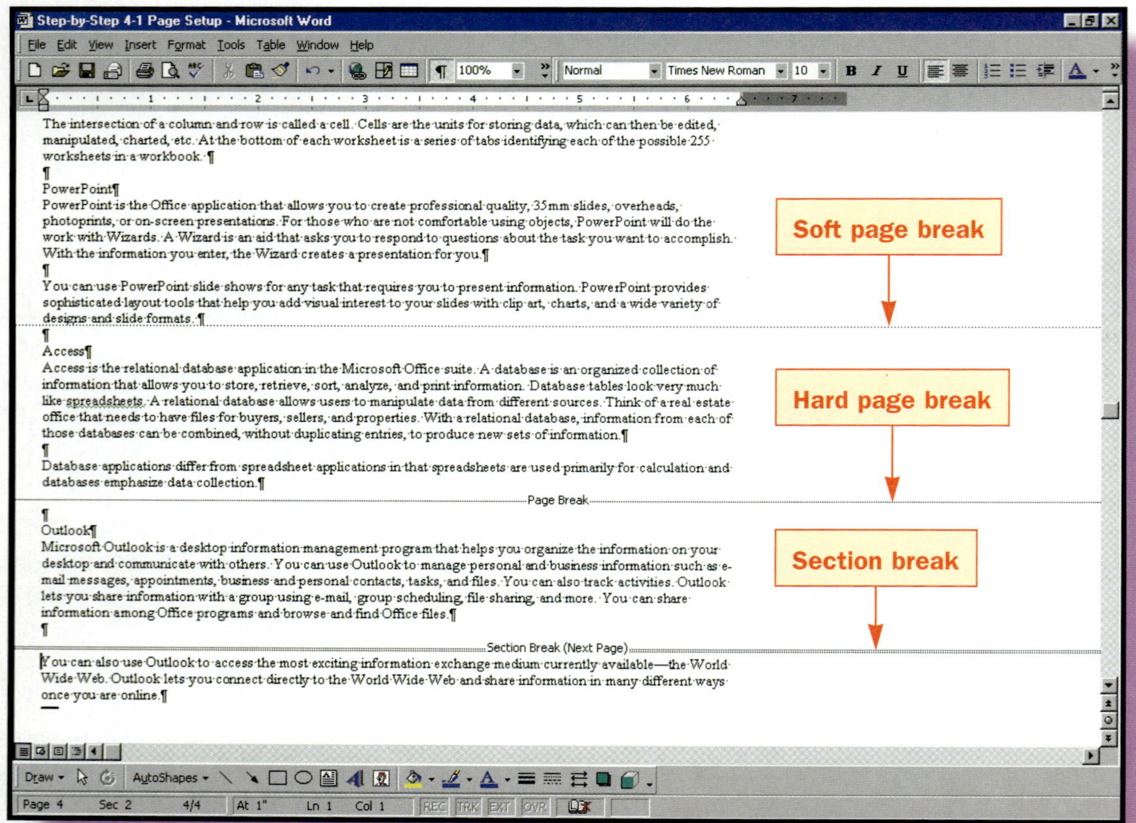

Inserting a Page Break

You can insert a page break, called a **hard page break,** that tells Word where to begin a new page. When you insert a hard page break, Word always breaks the page at that point. You must go back and select and delete the hard page break if you want to change where the page breaks. In normal view, Word displays a hard page break as a dotted line with the words **Page Break** (see Figure 4.4).

When you choose the Break command on the Insert menu to insert a hard page break, Word displays the Break dialog box (see Figure 4.5). You can also insert a hard page break by holding the Ctrl key and pressing the Enter key.

To remove a hard page break, click on it and press the Delete key.

Using Section Breaks

You can use a **section break** to control a document's layout by telling Word to start a new Section. A section can be as small as a single paragraph or as long as an entire document. You can format each section differently.

Use the Break command to start a new section in a document (see Figure 4.5). You can specify that the new section start on the next page or on an odd or even page. You can also request Continuous to have the new section start on the current page. In normal view, Word displays a double dotted line where the section break occurs. The words **Section Break** and the kind of section break appear on the dotted line.

You can also use the Layout tab in the Page Setup dialog box (Figure 4.6) to designate how new sections are laid out. Use the Section Start box to specify whether a new section begins on a new page, on an odd-numbered page, on an even-numbered page, with a new column, or on the same page as the preceding section.

To remove a section break, click it (in normal view) and press the Delete key.

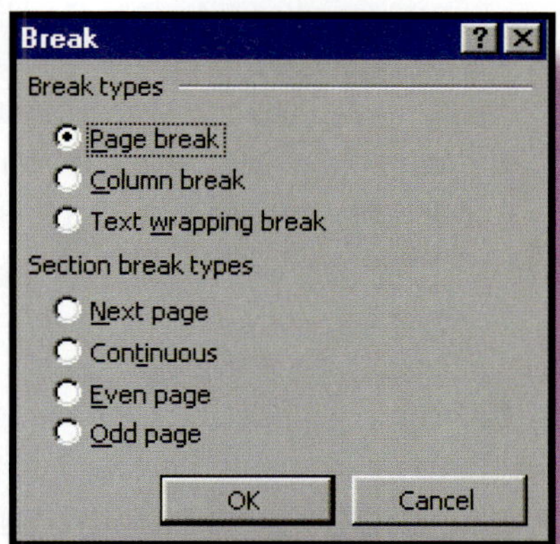

FIGURE 4.5
Insert a page or section break in the Break dialog box.

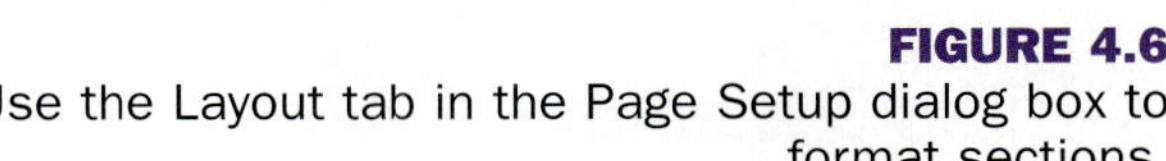
Hot Tips

Whenever a page break at a certain position is not required, be sure to let Word break the pages rather than your doing it yourself. When you edit the document, you will not have to worry about manually changing the page breaks.

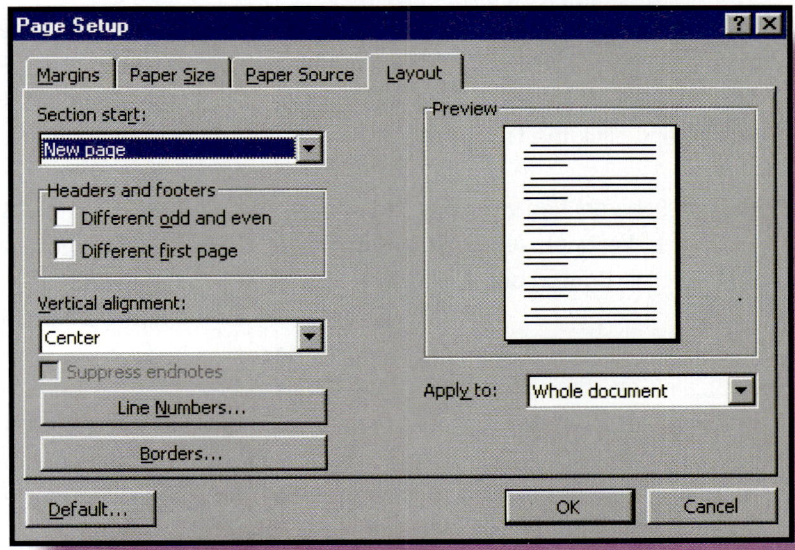

FIGURE 4.6
Use the Layout tab in the Page Setup dialog box to format sections.

1. To return to normal view and see a soft page break, click the **Normal View** button at the left side of the Horizontal scroll bar and scroll down through the document until you see a dotted line.

2. To insert a hard page break, move the insertion point down to the paragraph mark above the **Outlook** heading, click the **Insert** menu, click **Break,** be sure **Page break** is selected, and click **OK.**

3. To delete the hard page break, click it and then press the **Delete** key.

4. To insert a section break, click the **Insert** menu, click **Break,** click the **Next page** option in the Section break types area, and click **OK.**

5. To see that the new section starts on the next page, click the **Print Preview** button on the Standard toolbar.

6. To return to normal view, click the **Close** button on the Print Preview toolbar.

Adjusting Vertical Alignment

The Vertical Alignment box on the Layout tab in the Page Setup dialog box (Figure 4.6) lets you choose to align a document or section at the top or the bottom of the page, center your text on the page, or for full pages, justify or distribute text equally between the top and bottom margins.

1. To display the Layout tab, be sure the insertion point is below the section break in the new section, click **File,** click **Page Setup,** and click the **Layout** tab.

2. To center the section vertically on the page, click the **Vertical Alignment drop-down** button, click **Center,** and click **OK.**

3. To see that only the new section is centered vertically on the page, click the **Print Preview** button on the Standard toolbar.

4. To return to the normal view, click the **Close** button on the Print Preview toolbar.

5. To return the vertical alignment to Top, click **File,** click **Page Setup,** click the **Vertical alignment** drop-down button, click **Top,** and click **OK.**

6. To remove the section break, click on the **section break,** notice the insertion point on the left side of the section break, and press the **Delete** key.

7. To save and close the document, click the **Save** button, and then click the document's **Close** button.

Applying Character Formats

Characters are letters, numbers, symbols, punctuation marks, and spaces. You can select a character and apply one or more character formats. Word displays formatted text as it will look when you print it.

The character formats you can apply are font and font size; font style (regular, italic, bold); and font effects such as underline, color, strikethrough, superscript, small caps, and even animation.

You can either use the Font command on the Format menu to access the Font dialog box, or click a button on the Formatting toolbar.

Changing Fonts and Font Sizes

The **font** is the design of a set of letters and numbers. Each set has a name. Here are some examples:

Times New Roman   **Arial**   Bernhard ModernBT   Courier

You can see a list of available fonts in the drop-down list in the Font dialog box (Figure 4.7). By default, Word uses the Times New Roman font. You change to a different font by selecting text and choosing one of the fonts listed in the Font dialog box. You can also choose to begin typing text in a new font by selecting the font at the insertion point.

Did You Know?

The Times New Roman font and fonts like it are easier to read than sans serif fonts (Arial) and are usually used for word processing documents.

FIGURE 4.7

Use the Font command to display the Font dialog box.

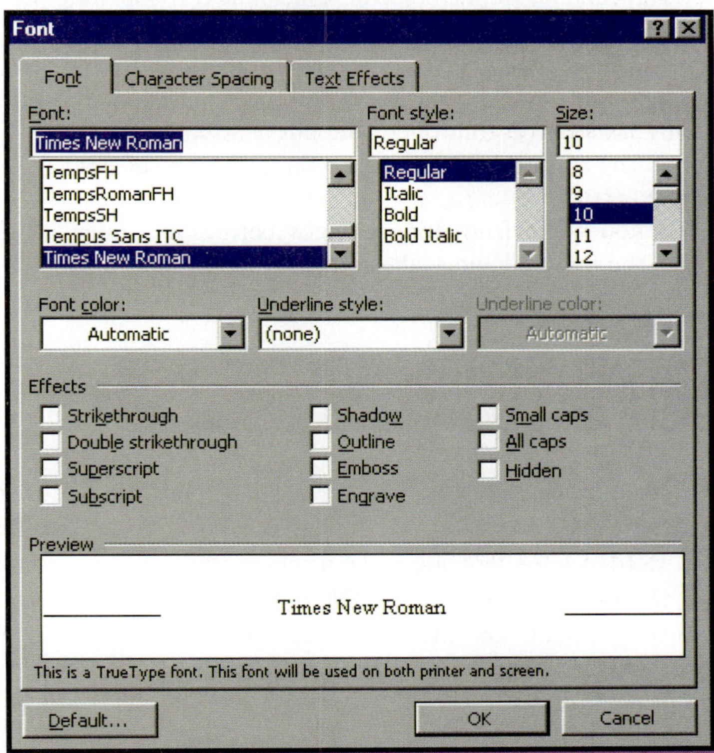

TrueType fonts are provided with Microsoft Windows. They are *scalable fonts,* which means they can be displayed and printed in any size. You can print them on any printer capable of printing graphics.

Font sizes are measured in points. Point size measures the height of characters. A **point** is approximately equal to 1/72 inch. A 10-point font is approximately 10/72 inch high. These examples show what different point sizes look like in the Times New Roman font.

8 Point   12 Point   24 Point   36 Point

You can change the font size by choosing a new size on the Size drop-down list in the Font dialog box. You can change the size of text you are about to type by choosing a new size at the insertion point location.

Applying Font Styles and Effects

Font styles are changes in the shape or weight of the font's characters. The four common font styles are regular, *italic,* **bold,** and ***bold italic.*** Not all fonts have all four styles available. To apply a font style to text, select the text and click a font style in the Font dialog box. You can apply only one style at a time.

Word offers a number of other ways to format characters. The Effects area of the Font dialog box contains 11 different formatting effects—from Strikethrough to Hidden. You can apply more than one effect at a time.

The Underline drop-down list in the Font dialog box contains nine different ways to underline text. Choosing the Word only underline option lets you <u>underline</u> <u>only</u> <u>words</u> and not the spaces between words.

You can change the color of selected text by opening the Color drop-down list. To apply a new color, choose a color on the palette.

The Font dialog box contains two additional tabs that can help you format your text. The Character Spacing tab lets you control the amount of space between letters. The Animation tab lets you add any of six animated effects to text.

If you make formatting choices before you enter text, all the text you enter takes on the same formatting.

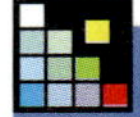

Concept Builders

The fonts and sizes you can use in your documents may depend on your printer.

Did You Know?

There are not many times when you need to underline words anymore. Instead use bold or italic styles to set text apart.

STEP-BY-STEP 4.5

1. Open **Step-by-Step 4-5 Fonts.**

2. To change the font size to 12 points for the whole document, click the **Edit** menu, and click **Select All;** then click the **Format** menu, click **Font,** click **12** in the Size box, and click **OK.**

3. To reformat the title, select **Microsoft Office,** click the **Format** menu, click **Font,** scroll up the font list to **Arial,** and click it.

4. To make other changes, click **Bold** in the Font style box, scroll to and click **18** in the Size box, click the **Font Color** drop-down button, and click **Blue.**

5. To make character spacing changes, click the **Character Spacing** tab, click the **Spacing** drop-down button, and click **Expanded.** In the By spin box, type **2**.

6. To add a text effect, click the **Text Effects** tab, click **Sparkle Text**, and click **OK.**

7. To apply a single underline to text, select the words **no relationship** near the end of the first paragraph following the Microsoft Office heading, click the **Format** menu, click **Font,** click the **Underline style** drop-down button, click the first **single line,** and

click **OK.**

8. To change the single underline to a words-only underline, be sure **no relationship** is still selected, click the **Format** menu, click **Font,** click the **Underline style** drop-down button, click **Words only,** and click **OK.**

9. To add a small caps effect to text, scroll down to find the **Word** heading, select the heading, click the **Format** menu, click **Font,** click **Small caps,** and click **OK.**

Using the Formatting Toolbar

You can use the Formatting toolbar (Figure 4.8) to apply many commonly used character formats. You can change the font and font size. You can use the Format Painter on the Standard toolbar to apply character formats from one formatted selection to another selection.

You can see the name of the font and the font size currently in use on the Formatting toolbar.

If either or both of those boxes are blank, you have selected text containing more than one font or font size.

Did You Know?

You can add or remove the bold, italic, or underline font style to or from a single word by positioning the insertion point anywhere within the word and clicking the font style button.

FIGURE 4.8
The Formatting toolbar lets you apply character formats to your document.

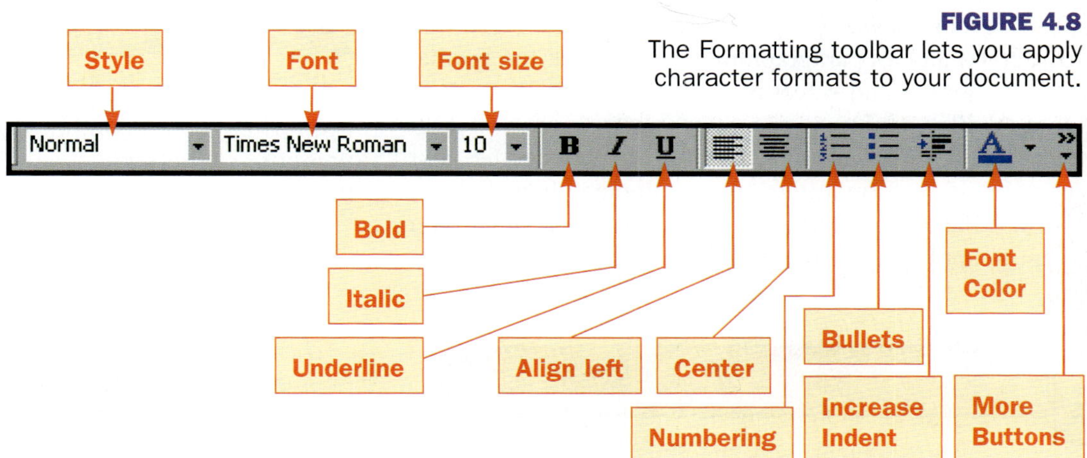

Removing Character Formatting

To remove formatting, select the text and perform the same steps you took to apply the formatting. For example, click the Bold button again to remove bold formatting from selected text.

1. To change the font for the **Word** heading, select the heading, click the **Font** drop-down button on the Formatting toolbar, and click **Arial.**

2. To add the bold style to the heading, be sure the heading is still selected, click the **Bold** button on the Formatting toolbar. Notice when you apply the Bold style, the toolbar button appears pushed in.

3. To add the italic style, be sure the heading is still selected, click the **Italic** button on the Formatting toolbar.

4. To change the size of the heading, click the **Font Size** drop-down button on the Formatting toolbar, and click **14.**

5. To change the underline style for the words **no relationship,** which are currently underlined with a Words only style, select the words, and click the **Underline** button on the toolbar.

6. To remove the underline, be sure the words **no relationship** are still selected, and click the **Underline** button again.

Using Format Painter

Once you have applied formatting to text, you can use the Format Painter button on the Standard toolbar to add the same formatting to other parts of your document. When you click the Format Painter, your mouse pointer displays a paintbrush.

To copy a *paragraph's* formatting, first select the paragraph and its paragraph mark, then click the Format Painter button, and select the text to which you want to apply the formatting.

To copy *character* formatting, select the text containing the formatting you want copied, then click the Format Painter button, and select the text to which you want to apply the formatting.

Concept Builders

Double-click the Format Painter button if you want to add the formatting to more than one selection. When you finish painting formats, click the Format Painter button or press the Esc key to turn off Format Painter.

1. To use the formatting for the **Word** heading for the other headings in the document, select the **Word** heading including its paragraph mark, and then double-click the **Format Painter** button.

2. To add the formatting to the **Excel** heading, scroll down through the document until you see the **Excel** heading and then click **Excel.**

3. To add the same formatting to the **PowerPoint, Access,** and **Outlook** headings

and toggle Format Painter off, click the paintbrush on each of the headings and then click the **Format Painter** button.

4. To save and close the document, click **Save** and click the **Close** button.

Using the Change Case Command

You can use the Change Case command on the Format menu to quickly change the case of text. The Change Case command affects character capitalization of text you have typed, but it does *not* affect characters you formatted with All Caps or Small Caps.

You must first select the text you want to change. Then choose one of the options in the Change Case dialog box (see Figure 4.9):

- *Sentence case* capitalizes the first word in each sentence.

- *lowercase* changes all characters to lowercase.

- *UPPERCASE* changes all characters to caps.

- *Title Case* capitalizes the first character of each word.

- *tOGGLE cASE* changes each character to the opposite of what it is.

Toggle case can help you fix things quickly if you have accidentally typed text with the Caps Lock feature.

FIGURE 4.9

The Change Case command gives you several options for changing the case of text.

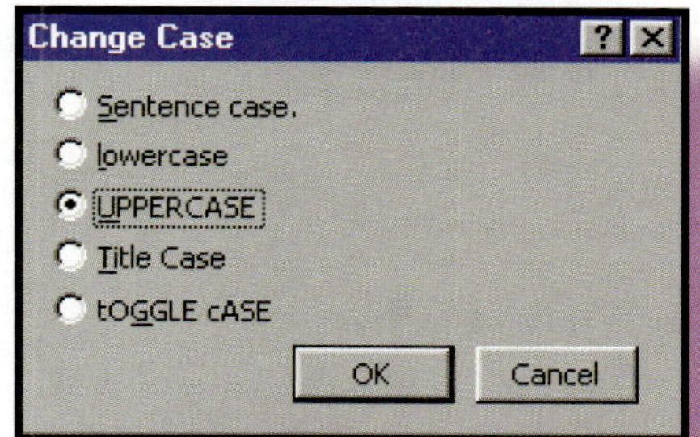

STEP-BY-STEP 4.8

1. Open **Step-by-Step 4-8 Case.**

2. To select all of the text, click the **Edit** menu and **Select All.**

3. To change to lowercase, click **Format,** click **Change Case,** and click **lowercase.** Then click **OK.**

4. To change to uppercase, click **Format,** click **Change Case,** and click **UPPERCASE.** Then click **OK.**

5. To change to title case, click **Format,** click **Change Case,** and click **Title Case.** Then click **OK.**

6. To use toggle case, click **Format,** click **Change Case,** and click **tOGGLE cASE.** Then click **OK.**

7. To return to the original, click **Undo** four times.

8. Close the document without saving.

Formatting Paragraphs

The alignment, indentation, spacing, and so forth, in your document depends on the formatting you apply to paragraphs—blocks of text. Word refers to any amount of text or other items followed by a paragraph mark as a **paragraph.**

To apply paragraph formatting to a paragraph, position your insertion point anywhere in the paragraph. Word will apply paragraph formats you select to the *entire* paragraph. You cannot apply paragraph formatting to just a selection within the paragraph.

The Paragraph command on the Format menu displays the Paragraph dialog box (see Figure 4.10). The options on the Indents and Spacing tab in the Paragraph dialog box let you control indentation from the left and right margins, spacing before and after paragraphs, line spacing within paragraphs, such special indents as first line indents and hanging indents, and alignment with margins.

You can also use the Formatting toolbar to apply some of these paragraph formats.

Setting Indents

Figure 4.11 shows several ways you can use indenting to set paragraphs off from other text in your documents.

You should not press the Tab key or the Spacebar when you want to indent lines of text. Nor should you try to control indentation by pressing the Enter key at the end of each line. Each of these methods make editing a Word document or converting a document to another file format very difficult.

You can set precise measurements for paragraph indents with the Paragraph command on the Format menu. Left and right indents are measured from the left and right margins. Negative indents run the text into the margins. You can also specify first line indents and hanging indents.

You can also control paragraph indents by dragging the indent markers on the Horizontal ruler (see Figure 4.11). The ruler contains three left indent markers and one right indent marker. The First Line Indent marker controls the indentation of the first line of a paragraph. The Hanging Indent marker indents all lines except the first one from the left.

The Indents and Spacing tab provides options for indentation and spacing.

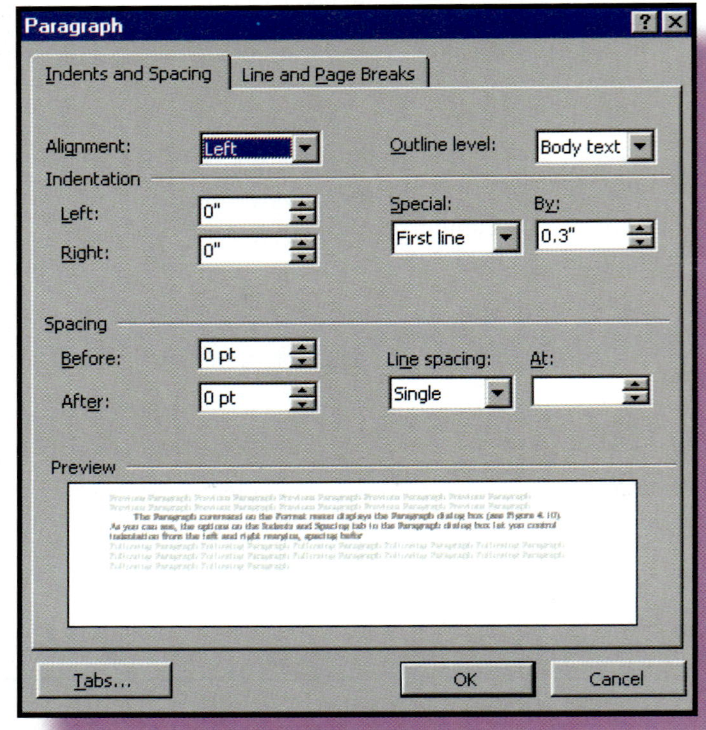

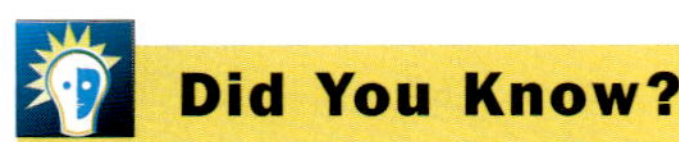

Hanging indents are often used in legal documents.

FIGURE 4.11
Examples of different types of indentations.

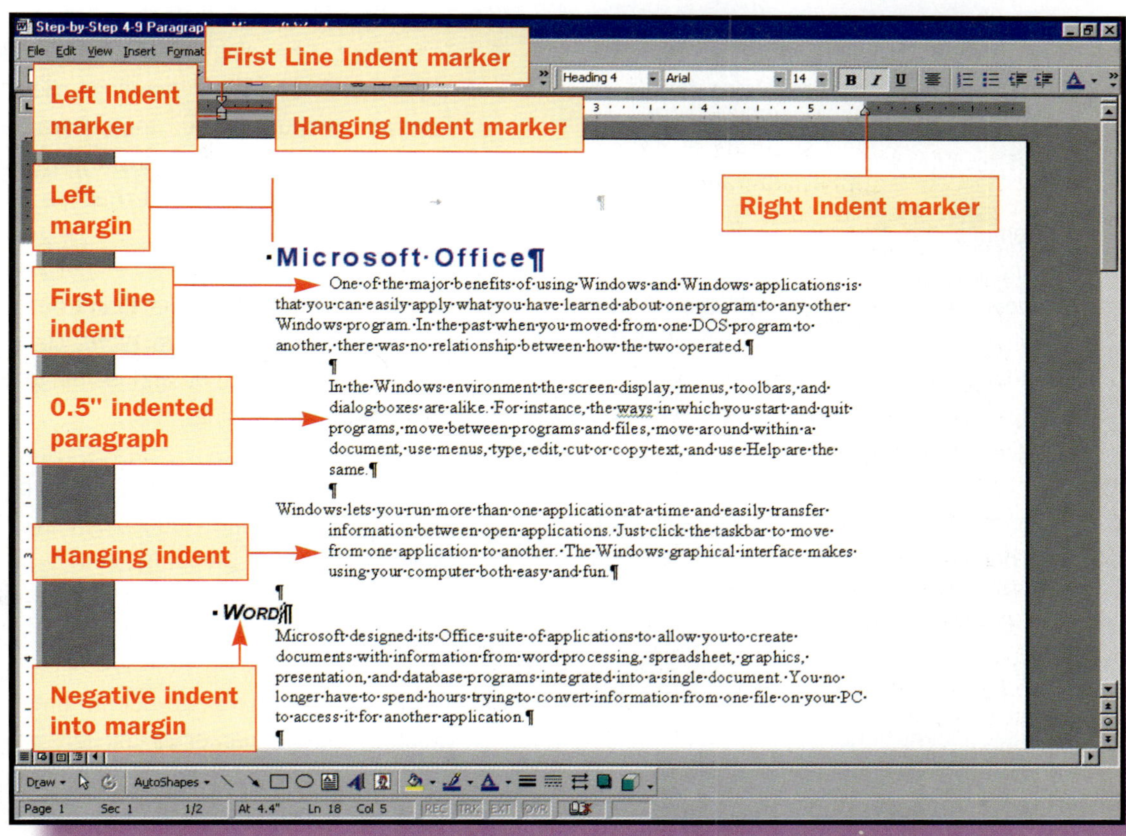

The Left Indent marker box beneath the Hanging Indent marker indents the entire paragraph from the left. The Right Indent marker indents a selected paragraph from the right. To use these markers, make sure the insertion point is in the paragraph you want to indent, and then simply drag the appropriate marker to the desired position on the ruler.

Use the Increase Indent and Decrease Indent buttons on the Formatting toolbar to set and remove indents quickly. Each time you use one of these buttons, you increase or decrease the indent by half an inch.

Word stores the paragraph formats in the end of paragraph mark, so be sure to include it if you copy or move text with formatting.

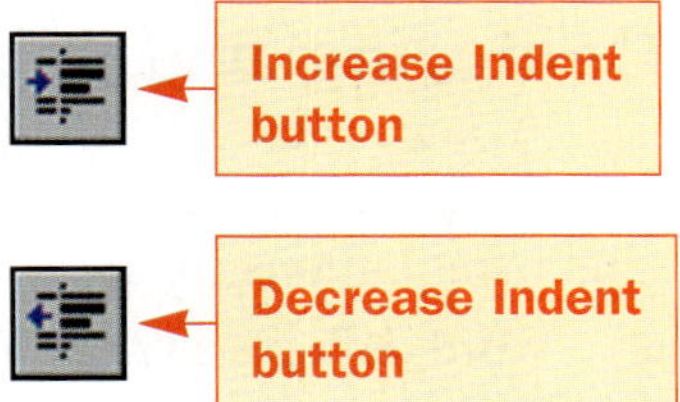

S TEP-BY-STEP ▷ 4.9

1. Open **Step-by-Step 4-9 Para.** To set the right margin, click the I-beam in the paragraph beginning **One of the major** and drag the Right Indent marker to 5.5".

2. To enter a first line indent for the first three text paragraphs in the document, drag the selection pointer in the left margin to select the first three paragraphs beginning **One of**

(continued on next page)

the major, click the **Format** menu, click **Paragraph,** click the **drop-down** button in the Special box in the Indentation section, click **First line,** and click **OK.**

3. To remove the first line indent from the second paragraph of text (beginning **In the Windows environment**), click the I-beam anywhere in the paragraph, then click the **First Line** Indent marker on the ruler, and drag it to the left until it aligns with the Hanging Indent marker.

4. To indent the entire second paragraph, click the I-beam anywhere in the paragraph, and then click the **Increase Indent** button on the Formatting toolbar. Notice Word indented the paragraph 0.5 inch. You may have to click the More Buttons button and click the Increase Indent button there.

5. To indent the paragraph 1 inch, click the **Increase Indent** button again.

6. To move back to the 0.5-inch indent, click the **Decrease Indent** button.

7. To indent the heading into the margin, click anywhere in the **Word** heading, click the **Format** menu, click the **Paragraph** command, click the **down** arrow in the **Left Indentation** spin box until it reaches **-0.5",** and click **OK.**

8. To paint the format on the **Excel** heading, click anywhere in the word **Word,** click the **Format Painter** button, and scroll to and click the **Excel** heading.

9. To set a hanging indent, click the I-beam anywhere in the paragraph beginning **The application that is probably used,** click the **Hanging Indent** marker on the ruler, and drag it to the 0.5-inch position.

10. To remove the hanging indent, drag the **Hanging Indent** marker to the left until it aligns with the **First Line Indent** marker.

11. Print the document. Save and close the document.

Centering and Aligning Text

You can left align, justify, right align, or center paragraphs in Word (see Figure 4.12). The easiest way to align text is to use the alignment buttons on the Formatting toolbar.

- Word defaults to *left aligned,* which lines up text flush with the left margin and leaves a ragged right edge.

- *Justified* aligns text flush with the left margin and flush with the right margin. Word adds extra space between words to even out the lines.

- *Right aligned* lines up text with the right margin and leaves a ragged left edge.

- *Center* centers the text between the margins.

INTERNET Use the Web toolbar to enter the following URL address: http://www.nasdaq.com. Display the latest price for Microsoft's stock.

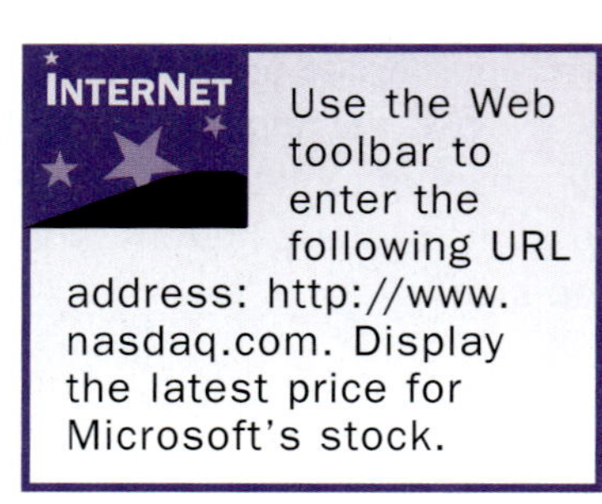

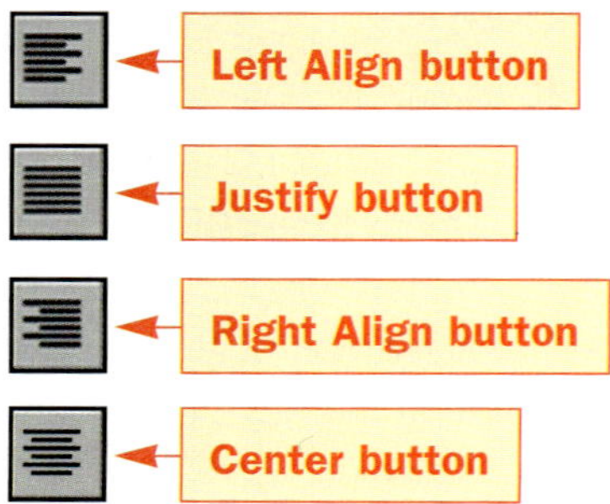

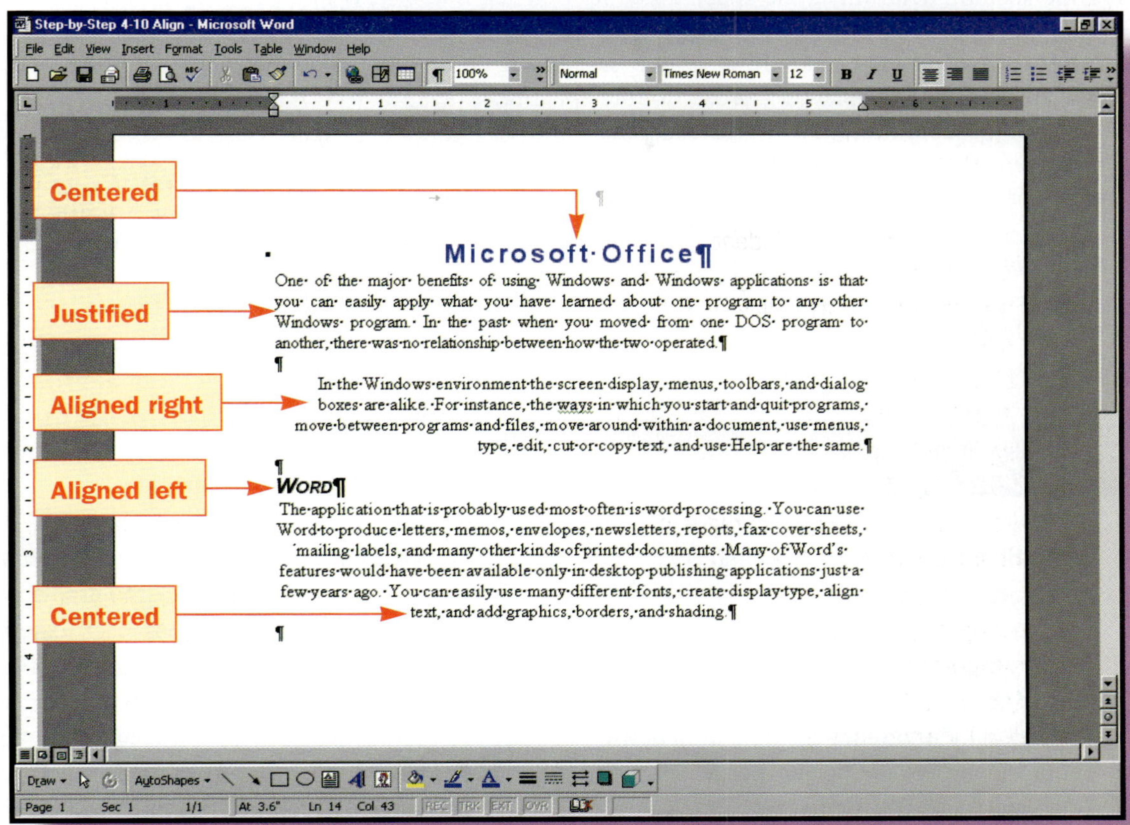

STEP-BY-STEP ▷ 4.10

1. Open **Step-by-Step 4-10 Align.**

2. To center the title between the margins, be sure the insertion point is in the paragraph with the words **Microsoft Office** and click the **Center** button on the Formatting toolbar.

3. To justify a paragraph, move the insertion point into the paragraph beginning **One of the major benefits**, and click the **Justify** button.

4. To align a paragraph with the right margin, move the insertion point into the paragraph beginning **In the Windows**, and click the **Align Right** button.

5. To realign the paragraph with the left margin, click the **Align Left** button.

6. To center the lines of a paragraph between the margins, move the insertion point into the paragraph beginning **The application that is**, and click the **Center** button.

7. Print the document. Save and close the document.

Setting Line Spacing

Line spacing determines the space taken up by each line of text in a paragraph. Word defaults to single line spacing.

The space allocated for single spacing is just a little taller than the point size used for the largest font size on the line. When you choose double-spacing, the line will be approximately twice the point size of the characters. If a line contains a large character, or a graphic, or a formula, Word increases the spacing for that line.

You can use the Paragraph command on the Format menu to designate line spacing to Single, 1.5 lines, Double, At least, Exactly, or Multiple line spacing.

Hot Tips

If you choose At Least, Exactly, or Multiple, you enter a value for the line size and Word no longer adjusts for font sizes used on the line.

S TEP-BY-STEP 4.11

1. Open **Step-by-Step 4-11 Spacing.**

2. To see spacing of 1.5 lines, position the insertion point in the paragraph beginning **One of the major benefits.** Click the **Format** menu, click **Paragraph**, click the **drop-down** button in the Line Spacing box, click **1.5 lines,** and click **OK.**

3. To see double-spacing, click the **Format** menu, click **Paragraph**, click the **drop-down** button in the Line Spacing box, click **Double,** and click **OK.**

4. To see line spacing of at least 15 points, click the **Format** menu, click **Paragraph,** click the **drop-down** button in the Line Spacing box, click **At least,** change **12** points to **15** points, and click **OK.**

5. To see exactly 14 points, click the **Format** menu, click **Paragraph**, click the **drop-down** button in the Line Spacing box, click **Exactly,** change **12** points to **14** points, and click **OK.**

6. To see multiple line spacing, click the **Format** menu, click **Paragraph**, click the **drop-down** button in the Line Spacing box, click **Multiple,** change **3** to **4,** and click **OK.**

7. To return to single-spacing, click the **Format** menu, click **Paragraph**, click the **drop-down** button in the Line Spacing box, click **Single,** and click **OK.**

Adding and Removing Space Between Paragraphs

You can add space before or after a paragraph without pressing the Enter key by entering measurements in the Spacing Before and Spacing After boxes on the Indents and Spacing tab in the Paragraph dialog box. You can, for instance, specify how much space should appear before and after a heading.

The Spacing Before and After feature is useful when working with lengthy documents.

STEP-BY-STEP ▷ 4.12

1. Notice that none of the headings have space between the heading and the text.

2. To add space between the **Word** heading and the text, click the I-beam in the heading, click the **Format** menu, click **Paragraph,** and

click the **up** arrow in the **Spacing After** box until **6 pt** shows. Click **OK.**

3. To paint the new spacing format on the other headings, double-click the **Format Painter,** and scroll to and click each of the headings.

Controlling Text Flow

When working with a document of a few pages, you may find that headings become separated from the text that follows them by soft page breaks.

The Line and Page Breaks tab in the Paragraph dialog box (Figure 4.13) lets you control how pagination is determined for each paragraph.

When Widow/Orphan control is toggled on, Word does not allow single lines to appear at the top or bottom of a page. You can use the Keep Lines Together option to specify that lines in a paragraph be kept together on a page. You can use the Keep With Next option to specify that selected paragraphs be kept together on a page. You can use the Page Break Before option to specify that a certain paragraph will always be at the top of a page.

FIGURE 4.13

The Line and Page Breaks tab controls pagination, line numbering, and hyphenation.

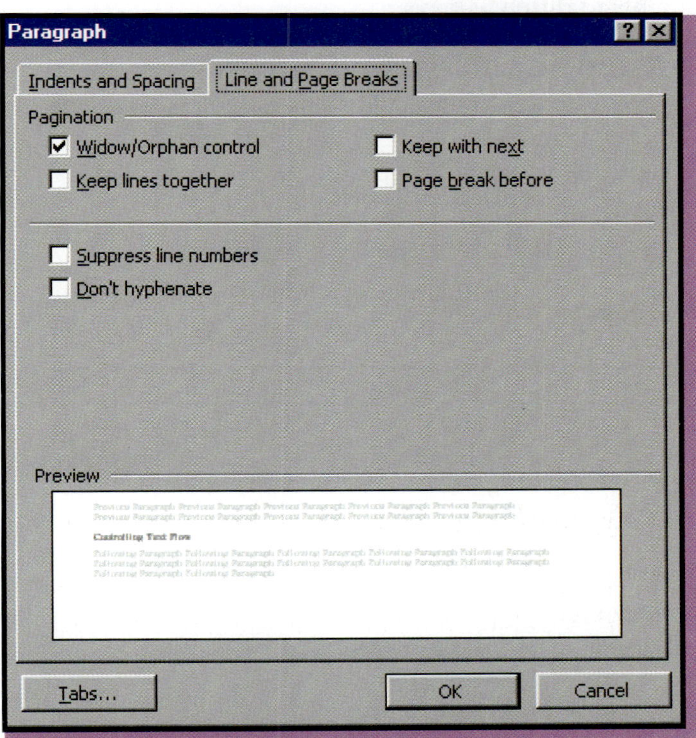

1. To turn on Widow/Orphan control, click the **Format** menu, click **Paragraph,** and then click the **Line and Page Breaks** tab. Click the **Widow/Orphan control** box. Click **OK.**

2. To specify that the headings stay with the paragraphs following them, click in the **Word** side heading. Click the **Format** menu, click **Paragraph,** and then click in the **Keep with next** box on the **Line and Page Breaks** tab. Click **OK.** Notice that a small black square appears next to the side heading to let you know that text flow options are active.

3. To use Format Painter to copy the new formatting to the other side headings, be sure the insertion point is somewhere in the **Word** side head, double-click the **Format Painter** button, and click each of the side heads. Press the **Esc** key. Notice the **Excel** side heading moves from the bottom of one page to the top of the next to stay with the following paragraph.

4. Print, save and close the document.

Using Tabs

Tabs are used to align text in a paragraph. For most tabular matter, you should use Word's Table feature. For short tabular entries, you can use tabs to align your text in a number of different ways.

Setting and Clearing Tabs

You can use either the tab stops on the Horizontal ruler (see Figure 4.14) or the Tabs command on the Format menu to change tab positions and the way text is aligned.

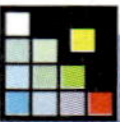

Concept Builders

To set tab stops in existing text, select the paragraph or paragraphs in which you want to set or change tab stops. Tabs you set are displayed on the ruler only when the insertion point is in the area selected for tabs. If you are at the beginning of a document and set tab stops, they will be stored in the paragraph mark.

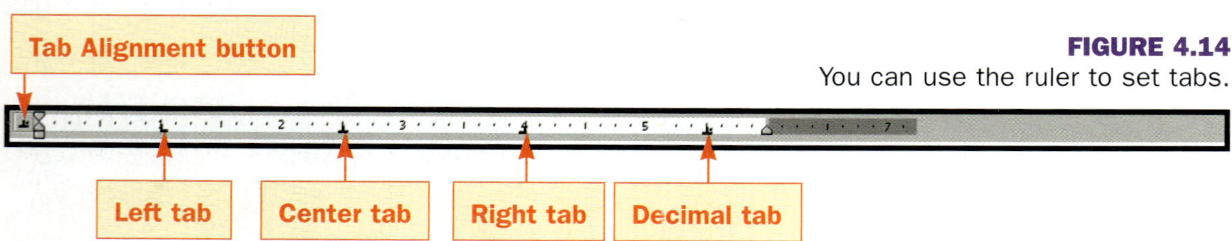

FIGURE 4.14
You can use the ruler to set tabs.

When you click the Tabs command on the Format menu, Word displays the Tabs dialog box shown in Figure 4.15. In this dialog box, you can set tabs and choose leaders. You will learn more about leaders later in this lesson.

By default, Word sets tab stops at 0.5-inch intervals from the left margin.

Word offers five types of tab stops:

- *Left* aligns text flush left at the tab stop.

- *Right* aligns text flush right at the tab stop.

- *Center* centers text at the tab stop.

- *Decimal* aligns characters on the decimal point at the tab stop.

- *Bar* aligns characters flush left and displays a vertical line between columns at the tab stop.

   To set a tab:

- Click the Tab Alignment button at the far left of the Horizontal ruler until you see the tab you want—left, right, center, decimal, or bar.

- Click the location on the ruler where you want to position the tab stop.

   To remove a tab stop, drag it off the ruler.

   To move a tab stop, drag it to another location on the ruler.

FIGURE 4.15
You can also set tabs in the Tabs dialog box.

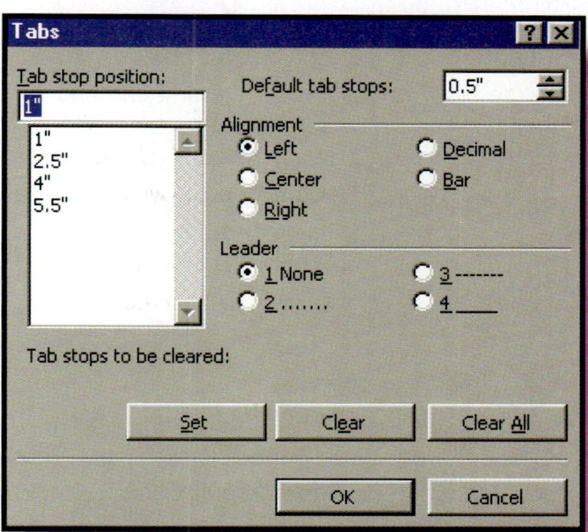

 **Hot Tips**

You can use a decimal tab to align whole numbers.

S TEP-BY-STEP ▷ 4.14

1. To create a new document, click the **New** button. Notice the left tab is displayed at the far left of the Horizontal ruler. (If it isn't, click the **Tab Alignment** button on the ruler until the left tab is displayed.)

2. To insert a left tab, click the approximate spot on the ruler where the left tab is set in Figure 4.14.

3. To display and set the center tab, click the **Tab Alignment** button at the left of the ruler. Notice Word now displays the center

tab. Click the approximate spot where the center tab is set in Figure 4.14.

4. To display and set the right tab, click the **Tab Alignment** button at the left of the ruler and click the approximate spot where the right tab is set in Figure 4.14.

5. To display and set the decimal tab, click the **Tab Alignment** button at the left of the ruler and click the approximate spot where the decimal tab is set in Figure 4.14.

(continued on next page)

6. To enter the data, type the text below. Tab to the first tab position on the first line and begin typing. After each entry on the line, press the **Tab** key, and type the next entry. Press the **Enter** key at the end of the line. Then press the **Tab** key and begin the second line.

```
Left        Center      Right        342.16

Left Tab  Center Tab  Right Tab  2.43
```

7. Close the document without saving.

Using Tab Leaders

Leaders are symbols or characters used to fill the empty space before a tab stop (see Figure 4.16). Leaders are usually dotted, dashed, or solid lines. Select the paragraphs in which you want the leaders and use the Tabs command on the Format menu to set tabs and specify the leader character.

FIGURE 4.16
Use the Tabs command on the Format menu to create dotted leaders.

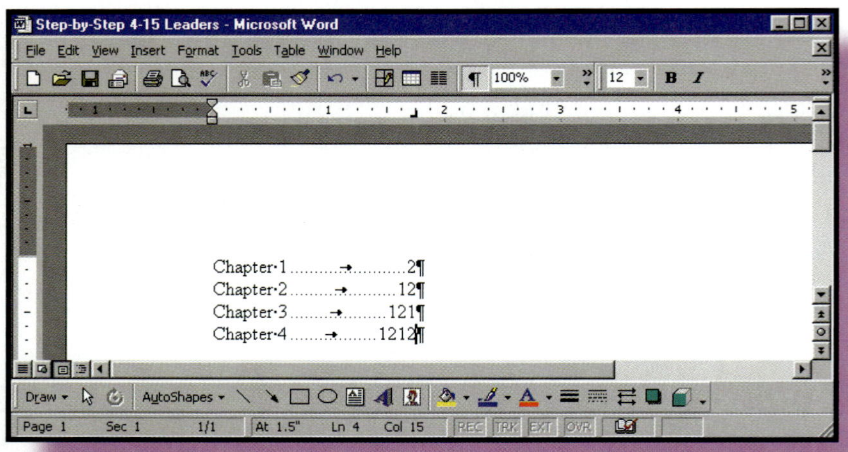

1. Open **Step-by-Step 4-15 Leaders.**

2. To select the entire file, click the **Edit** menu and click **Select All.**

3. To enter leaders, click the **Format** menu and click **Tabs.** Notice the tab position is already selected. Click the **2** option for dotted leaders, and click **OK.**

4. Close the document without saving.

Summary

You have learned a good many of Word's formatting features, including how to specify page size and orientation, set margins, control pagination and vertical alignment, apply character and paragraph formatting, and use tabs.

Try the activities on the following pages to test how well you remember what you learned. Don't be afraid to go back and look up procedures; you won't be able to remember everything you did. Using Help or looking back through this book will reinforce what you learned.

LESSON 4 REVIEW QUESTIONS

TRUE / FALSE

Circle the T if the statement is true. Circle the F if it is false.

T F   1. Sections let you use different margins or paper orientation within the same document.

T **F**   2. You can set custom sizes for paper with the Paragraph command on the Format menu.

T F   3. You must be in the print layout view to set margins with the Horizontal ruler.

T **F**   4. You can delete a soft page break that Word enters in the document.

T F   5. You must select existing text before you can apply character formatting.

T F   6. Font names describe the design of characters, and point sizes measure the height of characters.

T **F**   7. You should use underlining frequently to set words off from the rest of the text.

T F   8. You can specify that lines in a paragraph be kept together on a page.

T F   9. Any amount of text followed by a paragraph mark is considered a paragraph.

T **F** 10. The best way to indent whole paragraphs is with Tabs.

COMPLETION

Complete the following sentences by writing the correct word or words in the blanks provided.

1. You can use the _Page Setup_ command on the _File_ menu to change paper orientation from portrait to landscape mode.

2. You must be in _Page layout_ view to use the ruler to change margins.

3. You can use the _Tabs_ command on the _Format_ menu to add tabs and leaders.

4. You can use the *Change Case* command on the *Format* menu when you have accidentally typed text with the Caps Lock key on.

5. You can use the *Paragraph* command on the *Format* menu to change the line spacing from single to double.

6. You can set a(n) *decimal Tab* tab to align columns at the decimal points.

7. You can use the *Justify* tool to align text at both the left and right margins.

8. You can insert a(n) *section* break to change a page in your document from portrait to landscape mode.

9. You can use the *Center* tool to center a paragraph.

10. You can use the *Line Page Break Tab* to control how paragraphs break in a document.

LESSON 4 PROJECTS

PROJECT 4A

To practice what you've learned in this lesson, complete the following project:

1. Open **Project 4-1A**.

2. Print the document. Close the document.

3. Open and follow the formatting directions you find on the printed document of **4-1A**.

4. Print, save, and close the document.

PROJECT 4B

To practice what you've learned in this lesson, complete the following project:

1. Open **Project 4-B**.

2. Use fonts, font styles, font effects, and alignment to format the company name and address on the letter.

3. Insert a page break to move the table about new hardware and software to a new page.

4. Position tab markers to align the data in the table properly. Set leaders for the last three lines of the table—the Subtotal, Tax, and Total information.

Extra Challenges

Use Help to find information about line numbers. Read the information you find. Print a copy of each of the Help screens.

5. Add additional space between the column heads and the table body and between the table body and the Subtotal line.

6. Print the document. Save and close the document.

CRITICAL THINKING ACTIVITY

Find the symbols for the mouse, disk, and computer in the Symbol dialog box. You will have to search through the different fonts to find the symbols. Create a new document. Insert the symbols and change the font size for each symbol to 72 points. Print the document. Save the document as **Symbols,** and close the file.

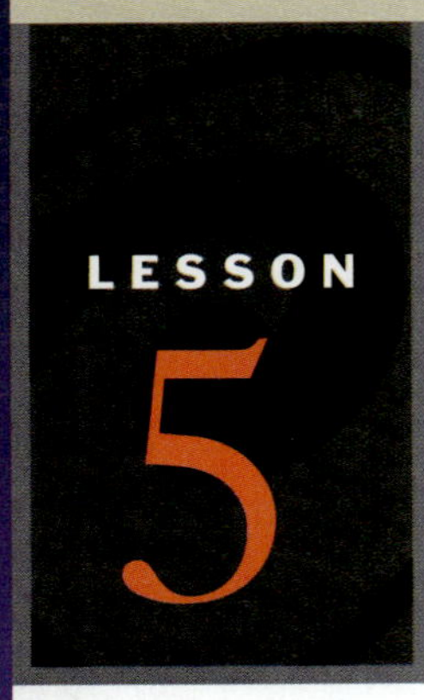

ENHANCING DOCUMENTS

Introduction

In this lesson you will learn to use features that can really enhance the appearance of your documents. You will work with bullets and numbering, add borders and shading, use Word's Style command, use heading numbering and drop caps, and format in newspaper-style columns.

Adding Bullets and Numbering to Lists

You can easily create bulleted or numbered lists with the Bullets and Numbering buttons or the Bullets and Numbering command on the Format menu.

Word automatically renumbers your lists when you insert, move, copy, or delete items.

Bullets are symbols that mark the beginning of each entry in a list.

Using the Bullets and Numbering Buttons

You can use the Bullets button to add bullets to a list. Use the Numbering button to add numbers to a list.

You can select an existing list and then click the Bullets or Numbering button to add bullets or numbers, or you can click the

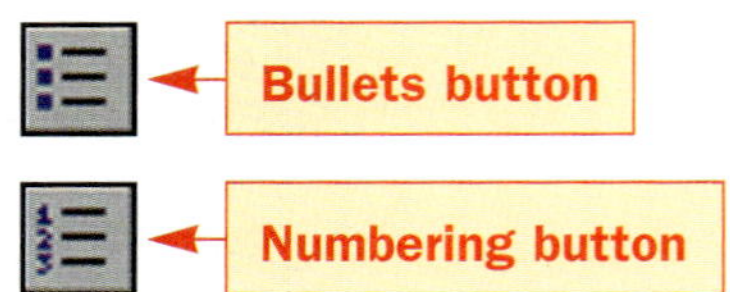

buttons before you type a list to have Word add the bullets or numbers as you type. When you finish typing the list, press the Enter key, and click the button again to turn off bullets or numbers.

If you want to add a blank line between numbered items (see Figure 5.1), you can press the Enter key twice. When you press the Enter key after the second item, Word automatically leaves a blank line and continues numbering from the previous item. You can also restart the numbering at 1 with the Bullets and Numbering command.

FIGURE 5.1
Use the Numbering button to add numbers to a list.

STEP-BY-STEP 5.1

1. Open **Step-by-Step 5-1 Bullet.**

2. To add bullets to the first list, drag in the in the left margin to select the four lines, and click the **Bullets** button.

3. To change the bullets to numbers, click the **Numbering** button.

4. To remove the numbering, click the **Numbering** button again.

5. To return to numbering, click the **Numbering** button again.

6. To insert a numbered item before the second item, position the insertion point before the word **This** in item 2, and type **This is an inserted item.** Press the **Enter** key.

7. To delete the item you just entered, click in the left margin to select the item, and press the **Delete** key.

8. To display nonprinting marks if they are not displayed, click the **Show/Hide ¶** button.

9. To add an item to the list, position the insertion point just before the paragraph mark at the end of the third item, press the **Enter** key, and type **This is item 4.** Press the **Enter** key.

10. To remove the extra number and turn off numbering, click the **Numbering** button.

11. To number the second list, select the three items in the list, and click the **Numbering** button.

12. To insert a blank line and add a fourth item, position the insertion point at the end of the third item, press the **Enter** key. Type **This is the fourth item for the second list.**

13. Print, save, and close the document.

115

Using the Bullets and Numbering Command

You can use the Bullets and Numbering command on the Format menu to modify the appearance of bulleted or numbered lists. You can change the bullet symbol or number format, the alignment of the bullets or the numbers, or the amount of space between a bullet or a number and an item in a list. You can restart the numbering at 1 or continue numbering from a previous list. You can see the formats available for bullets in Figure 5.2 and those for numbered lists in Figure 5.3.

You can use the Customize button to create a number format that includes parentheses or a format that starts list items with a word or phrase such as **Action Required.**

You will learn to use the Outline Numbered tab later in this lesson.

Notice the formats for creating bullets.

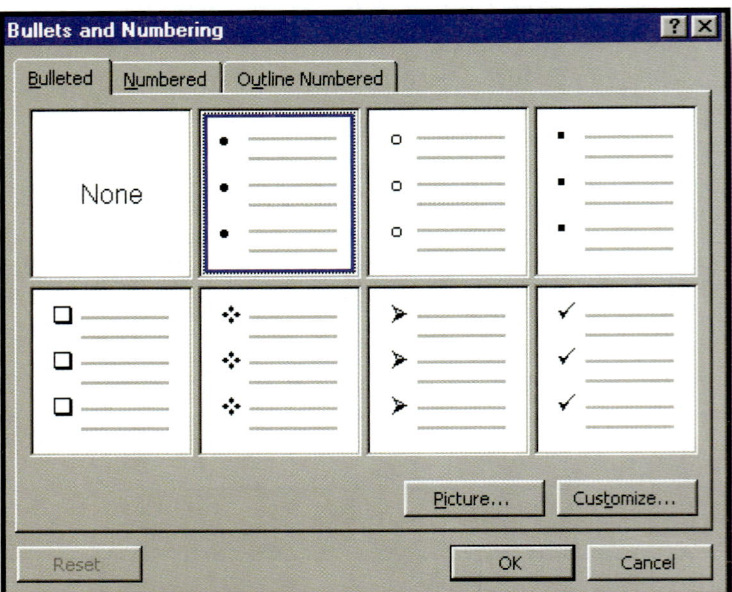

Notice the formats for creating numbered lists.

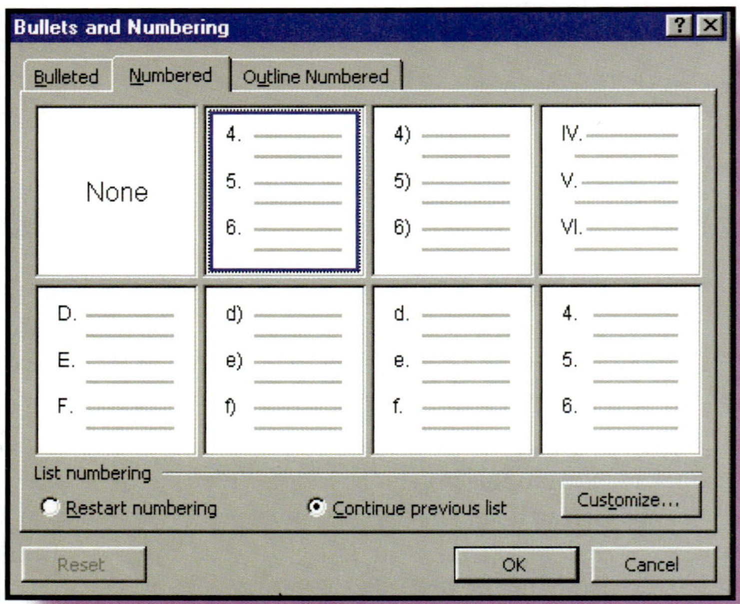

STEP-BY-STEP ▷ 5.2

1. Open **Step-by-Step 5-2 Number.**

2. To select the entire document, click the **Edit** menu, and click **Select All**.

3. To add numbering to the list, click the **Format** menu, click the **Bullets and Numbering**, click the **Outline Numbered** tab, click the first numbered format on the top row, and click **OK.**

4. To deselect the list and move the insertion point to the last paragraph mark, press the ↓ (down arrow) key.

5. To return the insertion point to the left margin, click the **More Buttons** button on the Formatting toolbar, if necessary, and click the **Decrease Indent** button twice.

6. To start a new main (Level 1) heading, click the **Numbering** button, type **Starting a New Level,** and press the **Enter** key.

7. To move to the next level, click the **Increase Indent** button. Notice Word changes the heading level.

8. To enter an item at this level and turn the numbering off, type **This is an example of how to enter text when outline numbering is turned on.** Then press the **Enter** key and click the **Numbering** button.

9. Print, save, and close the document.

Adding Borders and Shading to Text

You can add **borders,** or lines, around or to any side of selected text, and you can also shade text with a variety of colors and patterns. You can apply borders or shading to any amount of text, from a single character to an entire page.

To display the Tables and Borders toolbar (see Figure 5.4) you can click the Tables and Borders button on the Standard toolbar More Buttons list. Word automatically switches to print layout view.

You can use the Borders and Shading command on the Format menu to display the Borders and Shading dialog box (see Figure 5.5) for even more border style options and for shading, and page borders.

To apply a border line to only one side of the text, choose one of the options in the Preview area of the dialog box.

If you want to add a border to an entire page, display the Page Border tab. The settings, styles, and so forth, for this tab are the same as those on the Borders tab, except that the Apply to drop-down list allows you to choose how much of your document will have bordered pages.

Tables and Borders button

Hot Tips

Your Tables and Borders toolbar may appear on one line instead of two and be located somewhere else on your screen if a previous user has moved it.

FIGURE 5.4
The Tables and Borders toolbar contains buttons for adding borders.

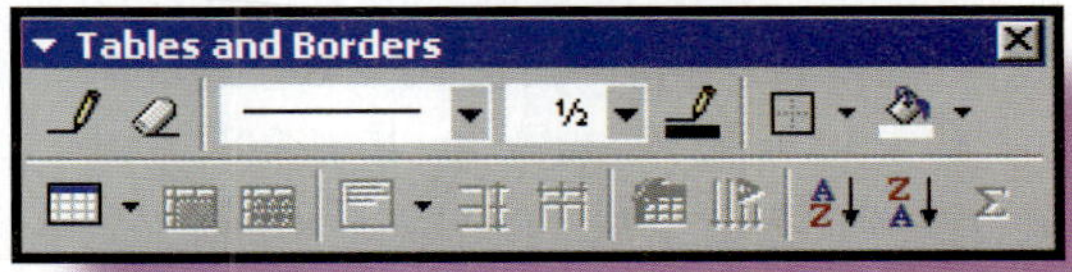

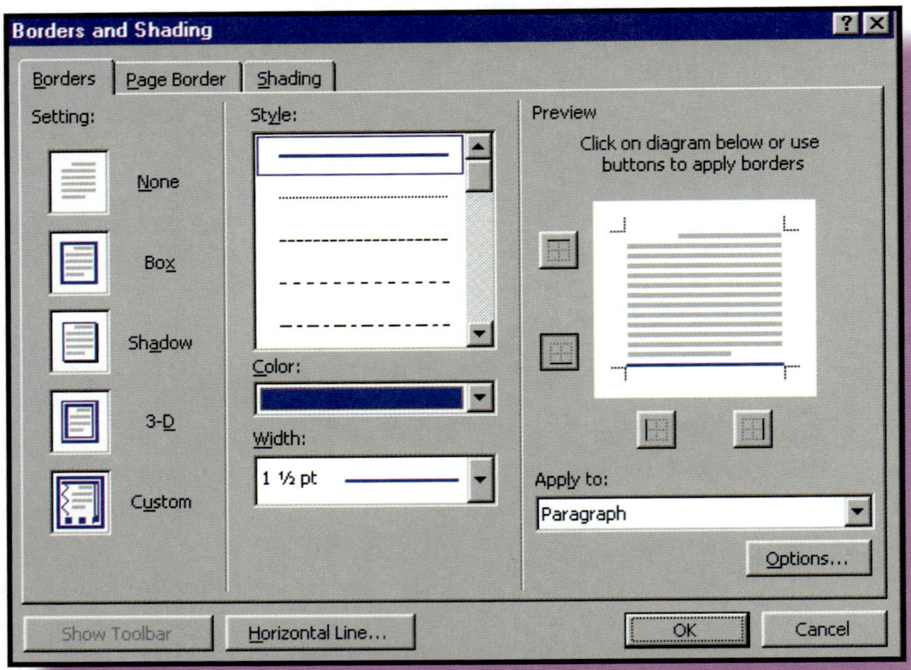

The Shading tab lets you choose a fill color and a pattern to shade selected text. When you apply a border or shading to an entire paragraph, it extends from the left indent of the paragraph to the right indent. To change the width of the bordered or shaded area in a short paragraph, such as a title, adjust the indent markers as you learned in Lesson 4.

Concept Builders

When using fill and patterns, be sure your text is still legible.

STEP-BY-STEP 5.3

1. Open **Step-by-Step 5-3 Border.**

2. To display the Tables and Borders toolbar, click the **Tables and Borders** button on the Standard toolbar.

3. To put a border around the title, select the title text. (Do not select the paragraph mark following the text.) Click the **Outside Border** button. Click outside the selection to deselect the title so you can see the border.

4. To modify the border, select the text again, click the **Format** menu, click **Borders and Shading**, click the **Borders** tab, and click **1½ pt** in the **Width** drop-down box.

5. To add shading, click the **Shading** tab, and choose a color or gray shade to fill the bordered area. Click **OK.** Click outside the selection to see the border and the shading.

6. Print, save, and close the document.

Using Styles

A **style** is a set of character or paragraph formats stored with a name. You can use the Styles feature to record paragraph and character formats and to easily apply that same formatting to other paragraphs or characters. You can also easily edit a style to change paragraphs and characters formatted with the style throughout the document.

All Word documents contain built-in styles. Use paragraph styles to format whole paragraphs and character styles to format such items as page numbers or text you want to emphasize.

You can easily distinguish between paragraph styles and character styles in the drop-down Style list on the Formatting toolbar (see Figure 5.6). Paragraph styles have a paragraph icon next to their names, and character styles have an underscored, lowercase a (<u>a</u>) next to their names.

The Style box displays the name of the style in effect at the insertion point. When you want to format headings or other common items, you can apply a style from the Style drop-down list (displayed in Figure 5.6) which shows the actual formatting for each style.

You may not see all of the built-in styles in the Style box. You can hold the Shift key while you click the drop-down button to display the entire list of built-in styles.

In Normal view, you can display the style names applied to text (see Figure 5.7) by opening the Tools menu, choosing Options, and displaying the View tab. In the Outline and Normal options, enter a Style Area width, such as 1".

To apply a *paragraph* style to a paragraph, you do not have to select the entire paragraph; just position the insertion point anywhere in the paragraph.

To apply a *character* style, you must select all of the text you want to format. You can also apply a character style for text you will enter. Choose the style you want to use for text you will enter at the insertion point, and then type the text.

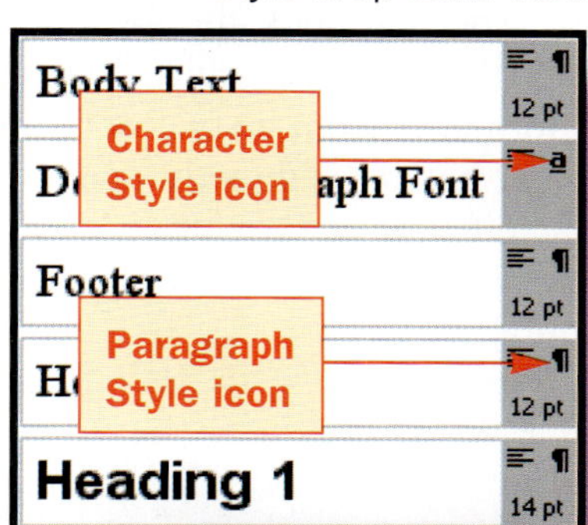
FIGURE 5.6
Choose a style from the Style drop-down box.

Concept Builders

By default, Word automatically applies the Normal style, 12-point Times New Roman, single line spacing, and left paragraph alignment.

FIGURE 5.7
Style names can be displayed in the margin when you display the View tab in the Options dialog box on the Tools menu.

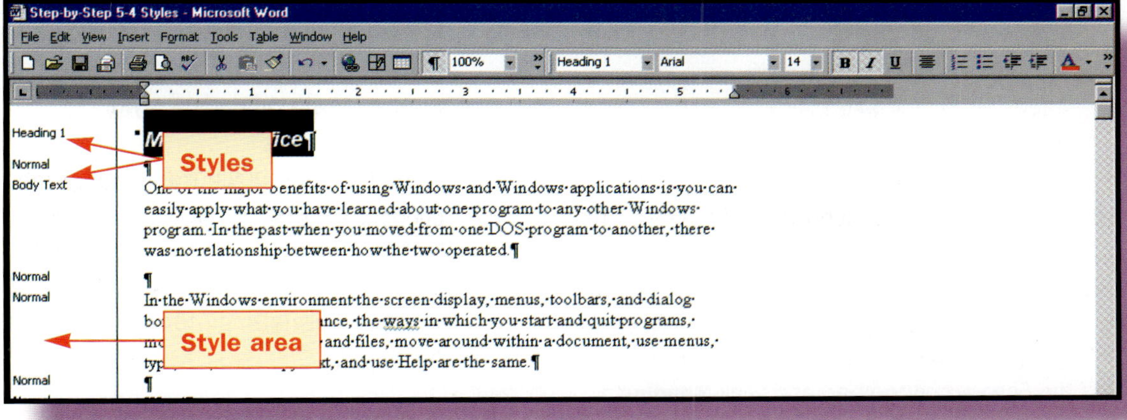

Determining How Formatting Was Applied

You can click the What's This? command on the Help menu and then click a character to find out whether its format is from a style or from direct formatting. If a format has been directly applied meaning you added it yourself with a formatting command or button, it will appear after the word **Direct.** You can see an example in Figure 5.8.

To make it easier to maintain consistent formatting in your documents, base new documents on a template; format all text with styles; and change formatting by updating styles.

FIGURE 5.8
ScreenTip shows the formatting used for this character.

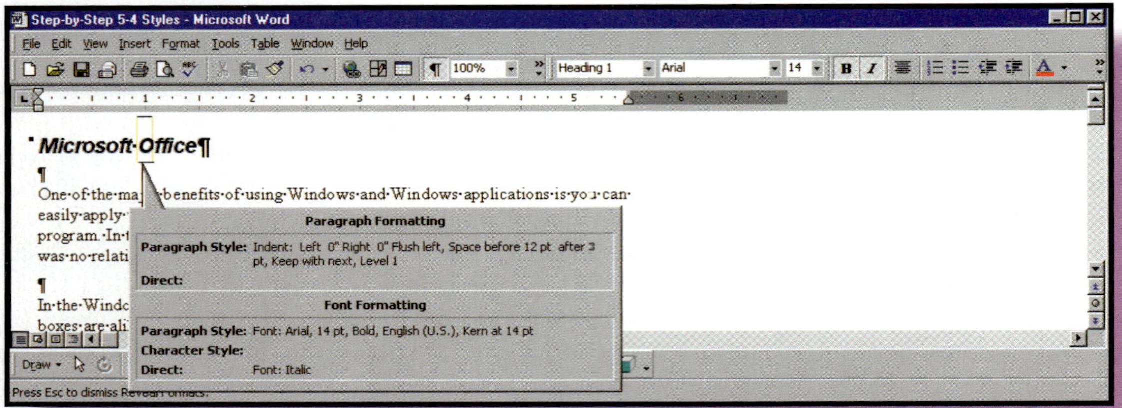

S TEP-BY-STEP ⟹ 5.4

1. Open **Step-by-Step 5-4 Styles.**

2. To change the paragraph beginning **One of the major benefits** to Body Text style, click anywhere in the paragraph, click the **Style** drop-down button on the Formatting toolbar, and click the **Body Text** style.

3. To move to the end of the document and start a new paragraph, hold the **Ctrl** key and press the **End** key and then press the **Enter** key twice.

4. To change the style before you begin to type, click the **Style** drop-down button on the Formatting toolbar, and click **Heading 1.**

5. To see the style, type your name, and press the **Enter** key twice. Notice the style at the final paragraph mark has returned to Normal because the Heading 1 style is set to return to Normal for the next paragraph. If nonprinting marks are displayed, a black mark appears before any paragraph formatted with a heading style.

6. To return to the beginning of the document and apply Heading 1 style to **Microsoft Office**, hold the **Ctrl** key and press the **Home** key, click the **Style** drop-down button on the Formatting toolbar, and click **Heading 1.**

1 2 0

7. To change the heading to italic using direct formatting, select the heading, and click the **Italic** button on the Formatting toolbar.

8. To see what formatting is applied to characters in the heading (see Figure 5.8), click the **What's This?** command on the **Help** menu, and click on characters in the heading. Check the ScreenTip and then press the **Esc** key.

9. To remove the Italic character formatting, be sure the heading is still selected, hold the **Ctrl** key and press the **Spacebar.** Notice the character formatting applied with the Italic button is removed and the paragraph formatting remains in effect.

10. Print the document. Save and close the document.

Modifying an Existing Style

The easiest way to change the appearance of text is to modify its style. When you modify and apply a style, all text formatted with the style is automatically formatted with the modified style. You can change the font and font size, and so forth, for built-in styles. Word updates text in the active document formatted with that style.

You can use the Formatting toolbar to modify a style (see Figure 5.9).

You can also use the Style command on the Format menu (see Figure 5.10) to modify a style. One style is often based on another.

FIGURE 5.9

You can display this dialog box from the toolbar.

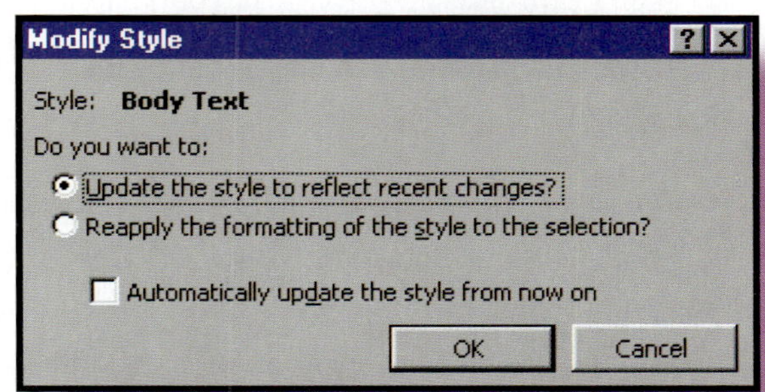

FIGURE 5.10

The Style command on the Format menu also lets you change a style.

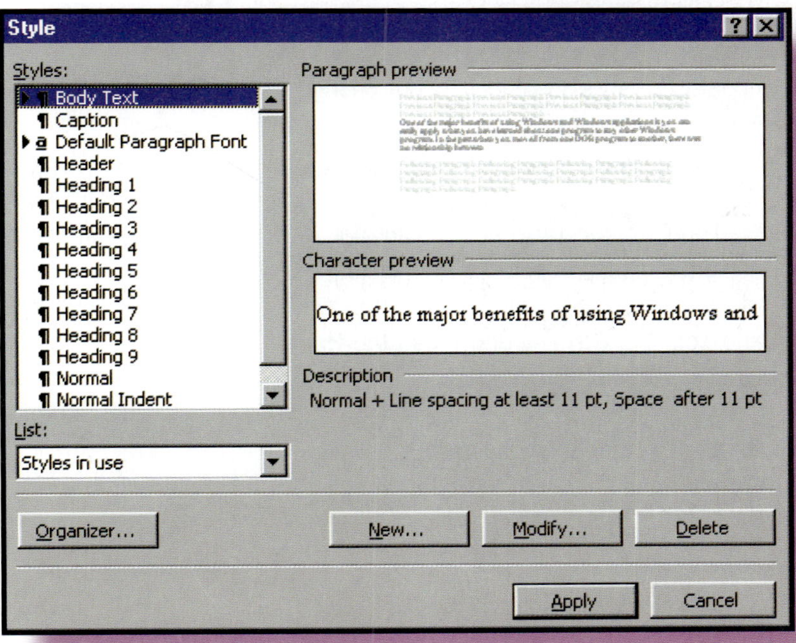

1. Open **Step-by-Step 5-5 Styles.**

2. To display the style names to the left of the text in your document, click the Normal View button on the horizontal scroll bar, click the **Tools** menu, click **Options,** click the **View** tab if it is not displayed, increase the number in the Style Area Width box to **1"** (not 0.1"), and click **OK.**

3. To see that Heading 1 and Body Text are the two styles used in the document, notice the left pane.

4. To be sure your insertion point is at the beginning of the document, hold the **Ctrl** key and press the **Home** key.

5. To see how easily you can change the Body Text style from the Arial font to the Times New Roman font, triple-click the first paragraph of Body Text, click the **Font** drop-down button, click **Times New Roman,** click the I-beam in the **Style** box on the Formatting toolbar, press the **Enter** key, and respond **OK** when asked if you want to update the style to reflect recent changes. Notice all the paragraphs formatted with Body Text style are reformatted.

6. To return to the original style format and move the insertion point to the beginning of the document, click the **Undo** button twice and hold the **Ctrl** key and press the **Home** key.

7. To display the Style dialog box, click the **Format** menu, and click **Style.** Notice the

Heading 1 style is selected in the Styles list. Notice the paragraph and character previews. Notice also the description of all the settings in the style.

8. To see the formats included in the Normal style, click **Normal on the Styles list** and notice the description of the style.

9. To see the description of the Normal Indent style, click it. Notice it is the Normal style plus a left indent.

10. To display the Modify Style dialog box, click **Heading 1** in the Styles box again, click the **Modify** button. Notice the name of the style, the style type, the style it is based on, the style for the following paragraph, the preview, and the description. Notice you can assign a shortcut key. Notice the Format button for accessing all of the paragraph and character formats. Notice also the Add to template option that you can turn on to use the updated style in new documents using the current template.

11. To change the font size for the Heading 1 style, click the **Format** command button in the Modify Style dialog box, click **Font,** scroll to click **16** in the Size box, click **OK** twice, and click **Apply.**

12. To undo the style modification, click **Undo.**

13. To remove the style names from the pane at the left of the document, click the **Tools** menu, click **Options,** return the Style area width to **0",** and click **OK.**

Creating a New Paragraph Style or Character Style by Example

You can format a paragraph with the font, font size, alignment, and other formats you want, and then create a new style using that paragraph as an example.

S TEP-BY-STEP ▷ 5.6

1. To format a paragraph for use as an example for a new style, triple-click somewhere in the first paragraph beginning **One of the major benefits,** click the **Font Size** drop-down button, click **12,** and click the **Bold** button.

2. To create a new style by example, click in the **Style** box, type the name **Bold,** and press the **Enter** key.

3. To apply the new style to the next paragraph, click anywhere in the paragraph, click the **Style** drop-down button, and click the **Bold** style.

4. To delete the style, click the **Undo** button on the Standard toolbar twice.

5. Close the document without saving.

Numbering Headings

You can use the Outline Numbered tab in the Bullets and Numbering dialog box to have Word number headings that are formatted with built-in heading styles. Word will number only those paragraphs where you have used a built-in heading style. Word starts the numbering at the beginning of the document. You must create a new section if you want to restart numbering within the document. You can also use the Increase Indent and Decrease Indent button to set up to nine levels for outline numbering.

S TEP-BY-STEP ▷ 5.7

1. Open **Step-by-Step 5-7 Heads.**

2. To see the Heading 1, Heading 2, and Heading 3 formatting, use the ↓ (down arrow) key to move through the document. Click each of the headings and notice the Heading 1, 2, and 3 styles in the Style box.

3. To number the headings and see the numbers, make sure the insertion point is in the first heading (Heading 1), click the **Format** menu, click **Bullets and Numbering,** click the **Outline Numbered** tab, click the second option from the right on the bottom row, and click **OK.** Then scroll through the document

4. Save and close the document.

Using Drop Caps

A **drop cap** is a large or dropped initial capital letter or a large first word used to add interest, such as at the beginning of a document. Word lets you create drop caps with the Drop Cap command on the Format menu (see Figure 5.11).

You must be in Print Layout view or Print Preview view to see the dropped cap.

FIGURE 5.11

You can create a dramatic-looking initial capital letter using the Drop Cap command.

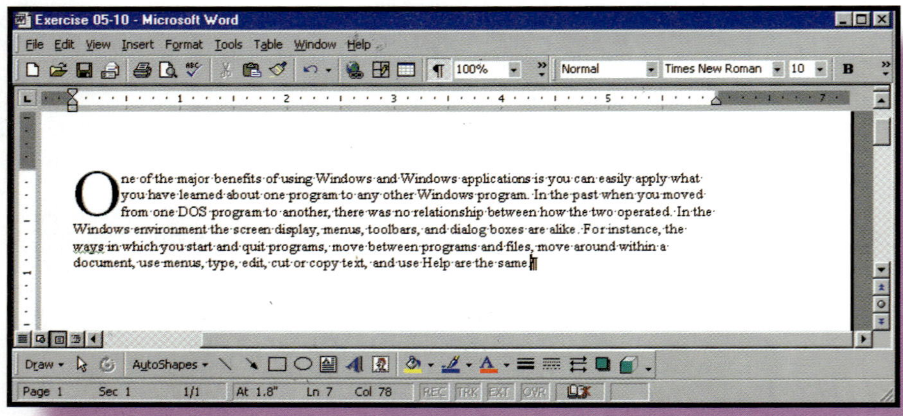

STEP-BY-STEP 5.8

1. Open **Step-by-Step 5-8 Drop.**

2. To drop the first character in the paragraph, *be sure the insertion point is in the paragraph,* click the **Format** menu, click the **Drop Cap** command, click the **Dropped** in the Position box, and click **OK.**

3. To remove the dropped cap, *be sure the insertion point is in the paragraph,* click the **Format** menu, click the **Drop Cap** command, click the **None** in the Position box, and click **OK.**

4. Close the document without saving.

Working with Newspaper-Style Columns

You can use the Columns command on the expanded Format menu to format all or part of your document with newspaper-style columns. The Columns command also lets you create columns of unequal width.

You can also use the Columns button on the Standard toolbar to create multiple columns of equal width.

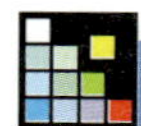

Use the Tables feature (which will be covered in Lesson 7) for side-by-side paragraphs used in resumes.

Text flows from the bottom of one column to the top of the next (see Figure 5.12) when you use the column format. You can vary the number of columns and the width of individual columns (see Figure 5.13).

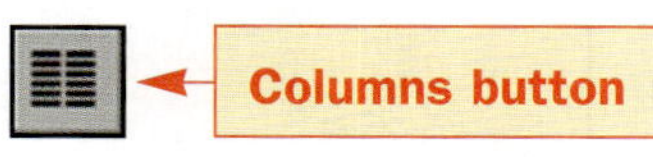

Word automatically adds section breaks at the beginning and the end of the text formatted for newspaper columns.

FIGURE 5.12

Newspaper-style columns can be created with the Columns command or the Columns button.

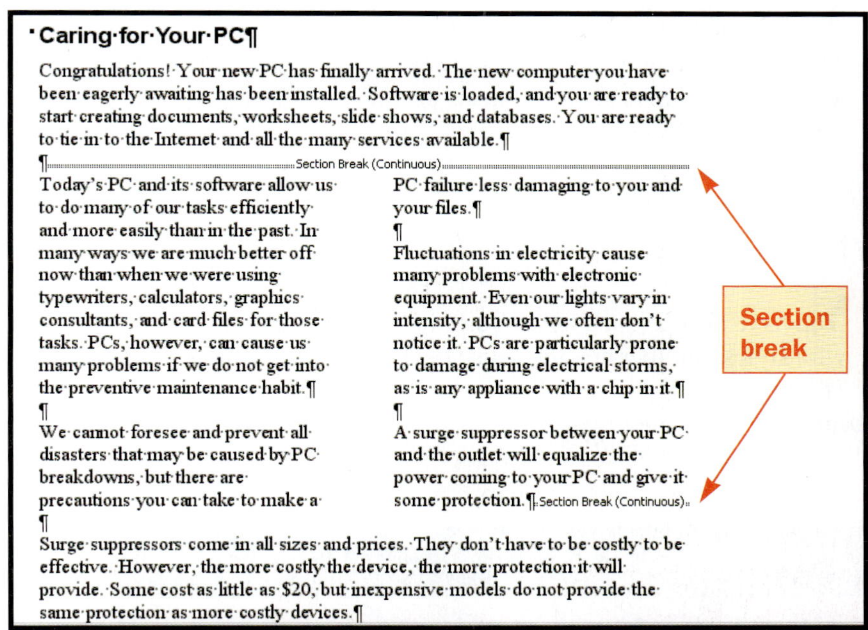

FIGURE 5.13

The Columns dialog box shows options for formatting columns.

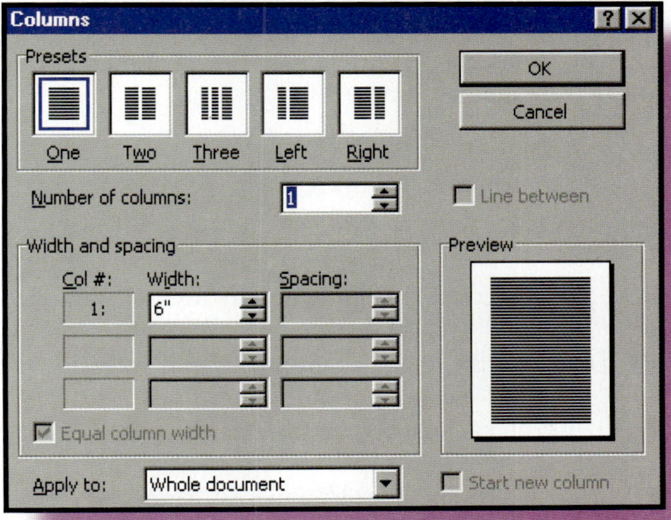

1. Open **Step-by-Step 5-9 Column.** To switch to Print Layout view, click the **Print Layout** view button.

2. To put the four paragraphs beginning with **Today's PC** in two-column format, select the four paragraphs, click the **Columns** button on the Standard toolbar, drag across **two columns,** and release (scroll up and down through the document).

3. To undo the column layout and delete the section breaks, be sure everything in the column section is selected, click the **Format** menu, click **Columns,** click **One,** and click **OK.** The click on each section break and press the **Delete** key.

4. Close the document without saving.

Summary

You have now learned how to use the bullets and numbering features, add borders and shading, work with styles, number headings, use the Drop Cap command, and create newspaper-style columns.

Try the exercises on the following pages to test how well you remember what you learned. Don't be afraid to go back and look up the answers, because that will help to reinforce what you learned.

LESSON 5 REVIEW QUESTIONS

TRUE / FALSE

Circle the T if the statement is true. Circle the F if it is false.

T **F** 1. You cannot leave a blank line between items in a numbered list.

T F 2. You can use the Increase Indent and Decrease Indent buttons to set up for an outline numbered list.

T F 3. You can select an existing list and use the Bullets button to add bullets to the list.

T **F** 4. You can have only one outline numbered list in a document.

T F 5. You can add a border to any text selection.

T **F** 6. You can remove a dropped cap by pressing the Esc key.

T F 7. You can display the style names used in your document in the left margin.

T **F** 8. You should use the columns feature for a resume with side-by-side paragraphs.

T (F) **9.** You can hold the Ctrl key and press the Enter key to remove character styles from a selection.

(T) F **10.** The Style box displays the style in effect at the insertion point.

COMPLETION

Complete the following sentences by writing the correct word or words in the blanks provided.

1. You can use the _Bullets & Number_ command to create an outline numbered list.

2. You can use the _Borders & Shading_ command to add color or pattern to a text selection.

3. A(n) _Style_ is a group of formats identified by a name.

4. You can automatically number headings if you use _Headup_ styles.

5. Word _renumbers_ your list as needed when you delete a numbered item from the list.

6. The _Style Box_ displays the name of the style in effect at the insertion point.

7. Word automatically applies the _Normal_ style when you enter text in a document.

8. You can use the _Columns_ command or button to create newspaper-style columns.

9. You can assign _shortcut / shift_ keys to a style.

10. You can use the _drop caps_ command to set off the first letter or word in a paragraph.

LESSON 5 PROJECTS

PROJECT 5A

To practice what you've learned in this lesson, complete the following project:

1. Open **Project 5-A.**

2. Add bullets shaped like diamonds to the first list and use the Numbering button to add numbers to the second list.

3 Print the document. Save and close the file.

Extra Challenges

Use Help to find out how to use shortcut keys with styles. Read and print the information you find.

To practice what you've learned in this lesson, complete the following project:

1. Open **Project 5-B.**

2. Put the text below the heading in three newspaper columns.

3. Print the document. Save and close the document.

CRITICAL THINKING ACTIVITY

SCANS

Use the Fax Recipient command on the Send To send to command on the File menu to start the wizard and prepare a cover sheet. Fax your **Project 5A** document and cover sheet to a friend.

USING TIMESAVING FEATURES

LESSON 6

OBJECTIVES

When you complete this lesson, you will be able to:

- Use the Replace command.
- Record and run a macro.
- Use the Comment feature.
- Track revisions in a document.
- Work with fields.
- Use Headers and Footers and Page Numbers commands.

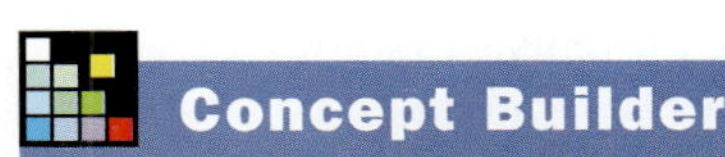

Estimated Time: 1½ hours

Introduction

In this lesson you will use many of Word's timesaving features. You will use the Replace command to quickly replace text or formatting throughout a document. You will record a series of actions to create a macro, and then run the macro to repeat the actions.

You will use the Comment feature, which allows you or others to put notes and voice comments in your document. You will use the Track Changes feature to view revisions made in a document. You will use fields to enter information contained in the system (such as dates, file names, and so on) in your documents. You will also use the Headers and Footers and Page Numbers commands to enter information that will repeat on each page.

Working with the Replace Command

Use the Replace command on the Edit menu to find and replace text, formats, and styles. This is a very useful feature if you have documents in which you must change names or other text or formatting.

Word gives you two ways to work with the Find and Replace dialog box. The collapsed dialog box can be used for simple find-and-replace operations. Use the More button to display the expanded dialog box (see Figure 6.1). The expanded Find and Replace dialog box lets you refine your find-and-replace operations by matching case, finding only specific formats, and using special characters.

Concept Builders

You can use the Undo button if you are not happy with the results of a find-and-replace operation.

You can see the expanded Find and Replace dialog box.

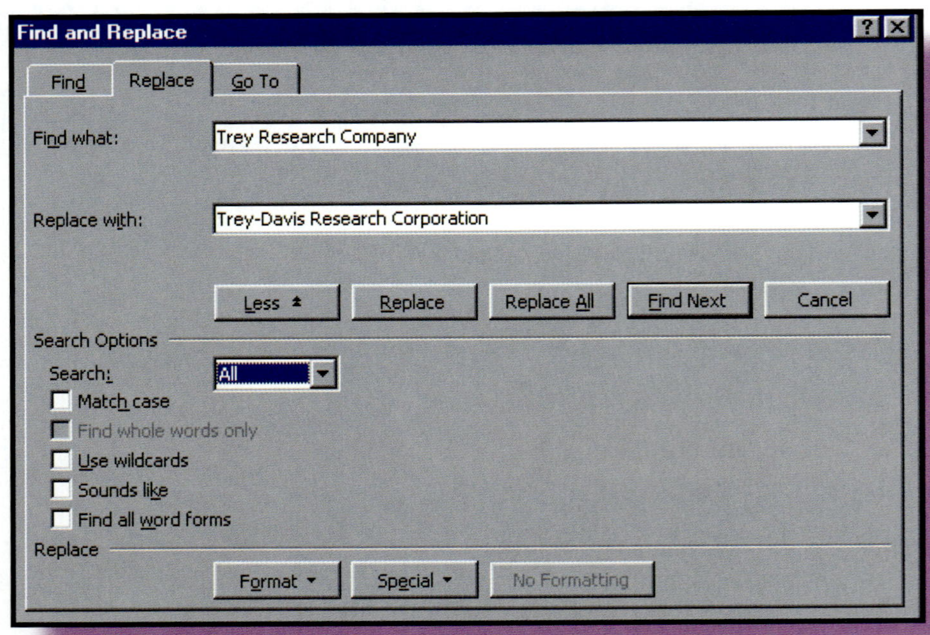

Word searches the entire document, including headers, footers, footnotes, endnotes, and comments. You can limit the search by selecting part of a document or by selecting Up or Down in the search drop-down list in the Search options area. If you use the Up option or Down option for the search, you limit the search to the main document and exclude headers and footers, footnotes, and so on.

If you want to replace an item with a large block of text or with graphics, copy the text or graphics to the Clipboard. Then find the item you want to replace, click the document to make it active, and use the Paste button.

If you need more information you can use Help to learn about advanced search criteria.

Replacing All Occurrences

You can use the Replace All button to replace all occurrences at once without confirming each. Be very sure when you use the Replace All button that you really want to replace all occurrences. For instance, you can run into trouble using Replace All when changing a person's name, such as Jackson to Johnson. If a company name or city name in the document contains the name Jackson, Replace All changes it to Johnson as well.

In the following exercise you will use the Replace All option. When replacing a name like Trey Research Company, it is not likely there will be unexpected results using that option.

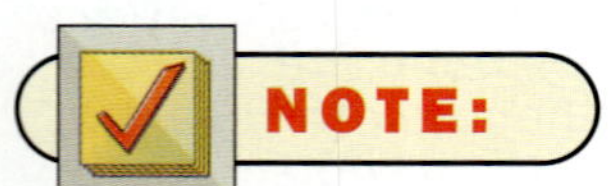

If your replace operation does not work properly, be sure you enter the text in the Find What box exactly as it appears in the document. Be sure, for instance, there are no extra spaces in the Find what text.

STEP-BY-STEP ▷ 6.1

1. Open **Step-by-Step 6-1 Replace.**

2. To open the Find and Replace dialog box, click the **Edit** menu and then click **Replace.**

3. To enter the Find what text, type **Trey Research Company.**

4. To enter the Replace with text, press the **Tab** key and type **Trey-Davis Research Corporation.**

5. To expand the Find and Replace dialog box if you have the collapsed one on your screen, click the **More** button in the dialog box. If any check boxes contain check marks, click them, and be sure the Search drop-down box displays All—not Down or Up.

6. To replace the several words all at once, click the **Replace All** button.

7. To close the box telling you three replacements were made and the dialog box, click **OK** and then click the **Close** button in the dialog box. Notice that because you did not specify formatting in the dialog box, the formatting in place for each of the original instances of **Trey Research Company** remained as it was.

Replacing One Occurrence at a Time

In the following exercise you will replace each occurrence of Janet Jackson's last name with Johnson. Because it is often likely such a find and replace operation could result in unwanted changes to the word Jackson, it is important to use the Find Next and Replace buttons to make just one replacement at a time.

STEP-BY-STEP ▷ 6.2

1. To begin another replace, be sure nothing is selected in your document, click the **Edit** menu, and click **Replace.** Type **Jackson** in the Find What box, press the **Tab** key to move to the Replace With box, type **Johnson,** and click the **Find Next** button.

2. To replace the first occurrence of Janet Jackson's last name, which is selected, with **Johnson,** click the **Replace** button.

3. To leave the selected name of Janet Jackson's company unchanged, click the **Find Next** button.

4. To replace Janet Jackson's last name, which is selected, click the **Replace** button.

5. To skip the company name again, Jackson Hole, and the letter writer's name, click **Find Next** three times.

6. To remove the dialog box telling you the search is finished and close the Find and Replace dialog box, click **OK** and click the **Close** button in the dialog box.

Replacing Formatting

You will now use the find and replace feature to find *Trey-Davis Research Corporation* with bold and italic formatting and replace it with the same text but with italic formatting only. You know from the first exercise that there are three instances of *Trey-Davis Research Corporation*. The first one is at the top of the page, and the other two are in the body of the letter. The two in the body of the letter have additional formatting.

If you cannot see the selected items because the dialog box covers them, move the dialog box by dragging its title bar. You can also click the Less button after adding formatting options.

S TEP-BY-STEP ▷ 6.3

1. To see the formatting applied to **Trey-Davis Research Corporation** in the body of the letter, click the **Help** menu, click the **What's This?** command, and click on **Trey-Davis Research Corporation** in the body of the letter. Notice Bold and Italic formatting were applied directly.

2. To remove the ScreenTip, press the **Esc** key.

3. To begin a replace operation to remove the direct bold formatting but keep the italic formatting, be sure nothing is selected, click the **Edit** menu, click **Replace**, and type **Trey-Davis Research Corporation** in the **Find what** box.

4. To add bold and italic to the search criteria so Word finds only the formatted occurrences of the text in the Find What box, click the **Format** button in the dialog box, click **Font**, click **Bold Italic** in the Font style box, and click **OK**. Notice the format criteria are entered directly under the Find what box.

5. To move to the Replace With box and enter the replacement text, press the **Tab** key and type **Trey-Davis Research Corporation**.

6. To format the replacement text with italic but not bold, click the **Format** button in the dialog box, click **Font**, click **Italic** in the Font style box, and click **OK.**

7. To replace the text with the different format and close the dialog box telling you Word made two replacements, click **Replace All** and click **OK.**

8. To remove the Format criteria from the Find What and Replace With boxes and close the dialog box, click the **Find What** box, click the **No Formatting** button in the dialog box, click the Replace with box, and click the No Formatting button. Then click the **Close** button in the dialog box.

9. Save and close the document.

Recording and Running a Macro

A **macro** is a recording of a series of Word commands. Macros can simplify repetitive tasks. You can make using a macro as easy as using a Word command by assigning it to a toolbar or to shortcut keys.

If you owned or worked for Trey Research Company when its name changed to Trey-Davis Research Corporation, you might have to use the Replace command on hundreds or even thousands of documents. A macro would certainly speed your task. You would need only to click a menu command or button or type a few keystrokes to run the macro for each document.

To display the Record Macro dialog box (see Figure 6.2), choose the Macro command on the Tools menu and then choose Record New Macro on the submenu, or double-click the REC button on the Status bar.

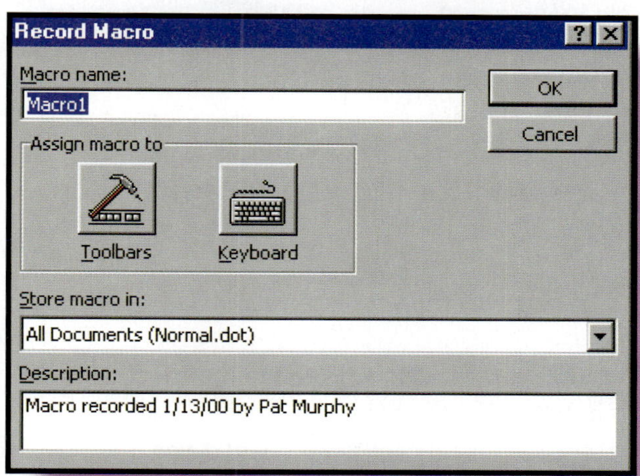

FIGURE 6.2

Use the Record Macro dialog box to create a macro.

NOTE:

To remind you that the recorder is on, Word attaches a recorder icon to your mouse pointer.

You can then enter a name for your macro and assign the macro to a toolbar or to keyboard shortcut keys. When you click OK, the recording begins, and Word displays the Stop Recording toolbar (see Figure 6.3).

You can use toolbar buttons to turn off the recorder and then turn it on again. You can use the Stop Recording button to signal you have finished recording.

When recording a macro, try to think of any prompts or dialog boxes that might interfere with your macro. For example, if your macro will use the Replace command, you must type the correct text in the Find What and Replace With boxes while you are recording the macro; otherwise, a prompt for which your macro does not have an action will create a problem with the macro.

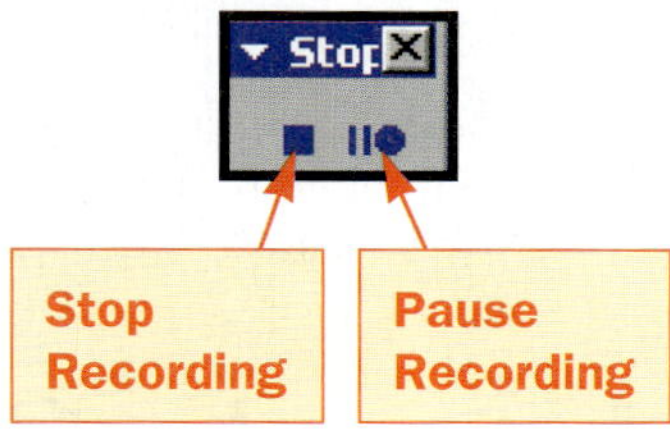

FIGURE 6.3

The Stop Recording toolbar appears when you begin recording a new macro.

It doesn't matter whether the correct text is already in the Find What and Replace With boxes when you display them as you are recording. The boxes are already empty when you turn on your computer each day, so you must retype the text to be sure entering it becomes part of the macro.

By default a macro you create is available in all your documents. If a template is attached to your document, you can store the macro in the attached template so that it is available only to documents that are based on that template.

The macro is not saved until you save the template in which it is stored. You can save the template by choosing the Save All command on the File menu or by clicking Yes when asked whether you want to save changes to the template.

You can use the Macros command on the Macro submenu to run a macro, or you can run the macro by using the toolbar button or shortcut keys you assign to the macro.

To delete a macro, click the Tools menu, click Macro, and then click Macros on the submenu. Find the macro name in the list of macros, and use the Delete button.

1 3 3

1. Open **Step-by-Step 6-4A Macro.**

2. To start the macro recording process, double-click the **REC** button on the status bar.

3. To name your macro, type your initials.

4. To assign shortcut keys to the macro, click the **Keyboard** button in the Assign Macro To area. In the Customize Keyboard dialog box, hold the **Alt** key and press **R.** Then click the **Assign** button, and click the **Close** button. Notice the Stop Recording toolbar and the recorder attached to your mouse pointer. The recorder is now on.

5. To begin recording the find-and-replace operation, hold the **Ctrl** key and press the **Home** key, click the **Edit** menu, click **Replace,** type **Trey Research Company,** and click the **No Formatting** button if there are formats displayed under the Find what box.

6. To finish recording the find-and-replace operation, press the **Tab** key, type **Trey-**

Davis **Research Corporation,** click the **No Formatting** command button if there are formats displayed under the Replace With box, click **Replace All,** click **OK** to respond to the number of replacement message, and click **Close.**

7. To stop recording, click the **Stop Recording** button on the Stop Recording toolbar.

8. To test the macro on another document, open **Step-by-Step 6-4B Macro,** and hold the **Alt** key and press **R.** Notice how quickly Word replaced the original text.

9. To delete your macro, click the **Tools** menu, click **Macro,** click **Macros** on the submenu, click the macro with your initials, click **Delete,** and click the **Close** button.

10. To close both documents without saving the documents or the macro, hold the **Shift** key while you click the **File** menu, and click **Close All.** Respond **No** when asked whether to save the documents.

Using the Comment Feature

Word's Comment feature allows reviewers to comment on rather than change a document. **Comments** are numbered remarks (see Figure 6.4). You can display comments in a separate pane, or you can display a comment as a ScreenTip by displaying nonprinting marks and sliding the mouse pointer on the comment's reference mark until the ScreenTip appears. If you have the necessary hardware, you can include voice and pen comments.

When several reviewers comment on a document, Word enters each reviewer's initials so you can easily tell who made a comment.

Before you insert a comment, you must select the text about which you will comment. When you choose the Comment command on the Insert menu, Word opens the Comment pane where you type your remarks. Word takes as your initials the initials of the name in the User Information tab in the Options dialog box and adds them with the number of the comment as hidden text in the

FIGURE 6.4
Notice the Comment pane and also the ScreenTip.

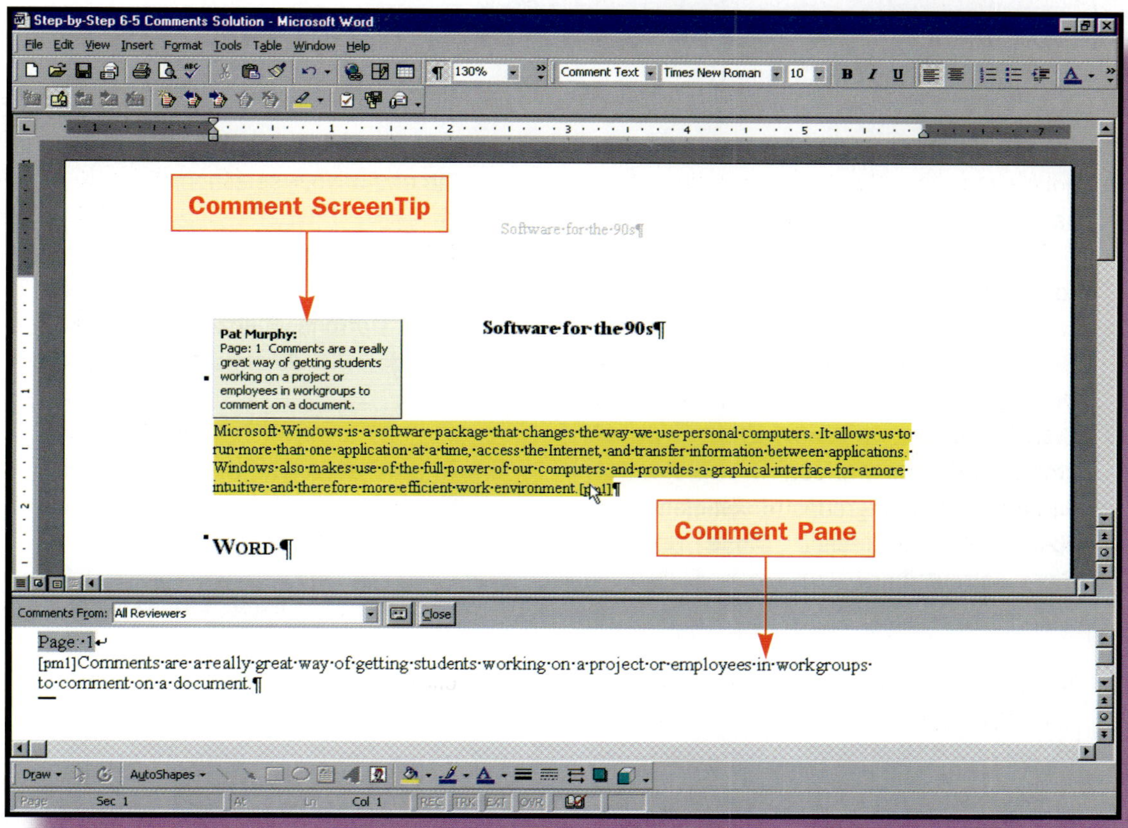

document. You can move from pane to pane by clicking in the pane in which you want to work to make it active.

Each comment has a comment mark in the document, which you can see when you use the Show/Hide ¶ button to display nonprinting marks. You can use the Comments command on the View menu to view the comment pane in a document. When the comment pane is open, it displays the comments corresponding to the part of the document displayed. Word highlights the text to which the comment refers. If nonprinting marks are displayed, you can double-click a comment mark to view the comment.

To put a copy of a comment into your document, select the comment, choose Copy on the Edit menu, position the insertion point where you want the comment, and click the Paste button on the Standard toolbar.

To delete a comment, select the comment mark in the document window, and press the Backspace key or the Delete key.

You can use the Print command to print only comments or to print a combination of the document and the comments. Word prints the comment numbers and the text if you print only comments. When you print the document and the comments, Word prints comment reference numbers in the document and the numbers and corresponding text at the end of the document.

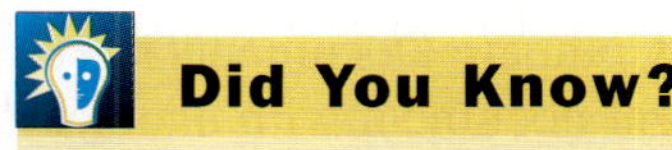
Did You Know?

When you copy, move, or delete a comment, Word automatically renumbers the comments.

1. Open **Step-by-Step 6-5 Comment.**

2. To select text on which you will comment, double-click in the left margin of the paragraph beginning **Microsoft Windows.**

3. To insert a comment and then close the comment pane, click the **Insert** menu, and click **Comment.** The comment pane opens, with the reviewer's initials in brackets. Type **Comments are a really great way of getting students working on a project or employees in workgroups to comment on a document.** Then click **Close** on the Comments toolbar.

4. To display nonprinting marks if they are not displayed, click the **Show/Hide ¶** button. Notice Word inserted the comment mark at the end of your selection.

5. To print the document and the comment, click the **File** menu, and click **Print.** Then click **Options,** click **Comments** in the **Include with document** list, and click **OK** twice.

6. To save and close the document, click the **Save** button and then click the document's Close button.

Tracking Changes in a Document

Word lets you track changes made in a document. This feature lets a document's author see and respond to changes made by other readers. Word uses a different color to mark each reviewer's changes. Use the Track Changes command on the Tools menu to display the Highlight Changes dialog box (see Figure 6.5).

The Track Changes submenu gives you three options for tracking revisions:

- Choose Highlight Changes to show revisions on the screen as you work and in printed documents.

- Choose Accept or Reject Changes to review changes made in a document. In the Accept or Reject Changes dialog box (Figure 6.6), you can find the next or previous change and can accept or reject all or selected changes.

- Choose Compare Documents to compare the current document with another version of the document and to mark differences between them on the edited copy. You can then review these changes and accept or reject them.

Concept Builders

If you are comparing documents and want to compare versions of the same document, you must use the Save As command to save the newer version as a separate file before using Compare Documents to compare them.

FIGURE 6.5
The Highlight Changes dialog box.

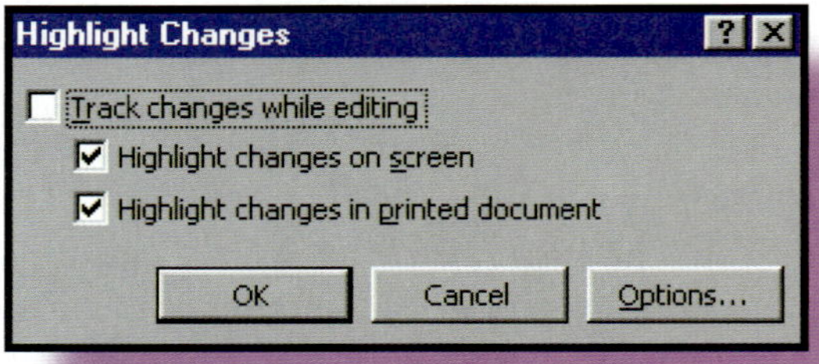

FIGURE 6.6
The Accept or Reject Changes dialog box.

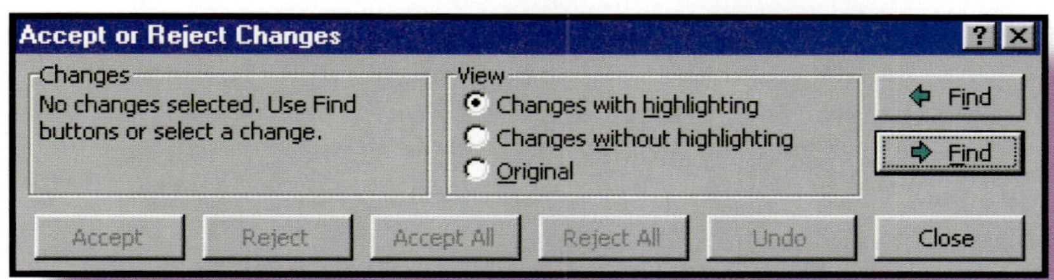

STEP-BY-STEP 6.6

1. Open **Step-by-Step 6-6 Track.**

2. To open the Highlight Changes dialog box, click the **Tools** menu, click **Track Changes,** and click **Highlight Changes** on the submenu. Click to place a check in the **Track changes while editing** check box, and click **OK.**

3. To enter a change, place the insertion point at the beginning of the second line of text.

Type **When you enter new text it is underlined and in color.** Press the **Enter** key twice.

4. To see how Word marks a deletion, delete the first instance of **a line through it** on the third line.

5. To see how Word marks edited text, change **blue** to **red** at the end of the same line.

6. Close the document without saving changes.

Working with Fields

Fields are codes that tell Word to insert information in a document. Word contains more than 70 fields you can use in your documents.

You can use the Date and Time command on the Insert menu to insert the date and time (see Figure 6.7). As you can see in Figure 6.7, you can choose the format for the date or time. If you turn on the Update automatically option in the Date and Time dialog box, Word automatically updates the date or time when you print the document.

FIGURE 6.7
The Date and Time command lets you select the format for the date and time.

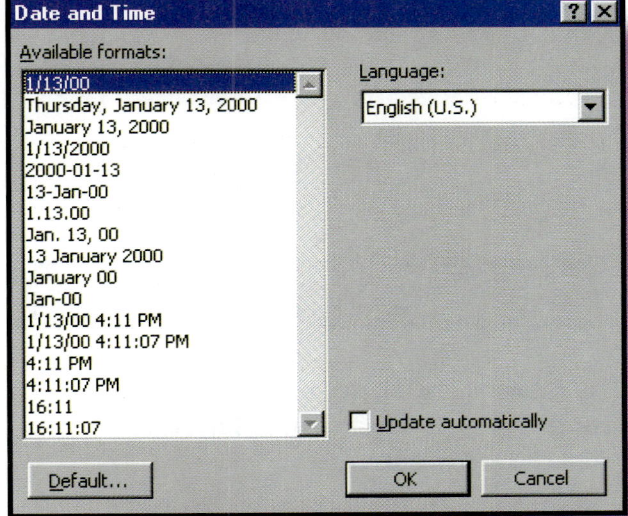

Field results are visible as text, graphics, or a combination of the two. Field codes are enclosed within field characters, which look like curly braces ({}). You can use the shortcut menu to view the field codes for a single field (Figure 6.8). You can display all of the field codes in selected text by holding the Shift key and pressing the F9 key.

You can update the date or time at any time by positioning the I-beam on the date, clicking the right mouse button to display the shortcut menu, and choosing Update Field. You can also update fields by selecting one or more fields (or the whole document) and then pressing F9.

You can also use the Field command on the Insert menu to insert other Word fields in your document (see Figure 6.9).

You can use the Date and Time category to insert such fields as the current date, the current time, the date a document was created, the date it was last printed, the date it was last saved, or the total time it was edited. You then use the Options button to select a format for a field.

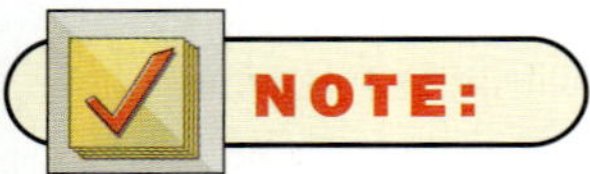

NOTE:

To update fields when you are printing, choose Options on the Tools menu, display the Print tab, and turn on the Update fields option.

Many people who use Word enter the FileName field as a footer in the document. That way the name of the file is displayed on all pages.

FIGURE 6.8

This document shows time and date field codes.

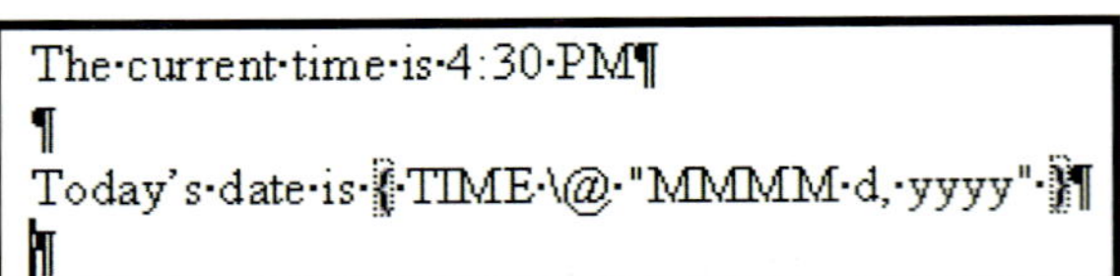

FIGURE 6.9

In the Field dialog box, you choose a field category.

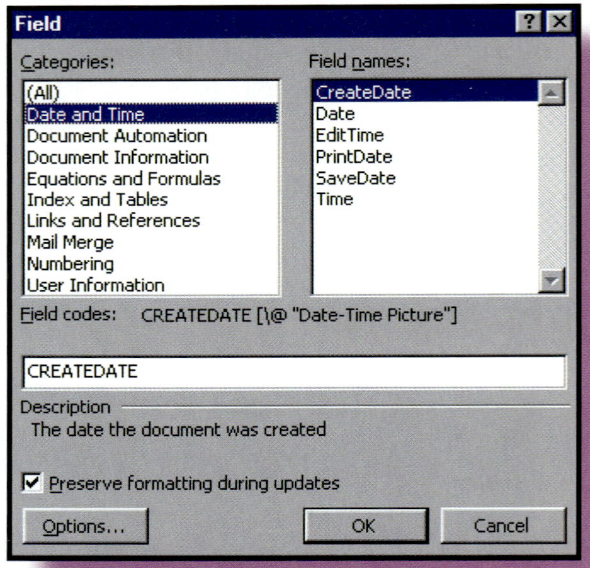

STEP-BY-STEP 6.7

1. To create a new document and enter some text, click the **New** button, type **The current time is,** and type a space.

2. To enter a time field, click the **Insert** menu, click the **Date and Time** command, and click the first time format. Be sure **Update Automatically** is checked, and click **OK.**

3. To enter the date, press the **Enter** key twice, type **Today's date is** and a space, click the **Insert** menu, click **Date and Time,** click the third format on the list, and click **OK.**

4. To display the field codes instead of the actual date and time, click the I-beam in the field, hold the **Shift** key and press the **F9** key.

5. To return to the original display, hold the **Shift** key and press the **F9** key again.

6. To enter the document's creation date, press the **End** key, press the **Enter** key twice, type **This document was created on** and a space, click the **Insert** menu, click **Field,** click the **Date and Time** in the categories list, and click **Create Date** in the Field names list.

7. To select the format for the date, click the **Options** button, click the third format, and click **OK** twice.

8. To update the time, position the I-beam over the **Time** field in the first line, click the *right* mouse button, and click **Update Field.**

9. Close the document without saving.

Adding Headers and Footers

A **header** or **footer** is text or graphics that is printed in the top or bottom margin of each page in a document. Headers and footers are usually simple document titles and page numbers. You can opt *not* to print a header or footer on the first page, and you can specify a different header or footer for odd and even pages. You can divide a document into sections and use different headers and footers in each section.

Use the Header and Footer command on the View menu to create headers and footers. Word automatically switches to print layout view and displays the Header and Footer toolbar (see Figure 6.10).

- Use the Insert AutoText button to see a list of text entries appropriate for headers and footers.

- Use the Insert Page Number button to insert the document's page number in the header or footer.

FIGURE 6.10
The Header and Footer toolbar lets you create headers and footers.

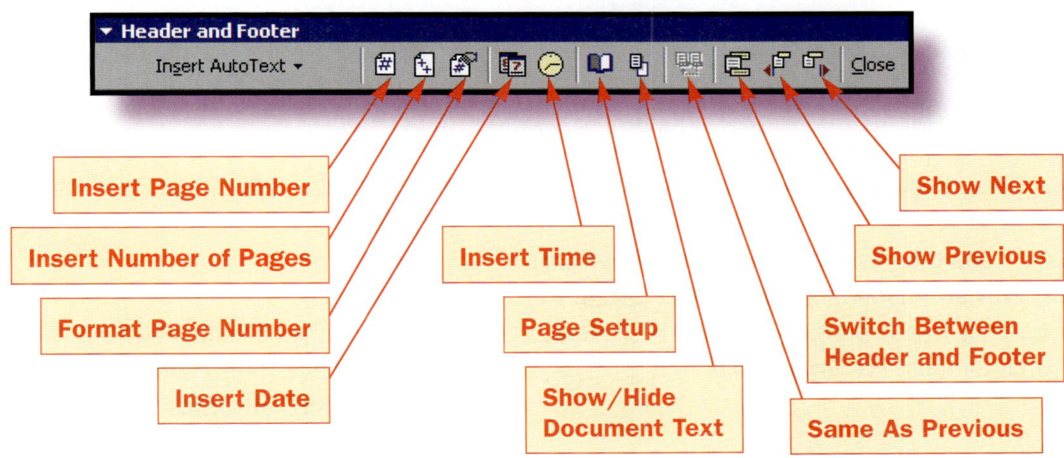

1 3 9

- Use the Insert Number of Pages button to insert the number of pages in the document.

- Use the Format Page Number button to change the way page numbers display.

- Use the Insert Date button to insert the current date field.

- Use the Insert Time button to insert the current time field.

- Use the Page Setup button to display the Layout tab in the Page Setup dialog box.

- Use the Show/Hide Document Text button to display or hide document text.

You can use the Header and Footer command on the View menu to insert a watermark, but it need not be placed at the top or bottom of a page.

- Use the Same as Previous button when you want to change the header or footer for a particular section. Clicking the Same as Previous button makes the header or footer the same as the header or footer in the previous section.

- Use the Switch Between Header and Footer button to switch between viewing the header and the footer.

- Use the Show Previous button (if you are working with different headers or footers on odd and even pages) to move to the previous header or footer.

- Use the Show Next button (if you are working with different headers or footers on odd and even pages) to move to the next header or footer.

The Page Setup button on the Headers and Footers toolbar lets you make layout decisions for headers and footers. On the Layout tab in the Page Setup dialog box, you can choose to create different headers or footers for odd and even pages or for the first page of a document. Display the Margins tab while in the Page Setup dialog box to specify how far from the edge of the page to print the header or footer.

The header and footer areas are marked with a nonprinting dashed line. Text and graphics in the document are visible but dimmed. You can type and format text in the header or footer area the same way you do in the document. There are two preset tabs in the header and footer areas: a center tab and a right tab. You can set other tabs.

A **watermark** is text or a graphic that appears on top of or behind text in your document. You can use a watermark to display a company logo or text such as the word **Confidential** in the background of each printed page.

S TEP-BY-STEP 6.8

1. Open **Step-by-Step 6-8 Headers.**

2. To see the whole document, click the **Print Preview** button, and display both pages. To return to the print layout view, click **Close** on the Print Preview toolbar.

3. To display Header and Footer view, click the **View** menu and then click **Header and Footer.**

4. To add the document title at the top right of each page, press the **Tab** key twice, and type **Microsoft Office.**

1 4 0

5. To switch to the footer area and enter the name of the file, click the **Switch Between Header and Footer** button, click the **Insert AutoText** button, and click **Filename**.

6. To enter the page number at the bottom right of each page, press the **Tab** key twice, and click the **Insert Page Number** button.

7. To remove the header and footer from the first page, click the **Page Setup** button, click to enter a check mark in the **Different First Page** option on the Layout tab, and click **OK**. Click **Close** on the Header and Footer toolbar.

8. To see the header and footer, click the **Print Preview** button and notice there are no headers or footers on page 1.

9. To return to print layout view, click the **Close** button on the Print Preview toolbar.

10. To delete the document title you added as a header, click the **View** menu, click **Header and Footer**, select Microsoft Office in the header, press the **Delete** key, and click the **Close** button on the Headers and Footers toolbar.

11. Print, save and close the document.

Inserting Page Numbers

You can use the Page Numbers command on the Insert menu to insert just page numbers as a header or a footer in your document (see Figure 6.11).

When you insert a page number with this command, you can specify whether you want it in the header or the footer area and whether it should be positioned at the left margin, in the center, or at the right margin.

You can specify a position and opt *not* to display the number on the first page of the document.

Use the Format button in the Page Numbers dialog box to display the Page Number Format dialog box (see Figure 6.12). You can choose from different numbering formats, include chapter numbers and separators, continue page numbering from a previous section, or enter a number other than 1 from which to begin the page numbering.

When you use the Page Numbers command to add page numbers to your document, Word inserts a Page field in the document and encloses it in the footer frame.

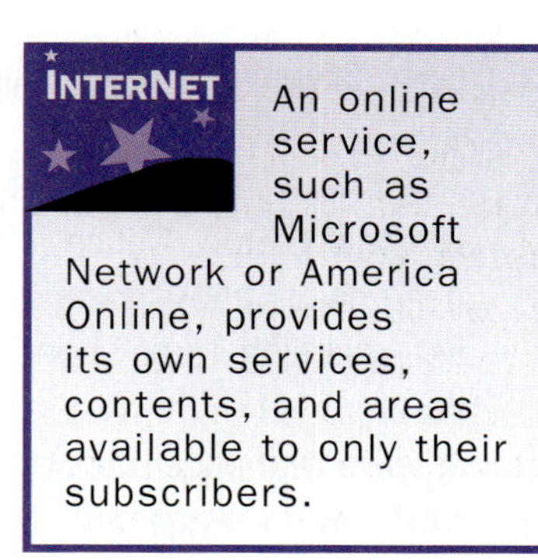

FIGURE 6.11
Add page numbers to your document with the Page Numbers command.

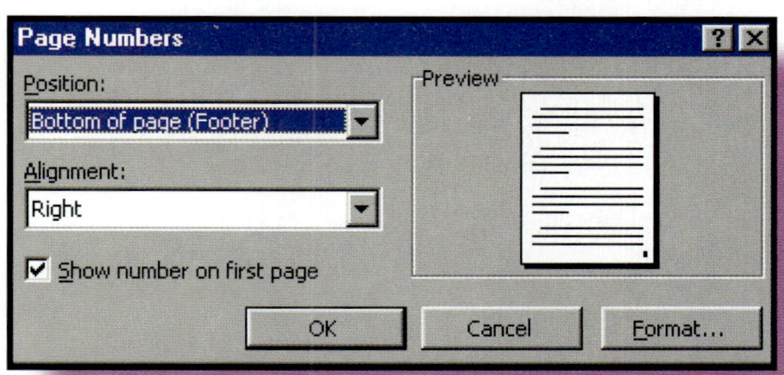

You can format page numbers in a variety of
ways with the Page Number format dialog box.

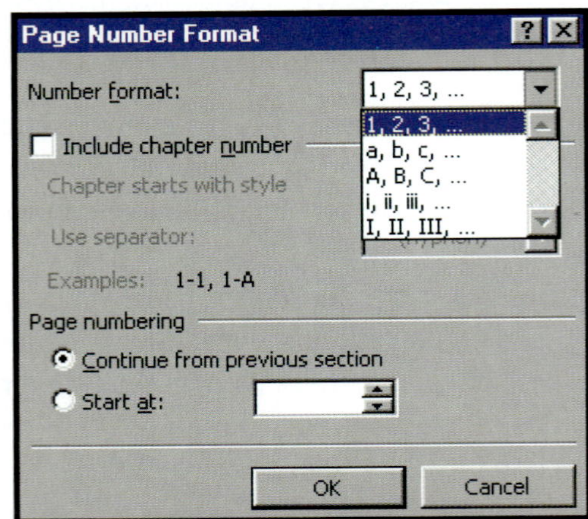

S TEP-BY-STEP 6.9

1. Open **Step-by-Step 6-9 Page.**

2. To preview the document, click the **Print Preview** button. Notice it is the same two-page document you worked with in the last exercise without any headers or footers.

3. To enter the page numbers, click the **Insert** menu, click **Page Numbers**, click **Top of page (Header)** on the Position list, click **Center** in the Alignment box. Be sure the **Show Number on First Page** box does not have a check mark. Click the **Format** button, and use the **up** arrow in the Page Numbering **Start at** box to display **1.** Click **OK** to return to the Page Numbers dialog box, and click **OK** again.

4. To see the page number on page 2, click the **Print Preview** button, and click the **Magnifier** pointer at the top right of the second page.

5. To delete the page number header, click the **View** menu, click **Header and Footer,** click the page number in the Header and click. Then click again when you see the double-crossed arrows and press the **Delete** key.

6. Print the document. Save and close the document.

Summary

You have now learned to use the Replace command, record and run a macro, use the Comment feature, track changes in your document, work with fields, and add headers and footers to your documents.

Try the exercises on the following pages to test how well you remember what you learned. Don't be afraid to go back and look up the answers, because that will help to reinforce what you learned.

LESSON 6 REVIEW QUESTIONS

TRUE / FALSE

Circle the T if the statement is true. Circle the F if it is false.

T **(F)** 1. The Replace command cannot search for or replace styles.

(T) F 2. You can refine searches by using operators and expressions such as S??rch in the Find what box.

(T) F 3. When you use the Find and Replace feature, you should usually use the Replace All option.

T **(F)** 4. You can assign a macro only to a toolbar.

(T) F 5. When recording a macro, you need to anticipate prompts or dialog boxes that might interfere with the macro.

T **(F)** 6. The macro is saved as soon as you finish recording it.

T **(F)** 7. You must accept all changes when you use the Track Changes command.

T **(F)** 8. Comments allow reviewers to make changes to your documents.

(T) F 9. When you use the Date and Time command, Word updates the field to the current date or time when it prints a document.

T **(F)** 10. A footer is text that prints at the top of every page.

COMPLETION

Complete the following sentences by writing the correct word or words in the blanks provided.

1. You can turn on the _Match Case_ option in the Replace dialog box to find text with the same capitalization as the text in the Find What box.

2. You can use the _Find next_ button in the Replace dialog box to leave a selection unchanged.

3. You can use the _undo_ button if you are not satisfied with the results of a find and replace.

4. You can use the _Pause_ button on the Stop Recording toolbar to stop recording until you click the button again.

5. Before you enter a(n) _Comment_, you should select the text it refers to.

6. Your document's file name is one of the ___*fields*___ you can enter in your document.

7. You can create different ___*headers & footers*___ for odd- and even-numbered pages in your document.

8. Divide a document into ___*sections*___ to use different headers and footers in different parts of the document.

9. Word inserts a(n) ___*frame*___ when you use the Page Numbers button in Headers and Footers.

10. There are ___*two*___ tabs set in the header and footer area.

LESSON 6 PROJECTS

PROJECT 6A

SCANS **To practice what you've learned in this lesson, complete the following project:**

1. Open **Project 6-1A.**

2. Create a macro to print just page 2 of the document. Be sure to assign shortcut keys to the macro. Save the document and close it.

3. Open **Project 6-1B,** and run the macro.

4. Delete your macro from the macro list.

5. Save the document. Close the document.

PROJECT 6B

To practice what you've learned in this lesson, complete the following project:

1. Open **Project 6-B.**

2. Use the Date and Time command on the Insert menu to enter the date and time in the header. Use the Insert AutoText button on the Headers & Footers toolbar to insert the file name at the left margin in the footer. Enter the page number at the right in the footer.

Extra Challenges

Use Help to find information about what the problems might be if you have trouble printing headers or footers. Read and print the information.

3. Print, save and close the document.

PROJECT 6C

SCANS **To practice what you've learned in this lesson, complete the following project:**

1. Open **Project 6-C.**

2. Use the Replace command to replace all occurrences of **PC** with **personal computer.** You may have to turn on some options to get the exercise to work as easily as you might like. Don't give up until you work it out. Remember as long as you close a document *without saving it,* you can open the original as often as you like.

3. Write a paragraph at the end of the document telling your instructor how you finally decided to accomplish the task. If your computer is equipped to do so, add a voice comment to the paragraph.

4. Print the document. Use e-mail to send the document to your instructor. Save and close the document.

CRITICAL THINKING ACTIVITY

SCANS Create a macro to enter the file name in the footer for each document. Add the macro to a toolbar. Test the macro. Use the Customize command on the Tools menu to reset the toolbar.

Working with Tables

OBJECTIVES

When you complete this lesson, you will be able to:

- Create a table, insert text, and use AutoFormat.

- Edit table entries.

- Work with numbers in a table.

- Change the table structure.

- Format a table.

- Convert text to a table.

- Print a table.

Estimated Time: 2 hours

Introduction

With Word's Table feature, you can arrange rows and columns of numbers, text, or graphics without using tabs. The Table feature makes it very easy to prepare documents with side-by-side text, such as you might find in a resume. The Tables feature is a good way to create interesting page layouts containing text and graphics.

Creating Tables

Word offers several easy ways to create a table (see Figure 7.1). You can use the Insert Table command on the Table menu, the Insert Table button on the Standard toolbar, the Draw Table command on the Table menu, or the Draw Table button on the Tables and Borders toolbar.

Parts of a Table

Word displays gridlines and other marks and handles that are not printed (see Figure 7.2). In addition, tables have by default a black ½ pt, single-line border that will be printed. You can remove or change the border. You can turn gridlines off with the Hide Gridlines command on the expanded Table menu, but it is much easier to work in a table when you can see gridlines.

An end-of-cell mark identifies the end of text or graphics within a cell. An end-of-row mark identifies the end of a row. You can use the Show/Hide button to display the marks you see in Figure 7.2. Each table also has a table resize handle and a table move handle (see Figure 7.2).

Notice the Tables and Borders toolbar and the Insert Table button's drop-down grid for creating a table.

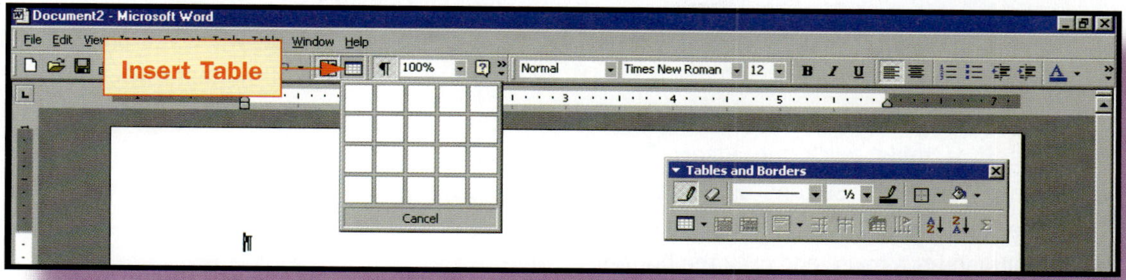

The initial structure of a simple table.

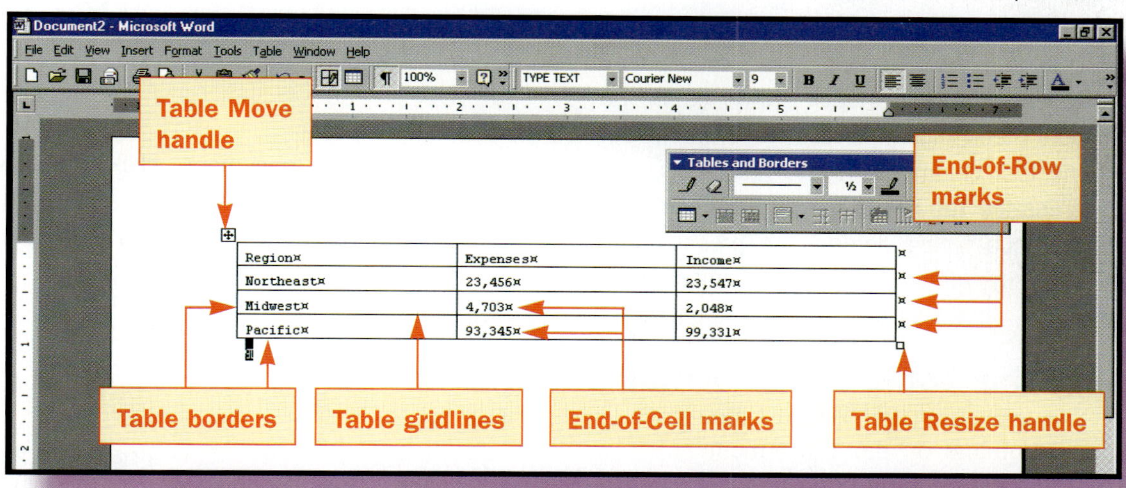

You can set the number of columns and rows when you insert a table, but there is no need because you can press the Tab key in the last cell to create a new row and move the insertion point into it. You can add spacing between table cells and add spacing between the boundary of a cell and the text inside.

Moving Around a Table

You move from cell to cell from left to right and then down to the next row by pressing the Tab key. You can move out of the table when you reach the last cell by pressing the ↓ (down arrow) key or by clicking the I-beam below the table.

Hold the Shift key and press the Tab key to move back a cell. Whenever you use the Tab key or hold Shift and press the Tab key to move within the table, Word automatically selects the contents of the cell into which you move.

You can use the arrow keys to move one character right or left or to move one line up or down.

Do not press the Enter key at the end of a row because that adds a blank line in the cell. If you press the Enter key, press the Backspace key to delete it.

1. To create a new document, click the **New** button.

2. To insert a table, click the **Insert Table** button on the More Buttons drop-down list on the **Standard** toolbar, drag across three columns and two rows, and click the bottom right box.

3. To display end-of-cell and end-of-row marks if they are not already displayed, click the **Show/Hide ¶** button.

4. To enter the information shown below, be sure the insertion point is in the first cell in the first column, type the first entry, and press the **Tab** key to move to the next cell. Continue typing entries and pressing the Tab key after each entry. Notice Word

creates a new row when you press the Tab key at the end of the last row.

Region	Expenses	Income
Northeast	23,456	23,547
Midwest	4,703	2,048
Pacific	93,345	99,331

5. To move out of the table when you reach the last cell, press the ↓ (down arrow) key. If you accidentally create a new row, don't worry about it. (You will learn how to delete rows later in this lesson.)

6. To save the document, click the **Save** button, type **Create Table,** be sure your folder is displayed in the **Save in** box, and click **Save.**

Using the Table AutoFormat Command

You can use the Table Auto-Format command on the Table menu or the Table AutoFormat button on the Tables and Borders toolbar to apply one of Word's table formats. As you can see in Figure 7.3, you can select each of the formats to see a preview of each format.

When you use the Table Auto-Format feature, Word applies borders, shading, font, color, and AutoFit formats and can apply special formats to the heading rows, the first column, the last row, and the last column (see Figure 7.4).

Use the Table AutoFormat dialog box to preview table formats.

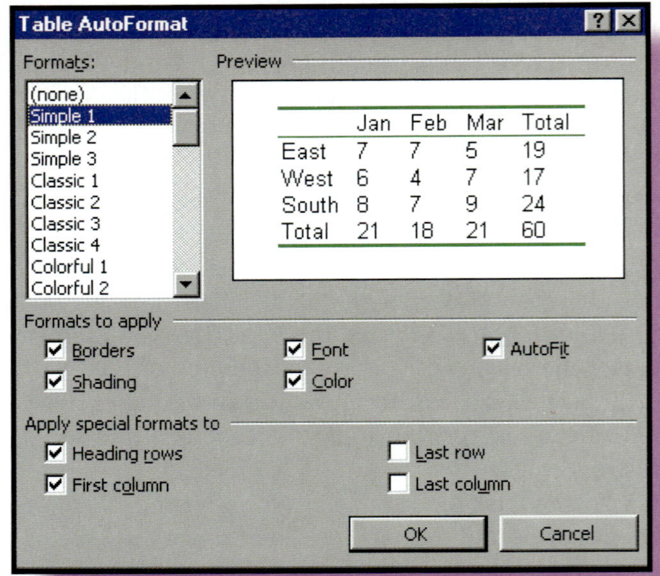

FIGURE 7.4
The Simple 3 table format.

Region¤	Expenses¤	Income¤
Northeast¤	23,456¤	23,547¤
Midwest¤	4,703¤	2,048¤
Pacific¤	93,345¤	99,331¤

STEP-BY-STEP 7.2

1. To work with the table commands, click the I-beam within the table.

2. To display the Table AutoFormat dialog box, click the **Table** menu, and click **Table AutoFormat.**

3. To see the kinds of formats you can apply, click the various formats and notice the previews.

4. To format the table, click **Simple 3** and click **OK.** Notice the numbers in the table are not lined up and the table is not centered between the margins. You will learn to set decimal tabs and position the table later in this lesson.

5. Save and close the document.

Using the Draw Table Tool to Create a Table

Word also lets you "draw" a table. Choose the Draw Table command on the Table menu, or use the Draw Table button on the Tables and Borders toolbar. Your pointer changes to a pencil. Use the pencil to draw just as you would use any pencil. You first drag the pencil from one corner of the table to the diagonally opposite corner. Then draw column and row lines. The Draw Table button helps you draw more complex tables (see Figure 7.5).

Concept Builders

Practice using the Draw Table and Eraser buttons until you are comfortable using them. They make creating tables easy.

FIGURE 7.5
This table was created with the Draw Table feature.

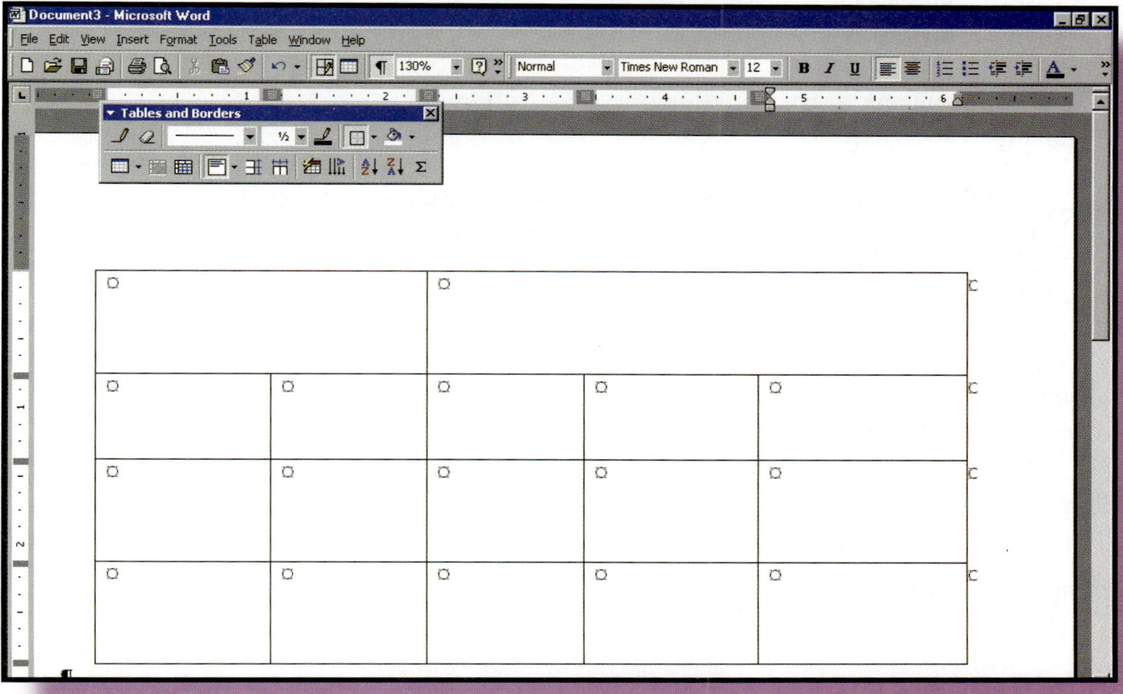

1. To create a new document, click the **New** button.

2. To display the Tables and Borders toolbar with the Draw Table button, click the **Tables and Borders** button on the Standard toolbar.

3. To draw a table the width of the page, click the **Draw Table** button to display the pencil pointer, click about an inch from the top left side of the page, and drag down and right until the rectangle is about two inches high.

4. To divide the table into four rows, click and drag the pencil pointer from the left border to the right border to draw three horizontal lines at approximately half-inch intervals. Don't worry if the rows are not evenly sized.

5. To divide the table into six columns, click the pencil pointer at the top of the table border and drag to the bottom five times.

6. To remove the last of the vertical lines you drew, click the **Eraser** button on the **Tables and Borders** toolbar, click the **eraser** pointer on one of the vertical lines, drag to the end of the line, and click again.

7. To remove the first, third, and fourth vertical lines in the top row of the table (see Figure 7.5), click the **eraser** pointer at the top of each, drag to the bottom of the cell, and click again.

8. To close the document without saving it, click its **Close** button and click **No** when asked to save changes.

Selecting Items in a Table

You can use the mouse, menu commands, or keystrokes to select within a table. Once you are comfortable using a mouse, you will probably use the mouse most of the time.

Table 7.1 contains instructions for selecting with the keyboard.

Did You Know?

When selecting in a table, be sure you don't see the drag-and-drop icon.

TABLE 7.1

SELECTING WITH THE KEYBOARD

TO	DO THIS
Select the next cell's contents	Press the Tab key
Select the preceding cell's contents	Hold the Shift key and press the Tab key
Select an entire table	Hold the Alt key and press 5 on the numeric keypad (with Num Lock off)
Extend a selection to adjacent cells	Hold the Shift key and press an arrow key repeatedly
Select a column	Position insertion point in top cell of column. Hold the Shift key and press ↓ until entire column is selected

Table 7.2 contains instructions for selecting with the mouse. See the labels in Figure 7.6 for various parts of the table.

You can also use the Select Row, Select Column, and Select Table commands on the Table menu to select within a table.

Hot Tips

If commands on the Table menu are dimmed, be sure your insertion point is in the table.

TABLE 7.2

SELECTING WITH THE MOUSE

TO SELECT	DO THIS
A cell	Click the cell selection bar at the left of the cell before the text
A row	Click the row selection bar to the left of the row outside the table
A column	Point to the top cell's top border. When the pointer changes to a filled down arrow (↓), click
Multiple cells, rows, or columns	Drag the I-beam pointer or the filled down arrow across the cell, row, or column; or select a single cell, row, or column and hold the Shift key while you click in another cell, row, or column

FIGURE 7.6
Parts of the table used for selecting with the mouse.

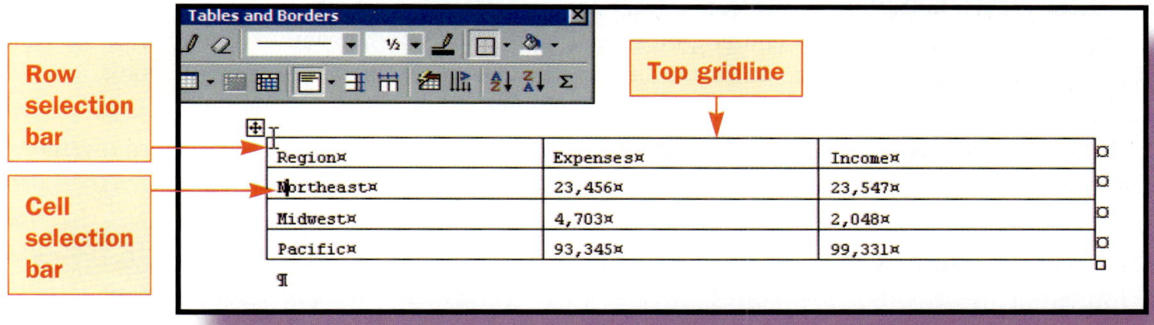

STEP-BY-STEP 7.4

1. Open **Step-by-Step 7-4 Select.** The insertion point should be in the first cell of the table.

2. To move to the next cell and select the cell's contents, press the **Tab** key.

3. To return to the preceding cell and select the contents, hold the **Shift** key and press the **Tab** key.

4. To cancel the selection and remain in the cell, press the → (right arrow) key.

(continued on next page)

5. To select the second row, click the **row** selection bar outside the table to the left of the second row.

6. To select the first cell in the first row, click the **cell** selection bar to the left of text in that cell.

7. To select the right column, point to the top right cell's top gridline, and click the filled down arrow (⬇) when it appears.

8. To select the first two cells in the second row, drag across the cells.

9. To cancel the selection, press the → (right arrow) key.

10. To select the entire table, click the **Table** menu and then click **Select Table.**

11. To cancel the selection, click anywhere in blank space.

12. To close the file without saving it, click its **Close** button and click **No** when asked to save changes.

Editing Entries in a Table

You can use many of the same techniques to edit text in a table that you use to edit other text in a document. The Cut and Paste commands, for example, work the same way within a table. You can also change the order of table entries with the Sort command on the Table menu.

Moving and Copying Text within a Table

You can move or copy text and graphics from one cell to another within a table with the Cut, Copy, and Paste commands or the drag-and-drop procedure you learned earlier in this book.

You should keep the following in mind when moving or copying within a table:

■ If you select and move only the text within a cell and not the end-of-cell mark, Word inserts the text at the drop point and Word does not change the text already in the cell.

■ If you select both the text and the end-of-cell mark, the text you move replaces the existing text and formatting.

■ If you select a whole row, including the end-of-row mark, Word inserts a new row for the row you move and moves all other rows down one.

Concept Builders

If you want to use the drag-and-drop feature to *copy* the contents of a cell, remember to hold the Ctrl key while dragging and dropping.

1. Open **Step-by-Step 7-5 Copy.**

2. To enter data in the second cell in the last row, click the I-beam in the cell and type **400.**

3. To move the contents of this cell to the last cell in the row, click in its **cell** selection bar to select the cell's contents including its

end-of-cell mark and then drag the selection to the last cell in the row.

4. To copy the contents of the last cell in the last row, click in the last cell's **cell** selection bar to select the contents, click the **Copy** button, click the I-beam in the second cell in the last row, and click the **Paste** button.

5. To see what happens when you don't select the whole cell, drag to select **400** in the second cell of the last row. Do *not* select the end-of-cell mark. Drag the selected number to immediately in front of the **400** in the third cell. Notice that Word inserted the number before the original number.

6. To undo the drop, click **Undo.**

7. To move the last row to a position above the row over it, click in the row selector bar to select the row including the end-of-row mark, drag the selection to the left of the row above it, and drop it. Notice the other row moved down to make room for the one you inserted.

8. Practice moving and copying selections from place to place until you are comfortable with all of the procedures.

9. Save and close the document.

Working with Numbers in a Table

Tables often contain numerical information. Word allows you to align and format numbers to display them correctly in the table cells. You can also perform some calculations in a table, just as you would in a spreadsheet.

Aligning Numbers

You can set decimal tabs in a table by clicking the Tab Alignment button (see Figure 7.7) until you see the decimal tab. Then click at the position in the ruler over the selected column where you want the decimal tab. It may take some moving of the tab if your numbers do not seem to fit in the cells. If you select two columns, Word automatically places a decimal tab in the corresponding position in the second column when you set the tab in the first.

Did You Know?

You need not have decimal places to align numbers at a decimal tab. Whole numbers will right align at a decimal tab.

FIGURE 7.7
Use the Tab Alignment button to set a decimal tab.

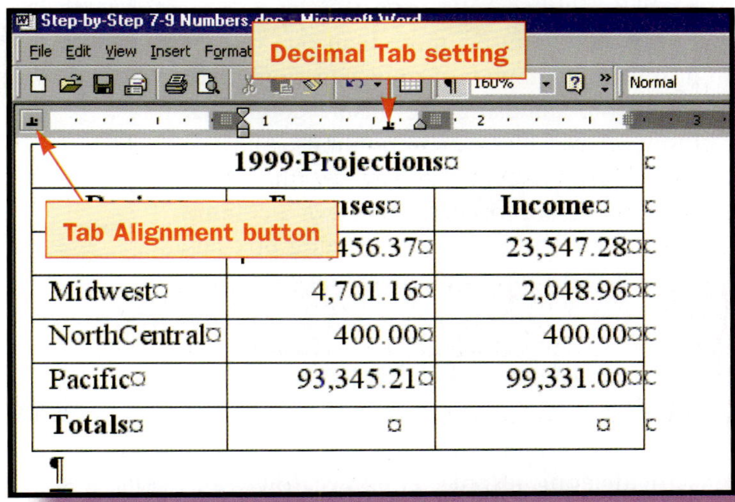

1. Open **Step-by-Step 7-6 Number.**

2. To display the Decimal Tab button, click the **Tab Alignment** button at the left side of the ruler until you see the **Decimal Tab** button.

3. To insert the decimal tab to align numbers in columns 2 and 3, select all the cells in those columns that contain numbers as well as the blank cells in the **Totals** row. Click the Ruler over column 2 in a position toward the right side of the column (use Figure 7.7 as a reference).

4. If your numbers do not align properly in the cell, click the **Undo** button on the Standard toolbar. You may have to reposition the decimal tab stop until the numbers are all aligned and fit properly in the cells.

5. Close document. Do not save.

Changing the Structure of a Table

Word makes it easy for you to change the structure of a table once you have created it. You can use menu commands or toolbar buttons to insert and delete rows and columns, merge and split cells, adjust column width and row height, and even split a table into two parts.

Inserting Cells, Rows, and Columns

You can use the options on the Table menu's Insert command to insert a table within a table, insert columns to the left or to the right of the current column, insert rows above or below the current row, or insert cells (see Figure 7.8). You can also use commands on the Insert Table drop-down list on the Tables and Borders toolbar to insert a table, columns, rows, or cells.

If you want to insert more than one row or column, select the number of rows you would like to insert before choosing the Insert command. Word inserts that many rows or columns.

If you select a cell, you can use the Insert Cells command to insert a cell, a row, or a column (see Figure 7.9). The Insert Cells dialog box lets you shift cells right or down or insert an entire row or column.

FIGURE 7.8
The Insert submenu options.

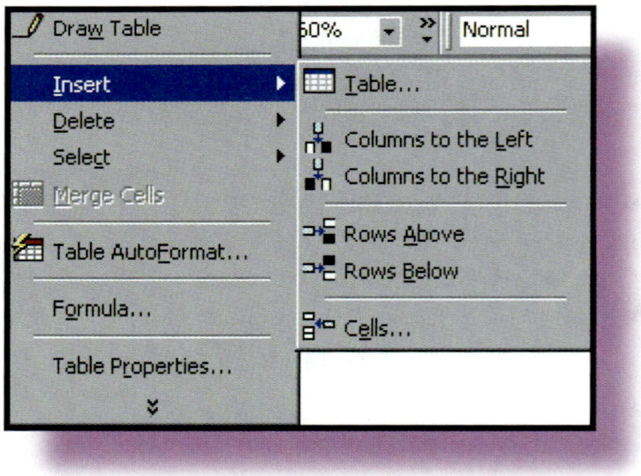

Deleting Tables, Columns, Rows, and Cells

The Delete command on the Table menu contains options for deleting a table, columns, rows, and cells. Select the area you want to delete and then choose the appropriate option (see Figure 7.10).

Did You Know?

To delete just the contents of a cell rather than the entire cell, select the text and press the Delete key.

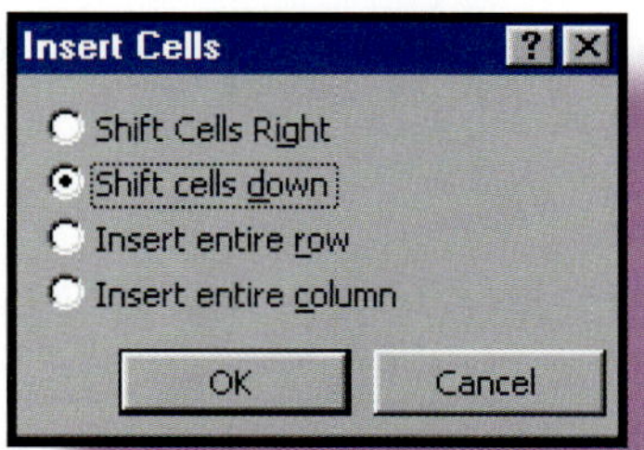

FIGURE 7.9
The Insert Cells dialog box lets you insert a cell, a row, or a column.

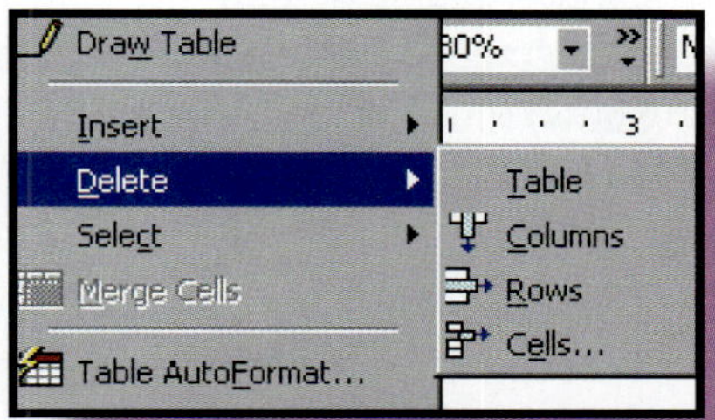

FIGURE 7.10
The Delete command on the Table menu contains options for deleting a table, columns, rows, and cells.

Merging and Splitting Cells

You can use the Merge Cells command on the Table menu to create a heading that spans several columns. You can also use the Split Cells command on the Table menu to split one or more cells. Word splits cells according to the number of paragraph marks they contain. If there is only one paragraph mark, the contents of the split cell are placed in the cell on the left and empty cells are inserted to the right. You can also use the Merge Cells and Split Cells buttons on the Tables and Borders toolbar.

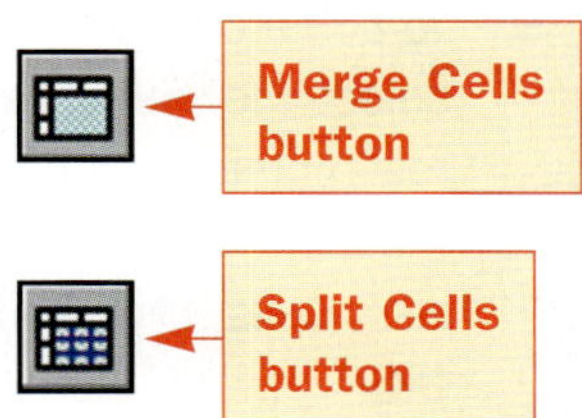

When you choose Split Cells on the Table menu or the Tables and Borders toolbar, Word displays the Split Cells dialog box (see Figure 7.11). There you can designate how to split the cell or cells. Notice Word lets you split a cell vertically into additional rows or horizontally into additional columns.

The Eraser button on the Tables and Borders toolbar can also help you to merge cells in your table. The Eraser button lets you "erase" any gridline in the table to merge cells vertically or horizontally.

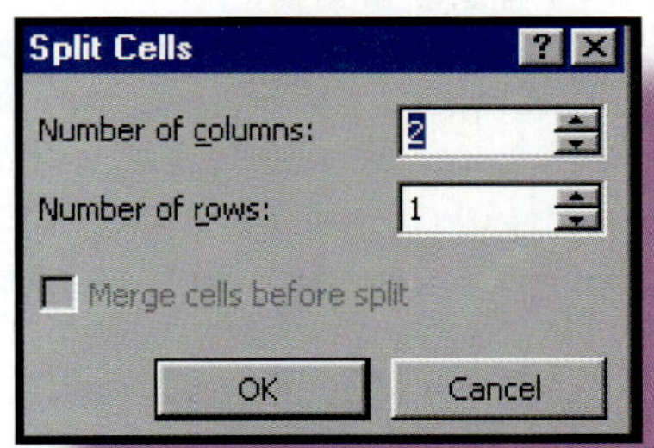

FIGURE 7.11
The Split Cells dialog box lets you split cells vertically or horizontally.

STEP-BY-STEP 7.7

1. Open **Step-by-Step 7-7 Struct.**

2. To insert a row in the table, click the I-beam anywhere in the last row of the table. *Be sure nothing is selected.* Click the **Table** menu, click **Insert**, and click **Rows Below.** Notice Word inserts the row and selects it.

3. To cancel the selection and keep the insertion point in the same row, press the ← (left arrow) key.

4. To delete the row you just inserted, click the **Table** menu, click **Delete**, and click **Rows.**

5. To insert a column to the left of the first column, position the insertion point someplace in the first column, click **Table**, click **Insert**, and click **Columns to the Left**. Notice a blank column is inserted before the first column.

(continued on next page)

6. To remove the column and display non-printing marks if they are not already on your screen, click **Undo** and then click the **Show/Hide ¶** button on the Standard toolbar.

7. If you are not using print layout view, click the **Print Layout View** button at the left of the horizontal scroll bar.

8. To add a cell to the right on the bottom row, select the **end-of-row** mark on the bottom row (outside the gridlines) by dragging over the mark, click the **Table** menu, click **Insert**, click **Cells**, click **Shift Cells Right**, and click **OK**.

9. To cancel the selection and scroll right to see the added cell, press the → (right arrow) key.

10. To delete the added cell, click the **Undo** button on the Standard toolbar.

11. To insert a new row at the beginning of the table, hold the **Ctrl** key and press the **Home** key. Then click **Table**, click **Insert**, and click **Rows Above**.

12. To merge the three selected cells and add a title to the table, click the **Table** menu and click **Merge Cells**. Then type **2000 Projections** in the merged cell.

Adjusting Column Width and Row Height

Word provides several ways for you to change the width of columns or the height of rows. You can rest your pointer on a boundary until it becomes a move pointer and then drag the boundary to the position you want. You can use the Table menu's Autofit options (see Figure 7.12). You can use the Table Properties command on the Table menu and display the Column tab (see Figure 7.13) to set a width, or display the Row tab (see Figure 7.14) to set a height. You can also double-click the right boundary of a row or column when the double-crossed arrows are displayed.

FIGURE 7.12
Notice the Table menu's Autofit options.

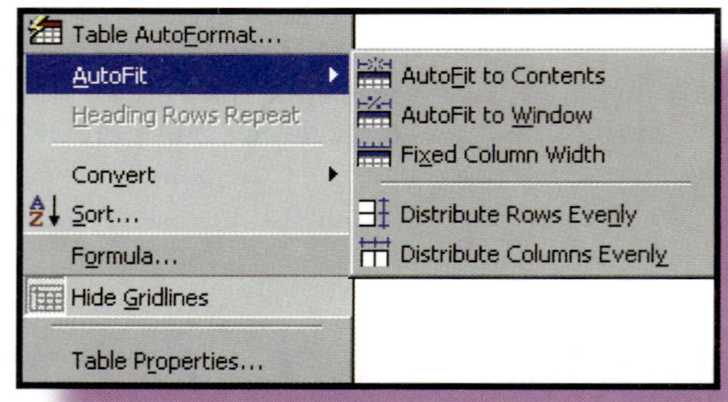

Positioning and Sizing a Table

You can use the table move handle to drag the table to another position and the table size handle to make the table larger or smaller. You must be in print layout view to see the move table and resize table handles.

By default, Word allows a row to break across pages.

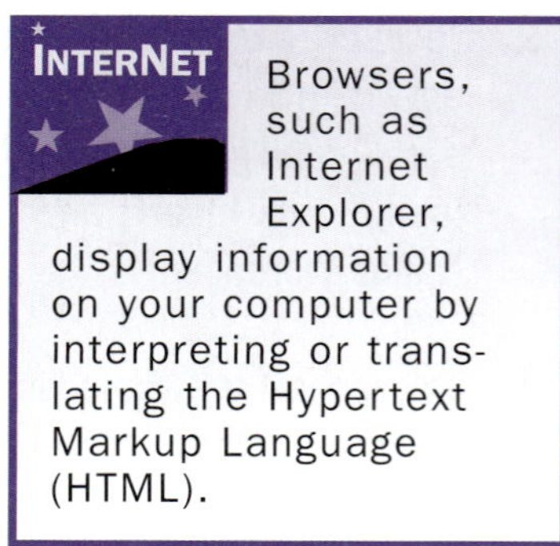

Browsers, such as Internet Explorer, display information on your computer by interpreting or translating the Hypertext Markup Language (HTML).

FIGURE 7.13
The Column tab lets you change spacing and column width

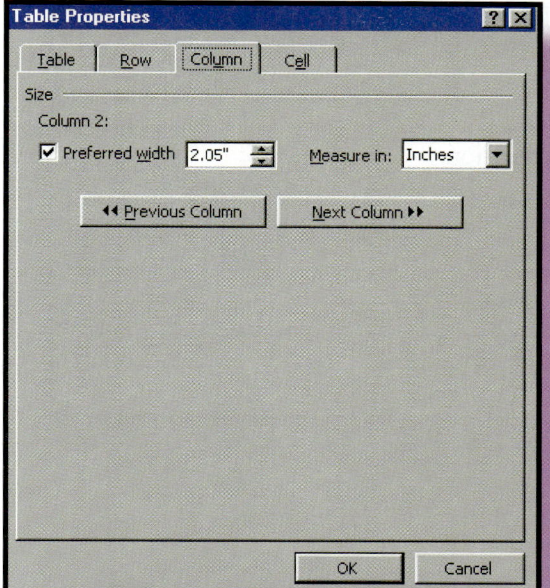

FIGURE 7.14
The Row tab lets you set the height of rows and make other changes.

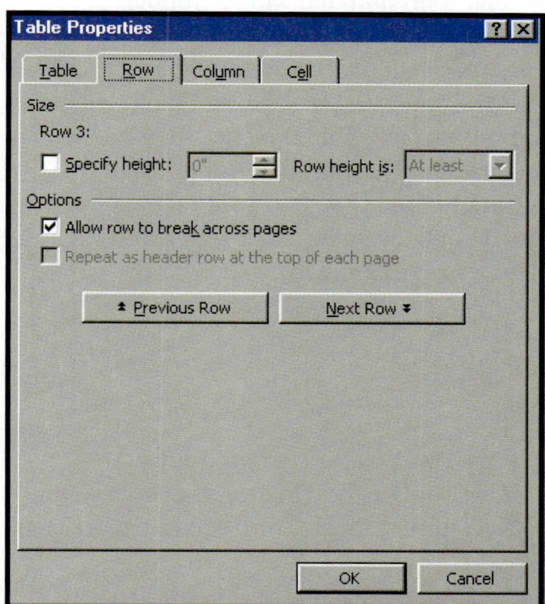

STEP-BY-STEP 7.8

1. To use the AutoFit feature to adjust column widths, select the bottom four rows of the table, click the **Table** menu, and click **AutoFit to Contents.**

2. To cancel the selection, click in blank space outside the table.

3. To make the whole table wider, point to the right vertical border. When you see the crossed arrows, drag about one inch to the right.

4. To make the second column wider, point to the boundary between the second and third columns. When you see the crossed arrows, drag until the two right columns are about evenly sized.

5. To insert a new row at the end of the table, position the I-beam in the last cell and press **Tab.**

6. To see how the Autofit to Contents option you chose works, type **NorthCentral** in the first cell of the new row. Notice the column expands automatically.

7. To move the table to the middle of the page, click and drag its move table handle. Release the handle when the table appears to be centered.

8. To increase the overall size of the table, point to its resize table handle. When the sizing arrow appears, drag down about one inch.

9. To undo the move and size, click the **Undo** button on the Standard toolbar twice.

Splitting a Table

To insert text between rows in a table, you can split the table. Simply position the insertion point in the row where you want the second table to begin and choose the Split Table command on the Table menu. Word inserts a blank line with a paragraph mark between the two rows (see Figure 7.15). To put the table back together, delete the paragraph mark.

Use the Split Table command in the first row of the table if you want to insert text before a table that is at the beginning of a document.

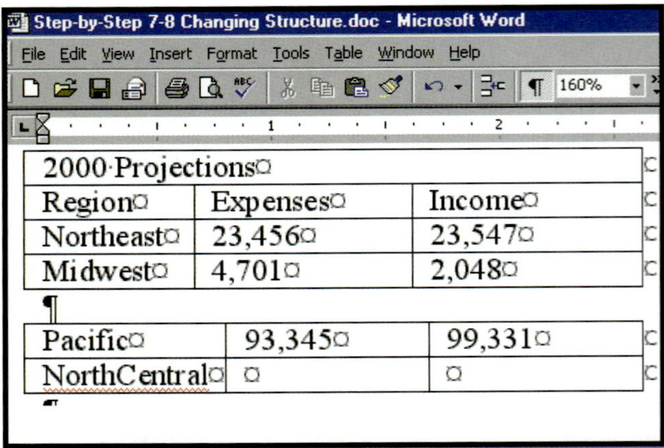

FIGURE 7.15
The Split Table command inserts a blank line with a paragraph mark.

2000 Projections¤			
Region¤	Expenses¤	Income¤	¤
Northeast¤	23,456¤	23,547¤	¤
Midwest¤	4,701¤	2,048¤	¤

¶

Pacific¤	93,345¤	99,331¤	¤
NorthCentral¤	¤	¤	¤

1. To split the table, position the insertion point in the fifth row of the table, and be sure nothing is selected. Click the **Table** menu, and then click **Split Table.** The table splits, and Word inserts a blank line between rows 4 and 5.

2. To rejoin the table, delete the paragraph mark on the blank line.

3. Save and close the document.

Formatting a Table

You can use any of the formatting methods you learned earlier in this book to format text in your table. You can align table entries as you do other text. You can apply borders and shading to cells, rows, or columns.

Aligning and Formatting Text and Tables

You can apply any of the standard text alignments—Align Left, Center, Align Right, and Justify—to entries in table cells. The Tables and Borders toolbar gives you access to several other alignment options. You can align the text in a cell at the top, middle, or bottom of a cell with the Align Top, Center Vertically, and Align Bottom buttons. You can also change the orientation of text from horizontal to vertical with the Change Text Direction button.

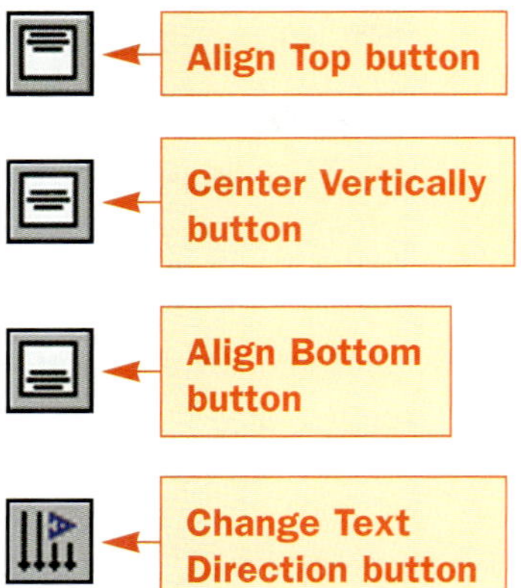

You can apply fonts, font styles, and font sizes to table text the same way you do for any other text in a document. You can even change the direction for the text.

You can also change the alignment of the entire table on the page by selecting it and clicking one of the toolbar alignment buttons.

You can also use the Table Properties command on the Table menu to format tables.

Adding Borders and Shading to a Table

The Tables and Borders toolbar makes it easy to change borders and add shading to any table cell, row, or column, or to the entire table. With the Tables and Borders toolbar active, select the cell, row, or column for which you want to change borders or add shading. Use the Outside Border drop-down button to choose the border style for the cell. Use the Shading Color drop-down button to display a palette of gray shades and colors you can use in the selected cells.

STEP-BY-STEP 7.10

1. Open **Step-by-Step 7-10 Format.**

2. To center and bold the headings in the first two rows, click and drag in the **row** selection bar to select the two rows, click the **Bold** button on the Formatting toolbar, and then click the **Center** button on the Formatting toolbar.

3. To add Bold font style to characters in the last row of the table, click the **row** selection bar to select the row and click the **Bold** button on the Formatting toolbar.

4. To increase the size of the text in the first row, click the **row** selector bar to select the row, click the **Font Size** drop-down button on the Formatting toolbar, and click **14.**

5. To display the Tables and Borders toolbar, click the **More Buttons** drop-down button on the Standard toolbar and click the **Tables and Borders** button.

6. To change the gridlines for the top row, click the **row** selection bar to select the row, click the **Line Weight** drop-down button on the Tables and Borders toolbar, and click **1½ pt.**

7. To select the outline border style for the cell, click the **Outside Borders** button on the Tables and Borders toolbar.

8. To add shading to the first row, be sure the first row is still selected, click the **Shading Color** drop-down button on the Tables and Borders toolbar, and select a red color.

9. To change the direction for text on the second row, select the row and click the **Change Text Direction** button on the Tables and Borders toolbar.

10. To undo the direction change, click **Undo.**

11. Print the document. Save and close the document.

Sorting Table Entries

You can use the Sort command on the Table menu or the Sort buttons on the Tables and Borders toolbar to arrange items in a table in alphabetical or numerical order. You can see the Sort dialog box in Figure 7.16.

You can sort a table using one column, such as last names; then sort the table using data in a second column, such as first names; and then sort using data in a third column, such as middle names. If data are the same in the first column, data in the second will determine the sort order, and so forth (see Figure 7.17).

NOTE:

If you want to keep the original list intact, and save the sorted list also, use the Save As command to save the sorted list with a new name.

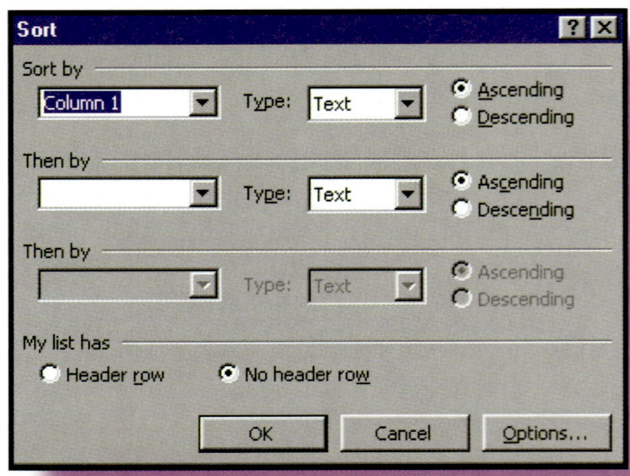

FIGURE 7.16
The Sort dialog box displays options for sorting a table.

FIGURE 7.17
Word can sort a table in alphabetical order or numerical order.

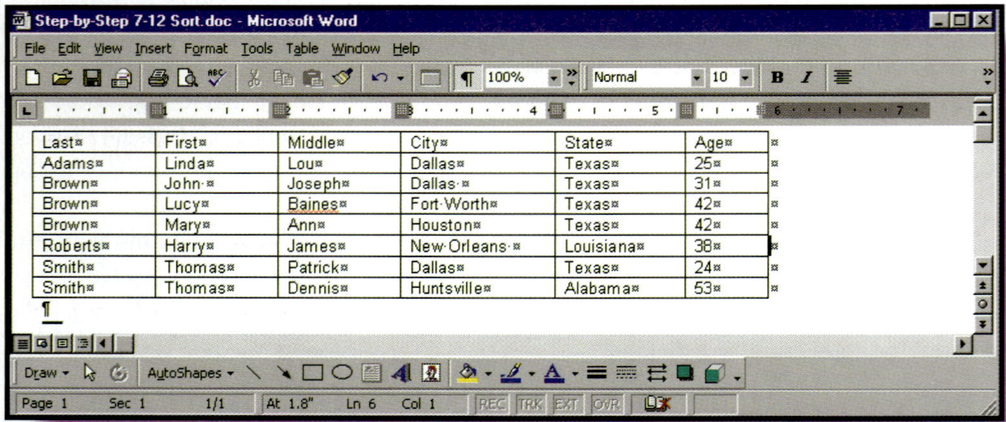

Last	First	Middle	City	State	Age	
Adams	Linda	Lou	Dallas	Texas	25	
Brown	John	Joseph	Dallas	Texas	31	
Brown	Lucy	Baines	Fort Worth	Texas	42	
Brown	Mary	Ann	Houston	Texas	42	
Roberts	Harry	James	New Orleans	Louisiana	38	
Smith	Thomas	Patrick	Dallas	Texas	24	
Smith	Thomas	Dennis	Huntsville	Alabama	53	

STEP-BY-STEP 7.11

1. Open **Step-by-Step 7-11 Sort.** Notice this table contains a list of last, first, and middle names; cities and states; and ages.

2. To display the Sort dialog box, be sure the insertion point is in the table, click the **Table** menu, and then click the **Sort** command. Notice that the **Sort by** box is correctly filled in already. You do want to

sort by last name (column 1), which is a text field, and you do want ascending order (from **a** to **z**).

3. To designate column 2, the first-name column, as the second column in the sort, click the **Then by** drop-down button, and click **Column 2.** Word automatically suggests **text** and **ascending** again.

160

4. To prevent your headers from being sorted with the list and sort the table, click the **My list has Header row** option and click **OK.**

5. Print the document. Close the document without saving it.

Converting Text to a Table

You can use the Convert command on the Table menu to convert text separated by paragraph marks, commas, tabs, or other characters to cells in a table. If the need ever arises, you can also reverse the process to convert a table to paragraphs or tabbed text.

When you click the Convert command and the Text to Table option, Word displays the Convert Text to Table dialog box shown in Figure 7.18. Here you can indicate how many columns your new table should have and can tell Word how to separate text into cells— by paragraphs, tabs, commas, or other mark.

You can also convert text to a table by selecting the text and clicking the Insert Table button on the Standard toolbar. When you use the Insert Table button, Word bypasses the Convert Text to Table dialog box and immediately creates the table.

FIGURE 7.18
Use the Convert Text to Table command to change text to a table.

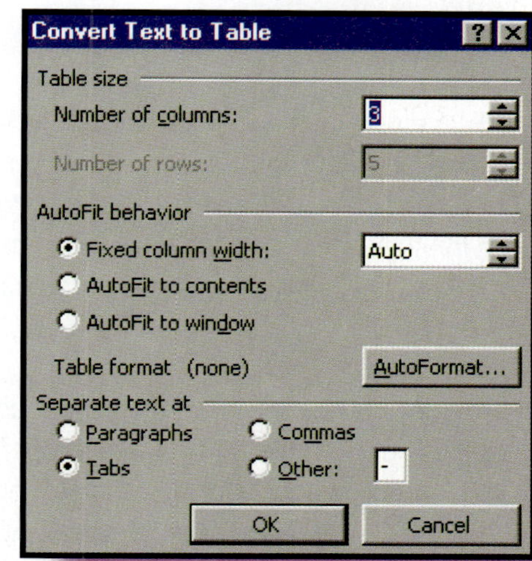

STEP-BY-STEP ▷ 7.12

1. Open **Step-by-Step 7-12 Convert.**

2. To convert the text to a table, select the text, click the **Table** menu, click **Convert,** and then click **Text to Table.** Notice the Number of columns spin box knows there are 3 columns separated by tabs. Click **OK.** Word places the text in a table.

3. To format the table, click the **Table** menu, click **Table AutoFormat,** click **Simple 2,** and click **OK.**

4. Print the document. Save and close the document.

Printing Options for Tables

You print a document containing a table with the Print command—the same way you print any other document. If you want to print one page of a document in landscape mode to accommodate a wide table, use the Break command on the Insert menu to insert section breaks before and after the table. You can use the Page Setup command on the File menu to change the orientation of the section containing the table.

161

For tables that run more than one page, you can use the Headings Rows Repeat command on the Table menu to designate that table header rows repeat on every page. Word automatically repeats the heading on all new pages created by soft page breaks but not on pages created with hard page breaks.

If your table is one or two rows too long to fit on one page, try decreasing the font size to make it fit on one page.

STEP-BY-STEP 7.13

1. Open **Step-by-Step 7-13 Print.**

2. To preview this two-page table, click the **Print Preview** button on the Standard toolbar. Notice the last row on the first page has separated and it runs over to the second page. Click the **Close** button on the Print Preview toolbar.

3. To prevent the row from splitting across pages, click **Table,** click **Table Properties,** click the **Row** tab, and then click to remove the check the **Allow row to break across pages** check box. Click **OK.**

4. To add the headings row to each page, hold the **Ctrl** key and press the **Home** key to move to the first row of the table. Click the **Table** menu, and then click **Heading Rows Repeat.**

5. To see how the heading on the first page of the table has been repeated on the second page, click Print Preview again. Notice Word has moved the partial row from the first page to the second page.

6. Print the document. Save and close the document.

Summary

You have now learned how to create a table, enter text and move around a table, and change a table's structure. You have learned how to edit table entries, work with numbers in a table, and format a table. You've learned how to convert text to a table, and you've explored printing options for tables.

Try the exercises on the following pages to test how well you remember what you learned. Don't be afraid to go back and look up answers or procedures, because that will help to reinforce what you learned.

LESSON 7 REVIEW QUESTIONS

TRUE / FALSE

Circle the T if the statement is true. Circle the F if it is false.

T (F) 1. Once you have created a table, you cannot easily restructure it.

(T) F 2. Gridlines print by default.

T F 3. When you hold the Shift key and press the Tab key to move back a cell, Word selects the cell's contents.

T **F** 4. You can insert only whole rows or columns in a Word table.

T **F** 5. You cannot use drag-and-drop procedures in a table.

T **F** 6. When you create a table, you must know the number of rows you need.

T **F** 7. You cannot set table headings to automatically repeat on each page.

T F 8. To rejoin a table you split, delete the paragraph mark where the table is split.

T F 9. You can use the Insert Table button to convert text to a table.

T F 10. The Formula command automatically recalculates totals if you change data in the cells.

COMPLETION

Complete the following sentences by writing the correct word or words in the blanks provided.

1. You can add a new row to a table by pressing _______*Tab Key*_______ in the last cell.

2. Use the _______*Draw Table*_______ tool to draw a table freehand.

3. Move back a cell in a table by holding the _______*Shift*_______ key and pressing the _______*Tab*_______ key.

4. Click _______*Selection*_______, click _______*Table*_______ and then click _______*Delete*_______ to delete a selected row.

5. The _______*end of cell mark*_______ identifies the end of text within a cell.

6. The _______*Table Autoformat*_______ command on the Table menu contains many preset table formats.

7. The _______*undo*_______ command or button is very useful when you get unexpected results during a procedure.

8. Set _______*Tab Alignment*_______ in a table to line up columns of numbers.

9. Use the _______*right align*_______ command on the Table menu to combine cells and center a heading over an entire table.

10. To repeat table headings use the _______*Table format*_______ command on the Table menu.

> ### Extra Challenges
>
> Use Help to find out how you create a blank line at the top of a table that is at the beginning of a document. Print the information you find.

PROJECT 7A

To practice what you've learned in this lesson, complete the following project:

1. Use the Draw Table tool to draw a table to organize some aspect of your home, school, or work life. If necessary, arrange column widths and row heights to accommodate the data you will enter.

2. Enter a few rows of data, including column heads, to show how the table will be used. Add shading and borders to improve the look or usefulness of the table.

3. Save the table with an appropriate name. Print and close the table.

PROJECT 7B

To practice what you've learned in this lesson, complete the following project:

1. Enter the following data in a table.

	1998 Sales			
	Qtr 1	Qtr 2	Qtr 3	Qtr 4
Jane Collins	38,456	56,934	34,457	36,421
Sue Jenkins	31,213	29,456	37,432	32,534
Joe Wong	25,421	32,365	34,343	33,893
Harry Haig	32,238	28,452	26,476	36,222
Totals				

2. Add decimal tabs to align numbers.

3. Use AutoFormat to format the table. Center the table between the margins.

4. Print the table. Save the table as **Formatted Table** and close it.

PROJECT 7C

SCANS

Send a resume (you will create it in the Critical Thinking Activity below) with a cover letter via fax or e-mail to your instructor or to a friend who might be able to help you find work.

CRITICAL THINKING ACTIVITY

SCANS

Use the Table feature to prepare your resume. Print the resume. Save and close the document.

WORKING WITH MAIL MERGE

Introduction

You can use the Mail Merge command on the Tools menu to personalize form letters, print addresses on envelopes or labels, and produce catalogs or any documents that combine standard text with unique information.

To create any type of mail merge document, you must merge a main document with a data source. The **main document** contains all the items that remain the same in each form letter along with merge fields. **Merge fields** tell Word where to print information from the data source. The **data source** contains the information that changes in each document.

In this lesson you will create a data source document, a form letter, and a merged document and labels.

Using Mail Merge Helper

You begin to create the two documents necessary for the mail merge with the Mail Merge command on the Tools menu.

The Mail Merge Helper dialog box (see Figure 8.1) prompts you through the steps necessary to create your documents. You must identify for Word the type of the document you intend to use for the main document (form letters, labels, envelopes, catalog), whether you will create it or use an existing document, and the data source. If you have existing documents to use with the Mail Merge feature, you would use those instead of creating new ones.

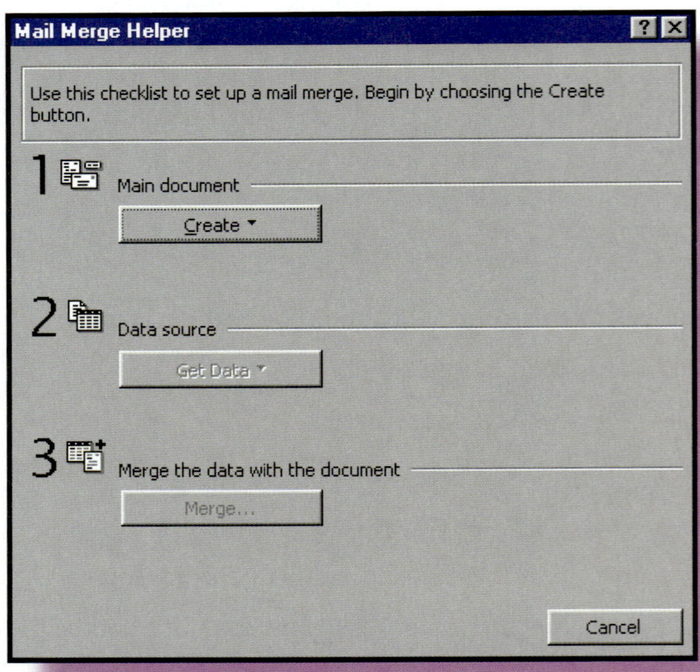

S TEP-BY-STEP ⇒ 8.1 

1. To see the Mail Merge Helper and to set up the files to use for the mail merge, be sure the Word application is open, be sure a blank document is open, click the **Tools** menu, and then click **Mail Merge.**

2. To begin, follow the directions at the top of the dialog box, and click **Create** in the Main document list box.

3. To create your form letters in a new document, click **Form Letters** and then **New Main Document.** Notice Word entered the unnamed new document as the name of the main document.

4. To follow the next prompt, click the **Get Data** button to specify a data source.

5. To create a new data source file, click **Create Data Source.**

Creating a Data Source

When you create the data source document, you actually set up a database. All the information about one person or thing in the database is called a **record.** Each piece of information in a record is called a **field.** Word already has a list of often-used fields.

1 6 6

It is wise to give some thought to the information you will need in a database before you begin. In the data source each record must have the same number of fields. Make sure to plan enough fields to hold even those records that have the most information. The Address2 field is a good example of a field that will be empty for most records but is very important when you have a record that contains a two-line address.

When planning fields for a person's name, be sure to use separate fields for the title (Mr., Mrs., Ms.), first name, last name, and any suffix that might be after a name (Jr. or 3d). That way, you can address the person either with a title and last name or with a first name.

You should always use the city, state, and postal code fields. If you have separate fields, you can sort by any of them. Then you can send a form letter to everyone in a certain city, state, or postal area.

In the Create Data Source dialog box (see Figure 8.2), you can add and remove fields, and use the Move up and down buttons to rearrange the order of fields. You can also access MS Query to select only certain records in your database for merging.

You can add the POSTNET bar code field to speed mail delivery.

FIGURE 8.2
Choose fields in the Create Data Source dialog box.

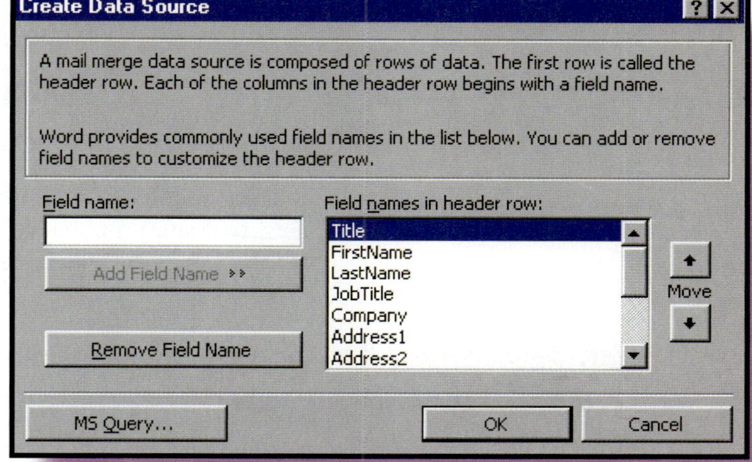

NOTE:

If a field is empty, Word does not leave blank space in the merged documents.

When you have created both the main document and the data source for the merge, Word displays the dialog box in Figure 8.3. Neither of your documents contains any information yet. You can either add new records to your data source or add merge fields to your main document.

FIGURE 8.3
You can choose to edit either the data source or the main document.

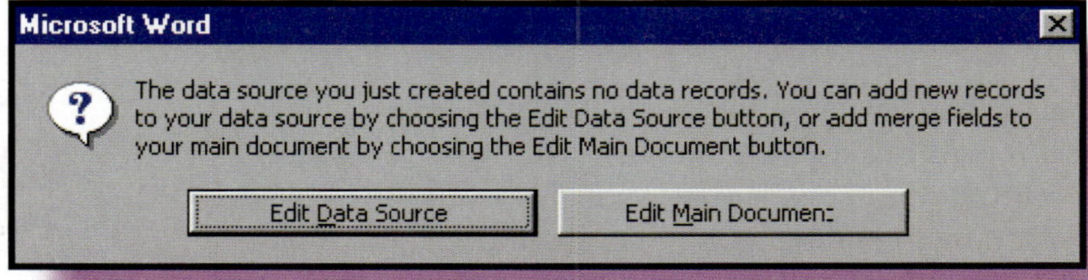

1. To remove the Country field, scroll down to and click **Country.** Then click **Remove Field Name.**

2. To find and remove the HomePhone field, scroll through the list, click **Home Phone,** and click **Remove Field Name.**

3. To add two fields because you are writing a form letter about a computer class and its date, type **Class** in the Field name box, and click **Add Field Name.** Then type **ClassDate,** and click **Add Field Name.** To signal that you are finished adding and removing field names, click **OK.**

4. To save the data source, type **Data Source** as the file name in the Save As dialog box. Be sure your data file folder is displayed in the Save in box, and click **Save.**

Editing the Data Source Document

The Data Form dialog box is displayed in Figure 8.4. To add records, click in the first field and type the data. Press the Tab key or the Enter key to move to the next field. When you finish entering all information for one record, click Add New to display a blank record. Word numbers records as you enter them.

FIGURE 8.4
Use the Data Form dialog box to enter a record.

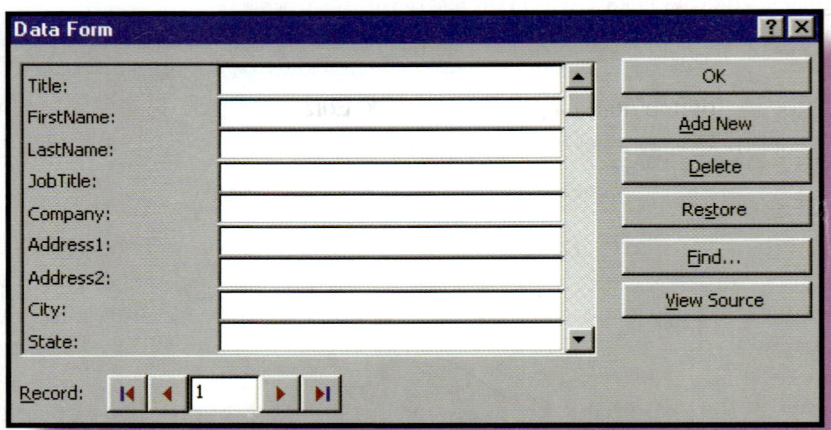

Use the Delete button to delete the current record. Edit a record by selecting the field you want to change and typing the new information. Use the Restore command button to return the original information to the field before you click Add New or Delete for a record.

Use the View Source button to view your records in table format and to access Word's menu bar to save the document after entering records (see Figure 8.5). You can

Hot Tips

Remember that all of the information for one person is called a record. Each piece of information about a person is called a field.

FIGURE 8.5
Data source records in table format.

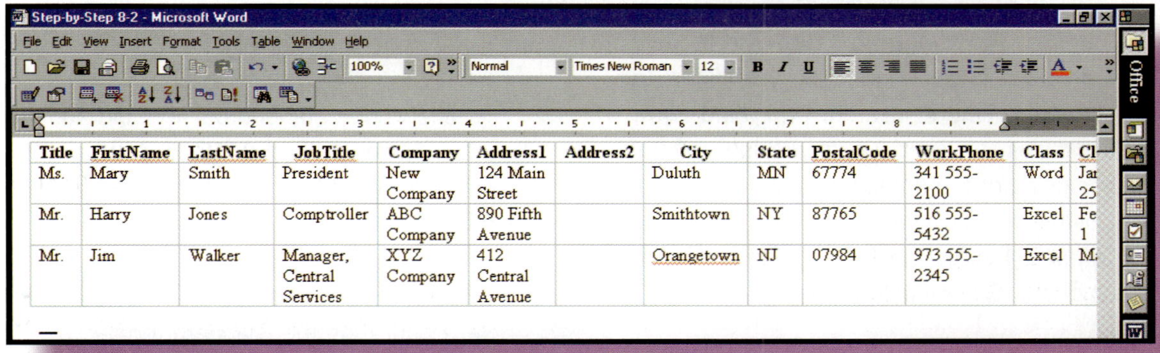

Title	FirstName	LastName	JobTitle	Company	Address1	Address2	City	State	PostalCode	WorkPhone	Class	Cl—
Ms.	Mary	Smith	President	New Company	124 Main Street		Duluth	MN	67774	341 555-2100	Word	Jar 25
Mr.	Harry	Jones	Comptroller	ABC Company	890 Fifth Avenue		Smithtown	NY	87765	516 555-5432	Excel	Fe 1
Mr.	Jim	Walker	Manager, Central Services	XYZ Company	412 Central Avenue		Orangetown	NJ	07984	973 555-2345	Excel	M.

use the Find button to search records using any of the fields to find a particular record.

When entering records, be sure to enter data in the correct field. Address2 will always be blank in this exercise. You can use the scroll bars to move to fields not displayed. Hold the Shift key and press the Tab key if you want to move back a field. After entering all information for one record, click the Add New button to display a blank record.

Did You Know?

When you press a key to move to a field with data in it, Word automatically selects the data in the field.

STEP-BY-STEP ▷ 8.3

1. To enter the following records, click **Edit Data Source.** Type the data shown below.

2. To find Mary Smith's record and change the date for her class, click **Find.** Type **Smith** in

Ms.	Mr.	Mr.
Mary	Harry	Jim
Smith	Jones	Walker
President	Comptroller	Manager, Central Services
New Company	ABC Company	XYZ Company
124 Main Street	890 Fifth Avenue	412 Central Avenue
Duluth	Smithtown	Orangetown
MN	NY	NJ
67774	87765	07984
341 555-2100	516 555-5432	973 555-2345
Word	Word	Excel
January 25	February 1	March 14

(continued on next page)

the Find What dialog box. Click the **In Field** drop-down button and click **LastName** to signal the field to search. Click **Find First.** Click **Yes** to continue searching at the beginning of the database.

3. To close the Find in Field dialog box, click one of its **Close buttons.**

4. To enter **March** instead of **January** in Mary Smith's ClassDate field, scroll down to display the field, double-click **January,** and type **March.**

5. To return to the original date, click **Restore.**

6. To see your data source in table format (see Figure 8.4), click **View Source.** The data may wrap around within a cell but will print properly.

7. To save the records you entered, click the **Save** button on the Standard toolbar.

8. To return to the Data Form and then close it, click the **Data Form** button on the **Mail Merge** toolbar and then click its **OK** button.

Preparing the Main Document

You can now enter the form letter in the main document. You type everything that remains the same for each of the letters in the main document, and you insert merge fields for each of the variable pieces of information.

You enter the fields with the Insert Merge Field button on the Mail Merge toolbar. When inserting merge fields, you must be careful to enter all spacing and punctuation that will be needed around the merged data. Merge fields are displayed in a document surrounded by chevrons (<< >>) (see Figure 8.6).

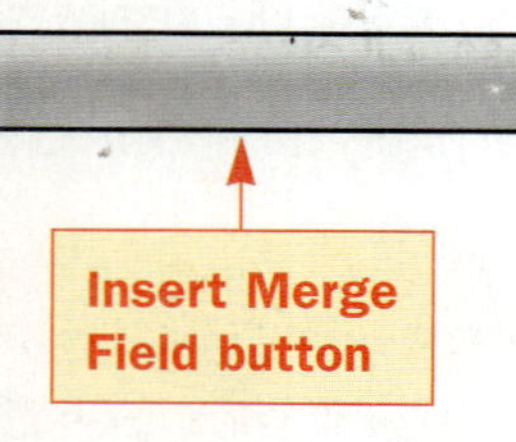

FIGURE 8.6
Merge fields are set off by chevrons in this document.

November 29, 2000

«Title» «FirstName» «LastName»
«JobTitle»
«Company»
«Address1»
«Address2»
«City», «State» «PostalCode»

Dear «FirstName»:

Thank you for enrolling in our class. All classes begin at 9 a.m. and end at 4 p.m.

We look forward to seeing you in our «Class» on «ClassDate».

Sincerely,

Pat Murphy

1. To prepare your main document and to insert the merge fields, click the **Mail Merge Main Document** button on Mail Merge Toolbar.

2. To position the insertion point 2.5 inches from the top of the page, click the Print Layout View button to be sure you can use the Click and Type feature and double-click at the 2.5 inch point on the Vertical ruler directly below the current left margin.

3. To enter the current date, click the **Insert** menu and then click the **Date and Time** command. Click the third format on the list showing the **March 24, 1999** format, and click **OK.**

4. To enter the first merge field, the recipient's title, press the **Enter** key four times. Click the **Insert Merge Field** button on the Mail Merge toolbar, and click **Title** in the drop-down list. Notice Word displays the field name in chevrons (<<>>).

5. To leave a space between the person's title and first name and enter the first name, press the **Spacebar.** Then click the **Insert Merge Field** button again, click **FirstName,** and press the **Spacebar.**

6. To enter the last name and move to the next line, click the **Insert Merge Field** button, click **LastName,** and press the **Enter** key.

7. To enter the job title and move to the next line, click the **Insert Merge Field** button, click **JobTitle,** and press the **Enter** key.

8. To insert the company name and move to the next line, click the **Insert Merge Field** button, and click **Company.** Then press the **Enter** key.

9. To enter the first line of the address and move to the next line, click the **Insert Merge Field** button, click **Address1,** and press the **Enter** key.

10. To enter the second line for the address and move to the next line, click the **Insert Merge Field** button, click **Address2,** and press the **Enter** key.

11. To enter the city, state, and postal code, click the **Insert Merge Field** button, click **City,** type a **comma,** and press the **Spacebar.** Then click the **Insert Merge Field** button, click **State,** and press the **Spacebar.** Then click the **Insert Merge Field** button, click **PostalCode,** and press the **Enter** key twice.

12. To enter the salutation and the body of the letter, type **Dear,** press the **Spacebar,** click the **Insert Merge Field** button, click **FirstName,** type a **colon,** and press the **Enter** key twice. Then type **Thank you for enrolling in our class. All classes begin at 9 a.m. and end at 4 p.m.**

13. To begin a new paragraph, press the **Enter** key twice. Type **We look forward to seeing you in our,** press the **Spacebar,** click the **Insert Merge Field** button, and click **Class.** Press the **Spacebar,** type the word **on,** press the **Spacebar,** click **Insert Merge Field,** and click **ClassDate.**

14. To enter the closing for the letter, press the **Enter** key twice. Type **Sincerely** and a **comma.** Press the **Enter** key four times. Type your name.

15. To save the main document, click the **Save** button, type **Step-by-Step 8-4 Main,** and click **Save.**

Using the Merge and Database Toolbars

When you open a main document that has been identified as a main document, Word displays the Mail Merge toolbar, shown in Figure 8.7.

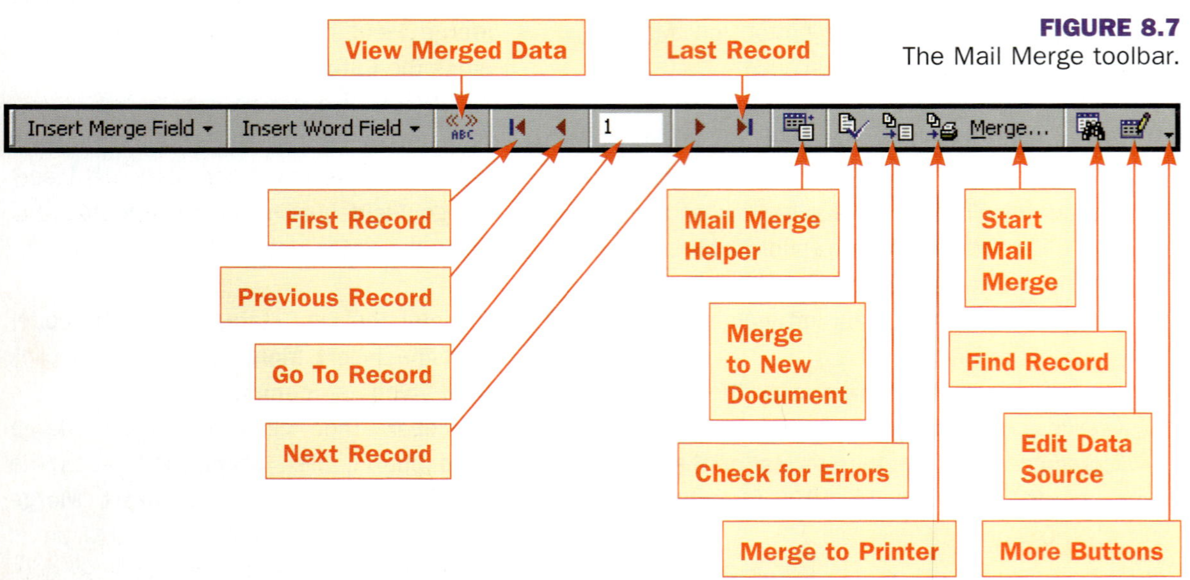

FIGURE 8.7
The Mail Merge toolbar.

When you view a data source document, Word displays the Database toolbar shown in Figure 8.8.

Use the View Merged Data button to look at the merged form letters for errors before you send them to the printer. You can also use the Print button or command to print the merged letter on the screen. You can use the First Record, Previous Record, Next Record, and Last Record buttons to see the merged form letters for each of the records in your data source.

It is wise to view merged data on the screen so you can be sure you've entered everything correctly before sending the entire job to the printer.

FIGURE 8.8
The Database toolbar.

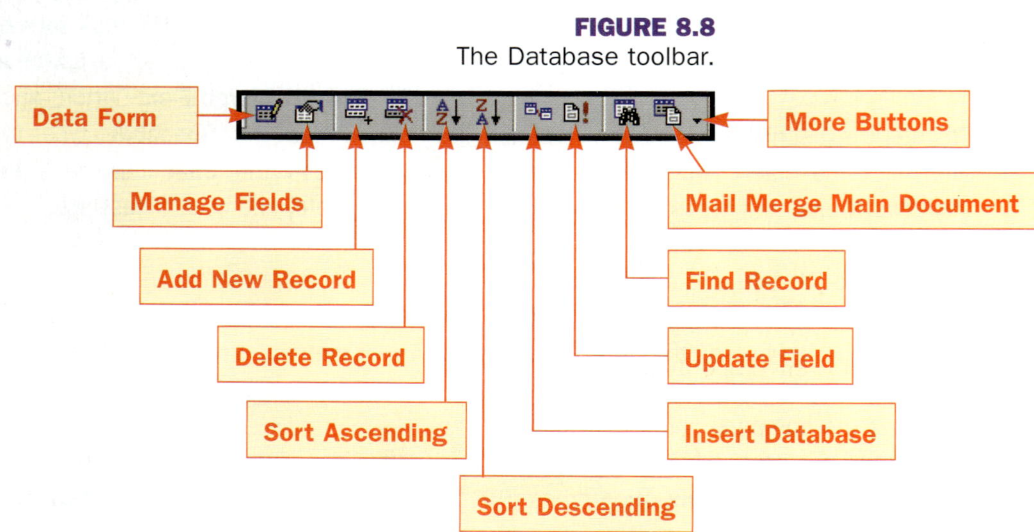

STEP-BY-STEP ▷ 8.5

1. To merge data, click **Merge.**

2. To see the merged form letter for record 1, click the **View Merged Data** button.

3. To see the merged form letter for record 2, click the **Next Record** button. Notice the last sentence needs to have the word **class** after the merged name of the class.

4. To return to the main document to make the correction for all letters there, click the **View Merged Data** button again.

5. To enter the word *class* and a space and save the change, click the **I-beam** before the word **on** after the **Class** merge field, and type **class** and a space. Then click the **Save** button.

Printing and Saving Merged Form Letters

You can merge to the printer or to a file. It is usually enough to merge to the printer and keep a copy of the main document and the data source file. You can use the Merge to Printer button on the Mail Merge toolbar to merge the form letters at the printer.

Producing Envelopes and Labels with Mail Merge

You can use the Mail Merge command on the Tools menu to produce envelopes or mailing labels for your form letters. You choose either Envelopes or Mailing Labels in the Create drop-down list in the Main Document area on the Mail Merge Helper (see Figure 8.9). You can use the same data source you used for the form letters.

Word uses information from your currently selected printer to print envelopes. You will need to know the type of envelope feeder your printer uses. You also have to specify the size of envelope you are using.

FIGURE 8.9
The Label Options dialog box offers a number of options.

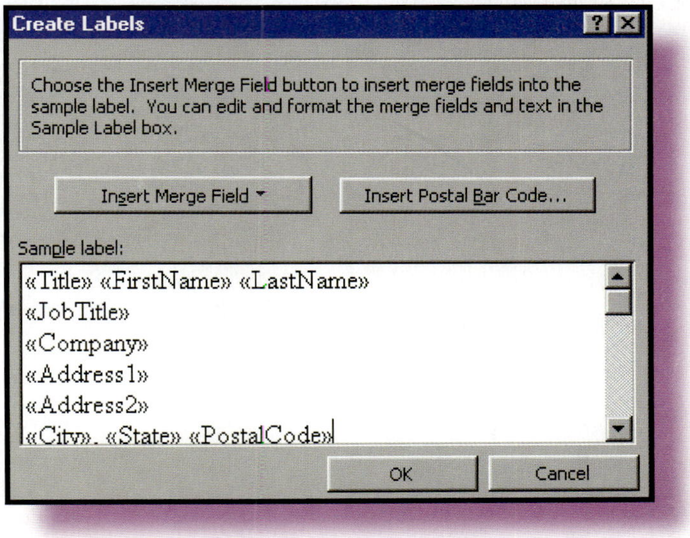

Word must know the type of labels you will use to set up for labels (see Figure 8.10). You will do the following exercise using options that may not apply to your printer so you can see how a mailing label merge document looks.

When you signal Word to merge the documents, the Merge dialog box appears (see Figure 8.11). You can merge to a new document, a printer, or to electronic mail.

You can see the merged label document in Figure 8.12. Word names the unsaved document Labels to distinguish the merged document from others.

FIGURE 8.10
The Create Labels dialog box with merge fields entered.

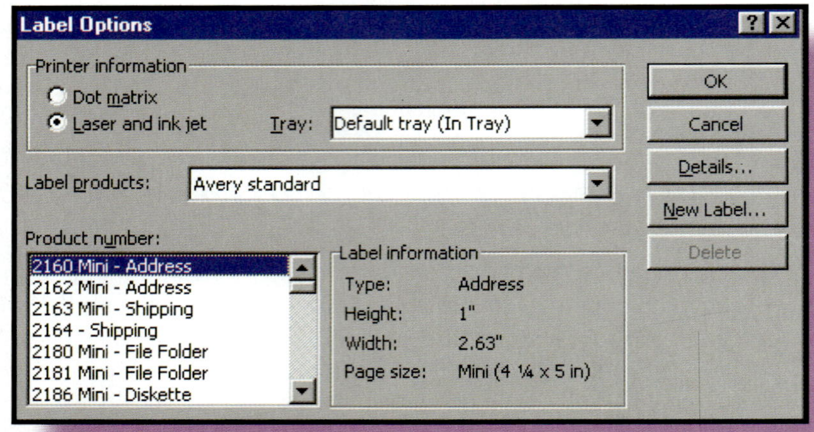

FIGURE 8.11
Clicking on Merge starts the mail merge.

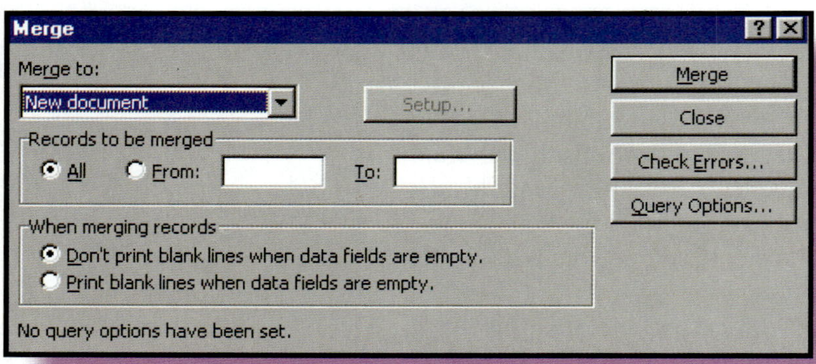

FIGURE 8.12
Notice the merged label document containing three records.

Ms. Mary Smith President New Company 124 Main Street Duluth, MN 67774	Mr. Harry Jones Comptroller ABC Company 890 Fifth Avenue Smithtown, NY 87765
Mr. Jim Walker Manager, Central Services XYZ Company 412 Central Avenue Orangetown, NJ 07984	

S TEP-BY-STEP ▷ 8.6

1. To merge the main document with the data source and print the three letters, click the **Merge to Printer** button on the **Mail Merge** toolbar, and click **OK.**

2. To create mailing labels, click the **Mail Merge Helper** button, in the Main document area click **Create,** and click **Mailing Labels.** When the dialog box appears, click **New Main Document.** Under **Data source,** click **Get Data,** click **Open Data Source,** and double-click the **Data Source** file in your folder.

3. To display the Label Options dialog box, click **Set Up Main Document.**

4. To signal the type of printer and select the tray, click **Laser and ink jet** and then click **Default tray (In Tray).** (The exact wording of this option may vary depending on the type of printer being used.)

5. To signal the type of labels to be used, click **Avery standard,** scroll to and click **5161 – Address** in the Product number box, and click **OK.**

6. To prepare the main document for the labels, enter the merge fields for the label so your sample label looks like the one in Figure 8.9. When finished, click **OK.**

7. To close the open documents, hold the **Shift** key and click **File,** and then click **Close All.** Respond **No** when asked to save changes.

Using a Data Source from Another Application

You can use data from another application such as Microsoft Excel, Microsoft Access, Paradox, or WordPerfect when working with Mail Merge. Use the Get Data button and then Open Data Source in the Mail Merge Helper dialog box. Type or select the file name of the data source, and then select the appropriate option in the List Files of Type box. Word provides converters for many types of files.

You may have to run the Office install program to add a converter for data from another application.

Selecting and Sorting Records

You can use the Query Options button in the Mail Merge Helper dialog box to select a particular set of data records for a merge. On the Filter Records tab in the Query Options dialog box (see Figure 8.13), you can specify what selection rules Word should use to retrieve (filter) the information you want.

In the Query Options dialog box you select a set of data records for a merge.

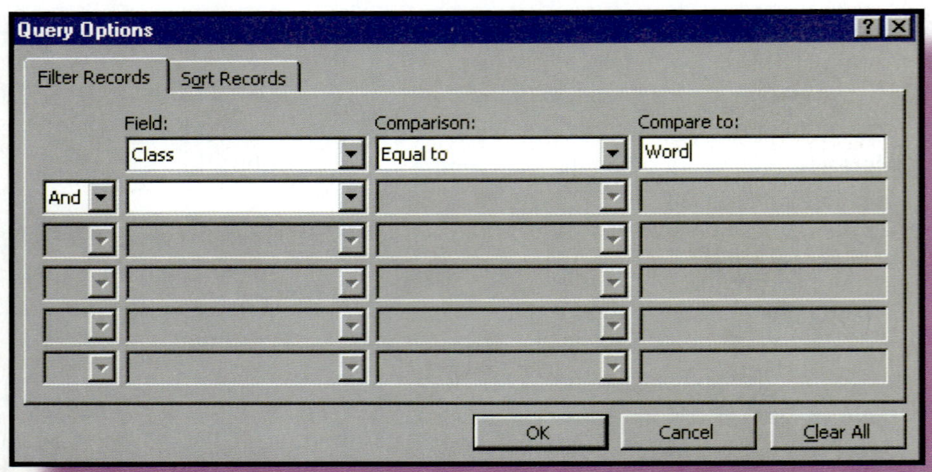

A selection rule is made up of three parts—a field name from your data source, a comparison phrase such as *equal to* or *is not blank,* and text or numbers to which you want the data field compared. You can specify as many as six selection rules to narrow the range of records selected.

You can also use the Sort tab in the Query Options dialog box to sort records in alphabetical or numerical order based on the contents of selected data fields. You could, for instance, put a large mailing in postal code order for the post office.

S TEP-BY-STEP ⇨ 8.7

1. Open **Step-by-Step 8-7 Merge.**

2. To display the Mail Merge Helper dialog box, click **Tools** and then click **Mail Merge.** Notice the Main document area and Get data area on the Mail Merge Helper contain the proper information because these documents have already been used in a mail merge.

3. To open the Query Options dialog box, click **Query Options** in the Merge area of Mail Merge Helper.

4. To see the list of fields in your data source, click the **Field** drop-down button.

5. To enter Class as the filter field, scroll to and click **Class.** Notice **Equal to** is already in the **Comparison** field and your insertion point is in the **Compare to** field.

6. To select just the records for Word classes, type **Word** and click **OK.**

7. To merge to a new document, click **Merge** in the **Mail Merge Helper** dialog box. Notice you are merging to a new document. Then click **Merge** in the **Merge** dialog box. You are now looking at the document, Form Letters. Word gives each form letters document a name and consecutive number. Scroll through and notice that only two form letters were merged.

Adding Records to a Data Source

You can use the Data Form dialog box to add data records. To open the Data Form dialog box, click the Edit button under Data Source in the Mail Merge Helper dialog box.

Adding or Deleting Data Fields in a Data Source

You can add, delete, and rename data fields in a data source document in the Manage Fields dialog box (see Figure 8.14). If you remove a field, all information in that field in *any* record is deleted. Use the Edit button under Data Source in the Mail Merge Helper dialog box to display the Data Form. Then use View Form and the Manage Fields button on the Database toolbar.

FIGURE 8.14
Add, remove, or rename fields in the Manage Fields dialog box.

STEP-BY-STEP 8.8

1. To make **Step-by-Step 8-7 Merge** active, click the **Step-by-Step 8-7** button on the **taskbar.**

2. To display the Mail Merge dialog box, click the **Mail Merge Helper** button.

(continued on next page)

177

3. To edit a data source document, click **Edit** in the **Data source** area and click **C:\...\Data Source.**

4. To see the source, click **View Source** in the **Data Form** dialog box.

5. To display the Manage Fields dialog box, click the **Manage Fields** button on the Mail Merge toolbar (second from left).

6. To add a field for a fee, type **Fee** in the Field Name box ,and click **Add.**

7. To remove the Address2 field, click **Address2** and click **Remove.**

8. To cancel the deletion and return to the data document, respond **No** and click **OK.**

9. Close all the open documents without saving changes.

Summary

You have now learned how to use Mail Merge Helper, how to work with a main document and a data source, how to use the Mail Merge and Database toolbars, how to merge to a new document and to the printer, how to print envelopes and labels, and how to use some advanced merge techniques.

Try the exercises on the following pages to test how well you remember what you learned. Don't be afraid to go back and look up answers, because that will help to reinforce what you learned.

LESSON 8 REVIEW QUESTIONS

TRUE / FALSE

Circle the T if the statement is true. Circle the F if it is false.

T **F** 1. The data source contains all items that remain the same in each letter along with merge fields.

T **F** 2. The main document contains the database.

T F 3. You should always separate the city, state, and Postal Code when entering fields in a database so you can sort and select using the individual fields.

T **F** 4. There is no need to have a field for a person's title (Mr., Mrs., Ms.).

T F 5. You can use the Move buttons in the Create Data Source dialog box to change the order of fields.

T **F** 6. You can type chevrons (<< >>) around the field names in a main document instead of using the Insert Merge Field button.

T F 7. There is usually no need to save a document with all merged form letters, because you have a copy of the main document and the data source.

T F 8. When you want to create envelopes or labels, you can use the same data source you used for the form letter.

T **F** 9. You cannot use data from other applications with Word's Mail Merge.

T F 10. You can add or remove fields from your data source after you have been using it for a while.

COMPLETION

Complete the following sentences by writing the correct word or words in the blanks provided.

1. The _____*main*_____ document contains the information that remains the same in each form along with merge fields for variable information.

2. You can use the same _*data sorce*_ for many different form letters.

3. You must use the Insert Merge Field button to enter _*merge fields*_ in your main document.

4. You can merge to a(n) _*file*_ or to the _*printer*_.

5. You can use the _*Query Option*_ button in the Mail Merge Helper dialog box to select records or to sort records for merging.

LESSON 8 PROJECTS

PROJECT 8A

To practice what you've learned in this lesson, complete the following project:

1. Perform a Mail Merge using **Project 8-A** as the main document and **Project 8-B** as the data source.

2. Print the merged memos and print labels for the recipients.

Extra Challenges

Use Help to get information about sorting merge records. Print some of the information you find.

PROJECT 8B

To practice what you've learned in this lesson, complete the following project:

1. Proofread the merged memos from **Project 8A** and then return to the main document file to correct the spacing problems in the class date in the first paragraph of the letter.

2. Merge and print the memos again and save and close the documents.

PROJECT 8C

Search the Web for information about using the Web. Print as much of the information as you think is valuable. Disconnect from your Internet service provider.

CRITICAL THINKING ACTIVITY

You are president of Northeast Computer Users. You know from calls you receive from the membership that there is a need to educate some of the members about the Internet.

Use Mail Merge to write a letter to six members you know have e-mail addresses and have been using the Internet. Ask them to share their knowledge with the rest of the group at meetings to be held in the near future. Send the merged letters electronically.

WORKING WITH GRAPHIC OBJECTS

Introduction

Word includes a number of sophisticated graphics tools that let you add visual interest to your documents. You can add clip art, pictures from other applications, AutoShapes from Word's Drawing toolbar, images from cameras or scanners, WordArt, text boxes, and charts.

When you work with some of these graphics tools, you are working with Word's OLE features. **OLE** stands for Object Linking and Embedding. You can use linked objects or embedded objects to add all or part of a file from another Microsoft Office or OLE-compliant application to your Word document. Some of the graphics you will use in this lesson are embedded objects.

When you embed an object in your file, the information from the source application is saved with your document, and you can modify it right in your document When you link an object, the size of your file does not increase, but a user must have access to the source document and it may take Word longer to load the graphic. The information is still stored in the source file, and Word displays a representation of the linked data. If the information in the source file changes, the information in your Word document changes.

Using the Picture Command

You can use the Picture command on the Insert menu to insert clip art, picture files, AutoShapes, Word Art, charts, and camera images. There are two types of graphics—pictures and drawing objects. Pictures are actually other files. They can be bitmaps, scanned pictures, photos, or clip art. Drawing objects are AutoShapes, curves, lines, or WordArt drawing objects that are part of your Word document.

You can use the Picture toolbar to insert and to modify pictures. You can insert picture files from other applications as long as you've installed a filter for the imported file. Check Word's online Help if you have any difficulty inserting a picture that is not part of the Microsoft Word software package. You may have to reinstall the Word software to add a filter.

You can use the images, sounds, and movies Microsoft provides in the Clip Gallery in any advertising, promotional and marketing materials, or product or service created with Word, provided the material, product or service is for noncommercial purposes. You may not sell any promotional and marketing materials or any products or services containing the images.

Inserting Clip Art

To display the Insert ClipArt dialog box, choose the Picture command on the Insert menu and then the Clip Art option on the submenu. The dialog box contains tabs for inserting pictures, sounds, and motion clips.

When you want to insert, replace, import, or organize clips, simply drag and drop or copy and paste them. When you select a clip, you will see the menu with Insert clip, Preview clip, Add clip to Favorites or other category, or find similar clips buttons (see Figure 9.1).

There are many more clip art files available for downloading from the Web.

FIGURE 9.1

Select a picture in the Microsoft Clip Gallery. Click a button to let Word know what to do with the selected clip.

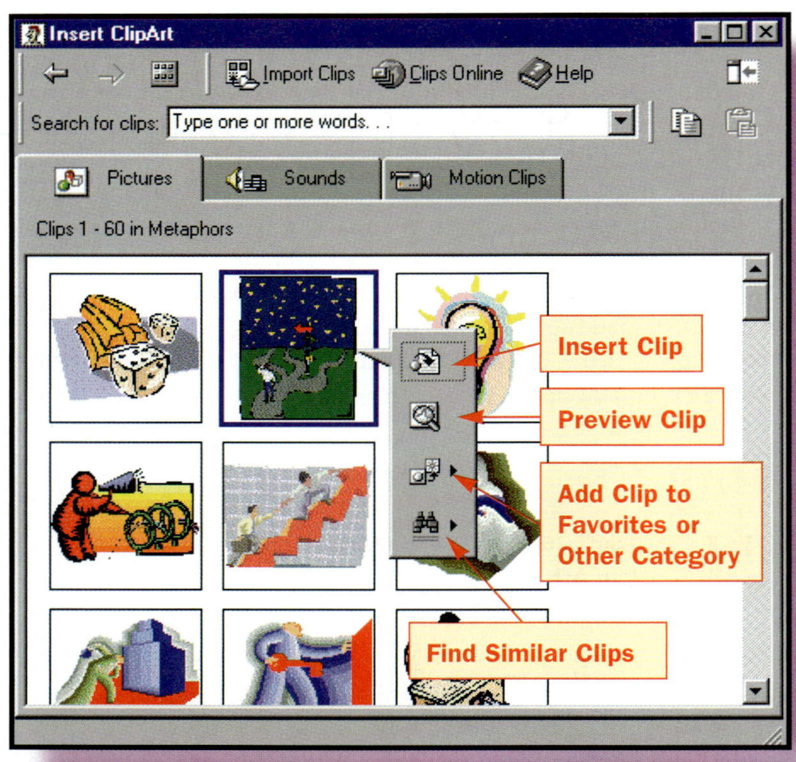

When you insert a picture, it appears in your document surrounded by small squares called sizing handles (see Figure 9.2). You use these handles to change the picture's size.

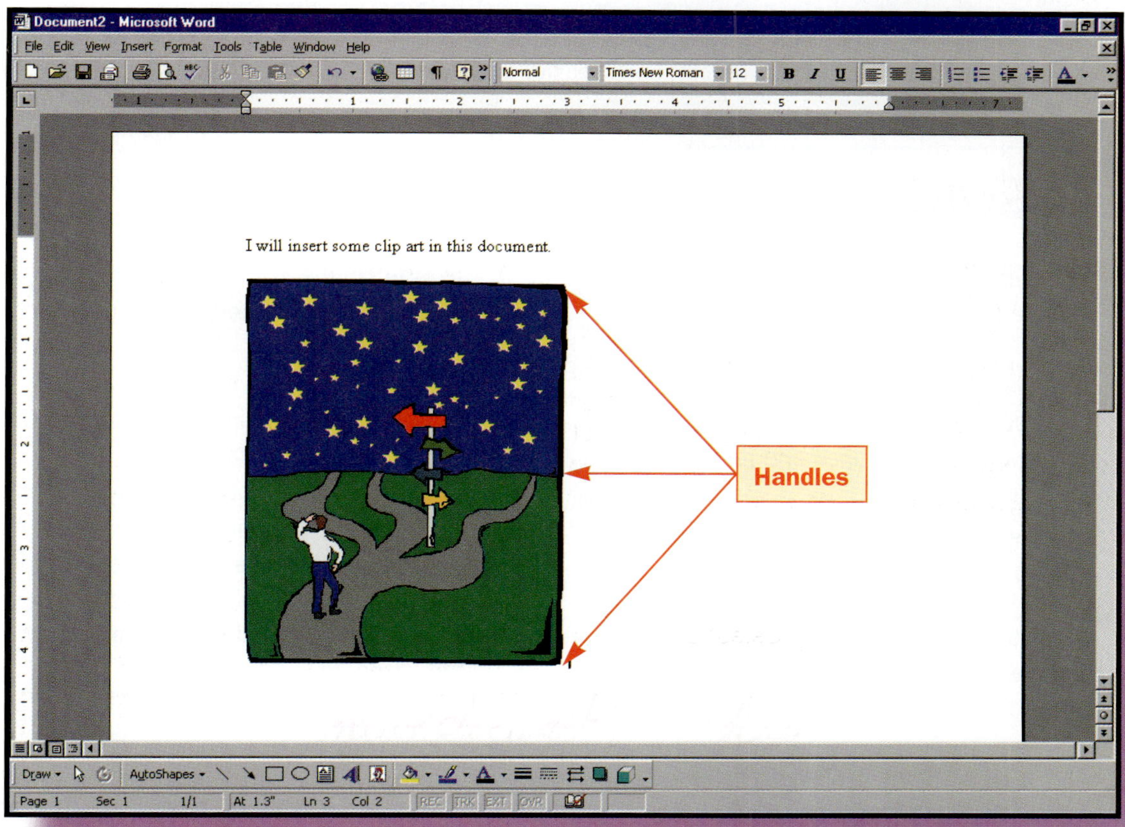

FIGURE 9.2
Word inserted the picture.

S TEP-BY-STEP ▷ 9.1

1. To open a new document, click the **New** button, type **I will insert some clip art in this document,** and press the **Enter** key twice.

2. To display the Insert ClipArt dialog box, click the **Insert** menu, click **Picture,** and then click **Clip Art.**

3. To insert a picture, scroll down to and click the **Metaphors** category, click the **decisions** picture (middle picture on top row), and then click **Insert clip.** Notice that Word inserted the clip art in your document.

Selecting and Sizing Graphics

Before you can modify or size a graphic, you must select it. To select a graphic, click it once. To resize a graphic proportionally, drag a corner handle. To resize a graphic by distorting it horizontally or vertically, drag a middle handle.

1 8 3

Some types of graphics require that you hold the Shift key while dragging a corner handle to size proportionally.

When a graphic is selected, you can copy, paste, and delete it the same as you would text.

STEP-BY-STEP 9.2

1. To select the picture, click anywhere on the picture.

2. To enlarge the picture proportionally, drag the handle at the lower right corner downward about an inch and release.

3. To return to the original size, click the **Undo** button on the Standard toolbar.

4. To stretch the picture horizontally, drag the middle handle on the right side of the picture to the right and release.

5. To return to the original size, click the **Undo** button on the Standard toolbar.

6. To stretch the picture vertically, drag the middle handle on the bottom of the picture down and release.

7. To return to the original size, click the **Undo** button on the Standard toolbar.

8. To delete the graphic and then return it to the document, press the **Delete** key, notice the picture has disappeared from the display, and then click the **Undo** button on the Standard toolbar.

Modifying Pictures

The Picture toolbar (see Figure 9.3) makes it easy to modify pictures.

When you select a picture, Word displays the Picture toolbar.

FIGURE 9.3
Notice the buttons on the Picture toolbar.

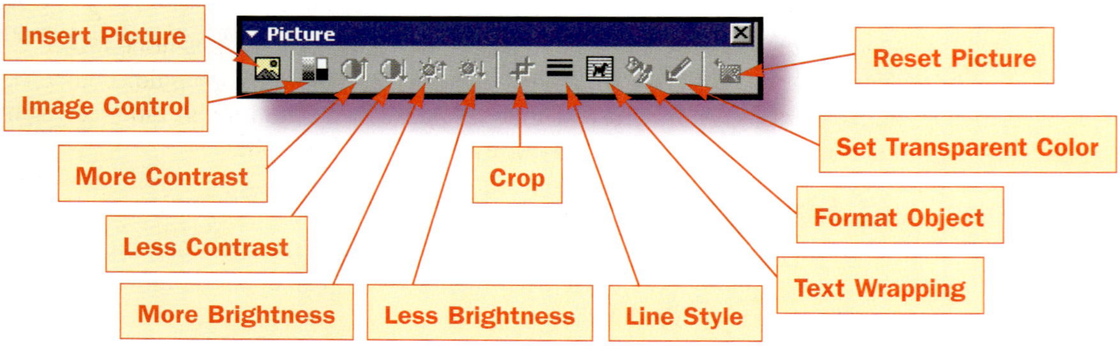

When a picture is selected, you can use the Picture command on the Format menu or the Format Picture button on the Picture toolbar to display the Format Picture dialog box. The Format Picture dialog box contains the following tabs:

- Colors and Lines lets you modify colors in fill and lines and designate arrow styles for clip art.

- Size lets you size, rotate, scale, and reset clip art.

- Layout lets you choose one of five ways text flows around or through a picture and the picture's horizontal alignment.

- Picture lets you crop to a precise size and control the color, the brightness, and the contrast of the image.

Concept Builders

Remember you can move a dialog box by dragging its title bar if it covers an area with which you want to work.

STEP-BY-STEP ▷ 9.3

1. To display the Picture toolbar if it is not already displayed, click **View,** click **Toolbars,** and click **Picture.**

2. To see the different ways you can display the graphic, be sure the picture is selected, click the **Image Control** button, and click **Grayscale.** Click the **Image Control** button again, and then click **Black & White.** Click the **Image Control** button again, and then click **Watermark.**

3. To return to the original setting, click the **Image Control** button, and click **Automatic.**

4. To adjust the contrast on the graphic, click the **More Contrast** button, and notice the change; click the **More Contrast** button again, and notice the change; and then click the **Less Contrast** button.

5. To crop the man, click the **Crop** button, and notice your mouse pointer is a cropping tool; position it on the middle handle on the left side of the picture, click and drag until the man is no longer visible, and then release.

6. To turn off the cropping tool, click the **Crop** button again.

7. To return to the full picture, click the Undo button.

8. To close the document without saving changes, click its Close button and respond No when asked whether to save changes.

Positioning a Picture

By default, Word inserts pictures inline with text. That means they are positioned directly in the text at the insertion point. Word assumes that text will not wrap around the graphic. You can change the way text surrounds a graphic in the Format Picture dialog box. The Layout tab (see Figure 9.4) contains five options for letting text flow around or even through a graphic.

The Advanced button on the Layout tab displays additional options for wrapping to one side or the other. You can also change the distance from the graphic to the text in spin boxes at the bottom of the dialog box. Figure 9.5 shows a watermark graphic behind the text.

You learned earlier that watermarks are text or graphics that are used as backgrounds on printed documents. You insert a watermark in a document's header.

When you use Portable Network Graphics (PNG) format for your pictures, your document takes less time to save, uses less disk space, and takes less time to download in a Web browser. To use the format, click the Tools menu, click Options, click the General tab, click Web Options, click the Pictures tab and click the Allow PNG as an output format option.

Use wrapping options to control how text formats around a graphic.

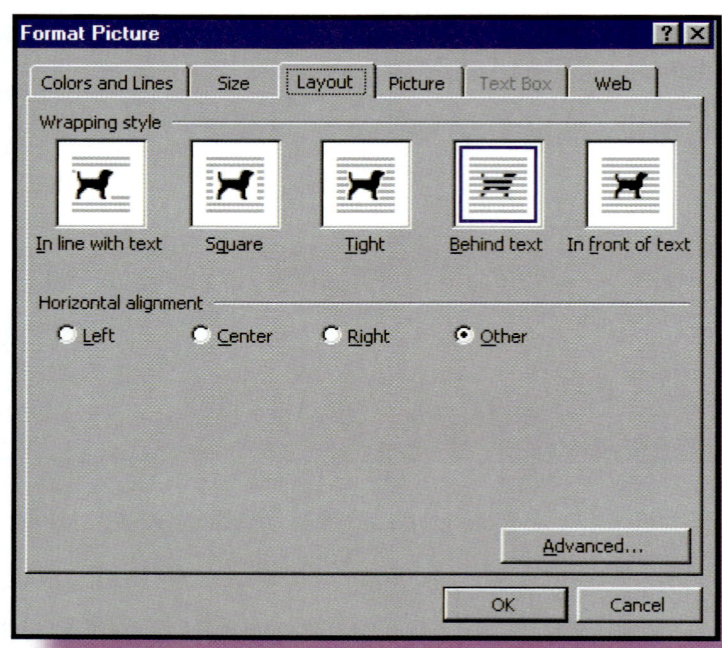

Notice the watermark behind the text.

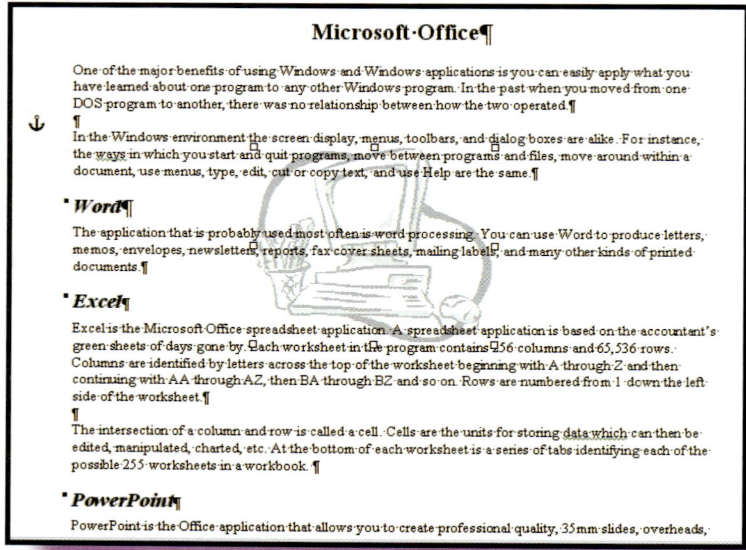

Copying and Pasting Graphics

You can copy and paste graphics with the Copy and Paste commands, just as you do text in a document. The copy of the picture will be the same size and will have the same wrapping and other formatting as the original graphic.

You can also use a shortcut method to copy a graphic: hold the Ctrl key while dragging the object.

Hot Tips

When you paste a copy of a graphic, the new copy appears on top of the original. Simply drag it to the desired position.

STEP-BY-STEP 9.4

1. Open **Step-by-Step 9-4 Posit.** If necessary, click the **Show/Hide ¶** button to display nonprinting marks.

2. To insert a picture, hold the **Ctrl** key and press the **Home** key, click the **Insert** menu, click **Picture,** click **Clip Art,** click the **Office** category, click the picture called **computers** (middle in second row), click **Insert Clip,** and click the **Close** button in the **Insert ClipArt** dialog box.

3. To change the wrap options, be sure the picture is selected, click **Picture** on the **Format** menu. Click the **Layout** tab, select the **Behind text** wrapping style, click the Center horizontal alignment option, and click **OK.**

4. To resize picture, click **Picture** on the **Format** menu. Click the **Size** tab, change the Height and Width values to **50%,** and click **OK.**

5. To position the picture, **drag** it up until the top of the dashed-line box aligns with the first line of text in the first paragraph.

6. To place a copy of the picture in the document, be sure the picture is selected, click the **Copy** button on the Standard toolbar**,** and then click the **Paste** button on the Standard toolbar.

7. To move the copy of the picture, **drag** it to the right side of the document.

8. To delete the second copy of the picture, be sure it is selected and press the **Delete** key.

9. To move the picture to the middle of the page in the first paragraph, be sure the picture is selected, and move your pointer around until you see the double-crossed arrows. Then drag the picture to the position you see in Figure 9.5.

10. To make the image a watermark, click the **Image Control** button and click **Watermark.**

11. To print the document, click the **Print** button on the Standard toolbar.

12. Save and close the document.

Working with WordArt

WordArt is a drawing tool that turns words into a graphic image. You can use the WordArt feature to create interesting text effects to enhance documents. WordArt lets you fit text into a variety of shapes, use unusual alignments, and add three-dimensional effects.

You can edit a WordArt drawing object the same way you edit other Word graphics. You can resize the WordArt graphic, add borders to it, and reposition it. You can return to edit the WordArt drawing object at any time by double-clicking the graphic.

To insert Wordart, use the WordArt option on the Insert menu's Picture command or the WordArt button on the Drawing toolbar. You can select text you want in the WordArt image before choosing WordArt, or you can type the text after you choose a WordArt style. When you click the WordArt command or button, Word displays the WordArt Gallery (see Figure 9.6) from which you can choose a style. You can then type text and choose fonts, font sizes, and font styles in the Edit WordArt Text dialog box (see Figure 9.7).

The WordArt toolbar shown in Figure 9.8 automatically appears with your WordArt drawing object. You can use toolbar buttons to modify your WordArt drawing object. You can add a new WordArt design, change the text in the current graphic, change the design and shape of the current graphic, change the color and pattern of the graphic, rotate the graphic, change the height of the text, change the orientation and alignment of the text, and change the spacing between characters.

FIGURE 9.6

Choose a WordArt style from the WordArt Gallery.

FIGURE 9.7

Type your text in this dialog box.

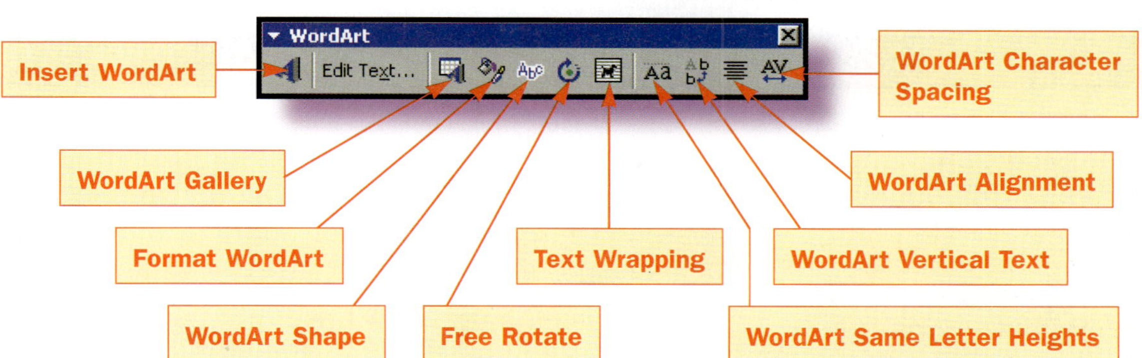

FIGURE 9.8
The WordArt toolbar.

STEP-BY-STEP ▷ 9.5

1. Open **Step-by-Step 9-5 Art.**

2. To display the WordArt Gallery dialog box, click **View,** click **Toolbars,** click **Drawing,** and click the **WordArt** button on the Drawing toolbar.

3. To choose a design, select the third WordArt design in the second column, and click **OK.**

4. To enter the text for the image in the Edit WordArt Text dialog box, type **ABC Computer** and click **OK.**

5. To position the WordArt graphic, point to any letter in the graphic. When the pointer becomes a double-crossed arrow, drag the graphic to the top left corner of the page.

6. To modify the color of the WordArt graphic, click **Format WordArt** on the WordArt toolbar. Click the **Color and Lines** tab, click the Fill Color drop-down button, click **Fill Effects** at the bottom of the color palette, click the Diagonal Up option, and click OK twice.

7. Print, save and close the document.

Working with Autoshapes and Drawing Tools

Word provides a set of predrawn shapes called AutoShapes. You can use AutoShapes as well as the other drawing tools on the Drawing toolbar to create, edit, and format objects (see Figure 9.9).

Drawing objects can be resized, rotated, flipped, colored, and combined with other shapes. Many AutoShapes have adjustment handles you can use to change one or more parts of the shape (see Figure 9.10).

Concept Builders

If you are not satisfied with a shape, press the Delete key while the shape is selected or use the Undo button immediately after creating it.

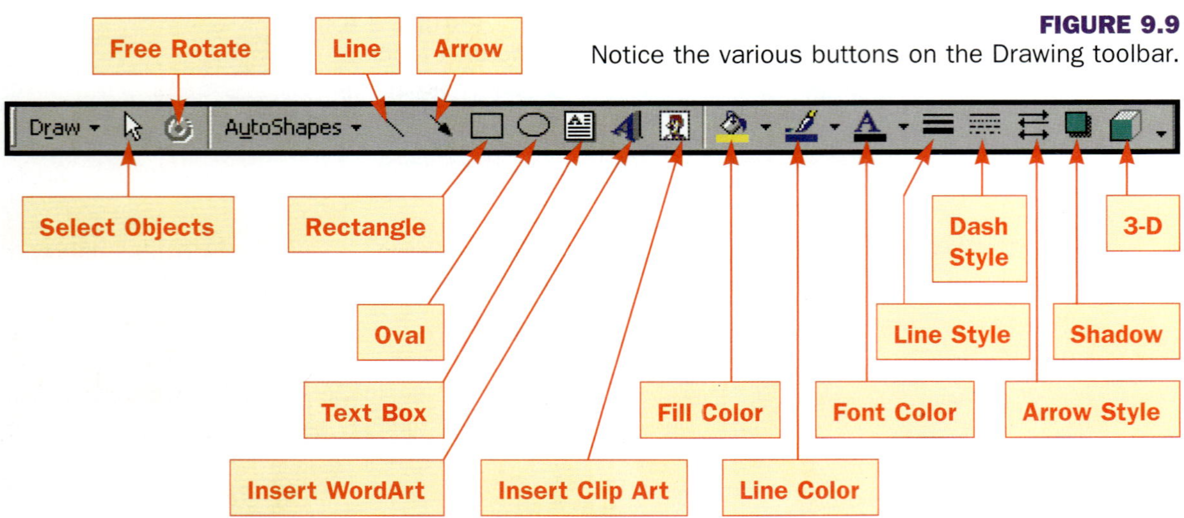

FIGURE 9.9
Notice the various buttons on the Drawing toolbar.

When you click the AutoShapes button on the Drawing toolbar, Word displays a pop-up menu containing lines, basic shapes, block arrows, flowchart elements, stars and banners, and callouts. When you click a category, Word displays a submenu of drawing options.

To insert an AutoShape in your document, simply click the shape you want to insert, position the crosshairs where you want to begin drawing, drag until the AutoShape is the size and shape you want, and release. The same applies to the drawing tools.

Hold the Shift key when using rectangular or oval drawing shapes or tools to draw squares or circles. To create a straight line, hold the Shift key while using line tools. To draw shapes from the center outward, hold the Ctrl key while dragging the crosshairs.

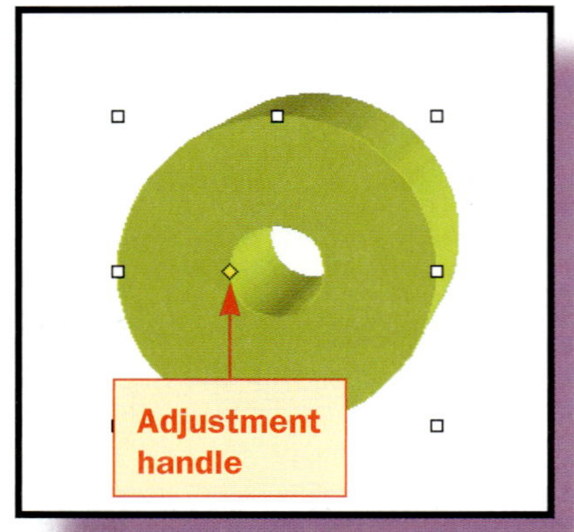

FIGURE 9.10
Notice the yellow adjustment handle.

STEP-BY-STEP ⟹ 9.6

1. To open a new document, click the **New** button.

2. To display the Drawing toolbar if you do not see it on your screen, click the **View** menu, click **Toolbars,** and click **Drawing** on the submenu.

3. To select the Donut shape, click the **AutoShapes** button on the Drawing toolbar,

click **Basic Shapes,** and click the **Donut** shape (second from the left in the fifth row). Word displays the crosshairs pointer.

4. To draw the donut, click the crosshairs at the top left of the document window, hold the **Shift** key and drag until the diameter of the donut is about 1½ inches. Notice the small yellow diamond attached to the inner circle of the donut.

5. To decrease the size of the inner circle, click the yellow diamond adjustment handle and drag it inward.

6. To move the donut, be sure it is still selected, move the mouse pointer until you see the double-crossed arrows, and drag to the center of the window.

7. To add a fill color to the donut's outer circle, be sure the donut is still selected, click the **Fill Color** button, and click a color.

8. To increase the weight of the donut's lines, be sure the donut is still selected, click the **Line Style** button, and click **3 pts.**

9. To add a shadow effect, be sure the shape is still selected, click the **Shadow** button, and click **Shadow Style 1,** the leftmost shadow option at the top of the pop-up menu.

10. To add a 3-D effect, be sure the donut is still selected, click the **3-D** button, and click **3-D Style 11,** the third option from the left on the third row.

Manipulating Objects

When you insert graphics in a document, Word layers them one on top of the other in the order in which they are inserted. You can use the Order command on the Draw pop-up menu to position graphics. You can Bring to Front, Send to Back, Bring Forward, Send Backward, Bring in Front of Text, or Send Behind Text.

You might want to combine shapes to create a drawing object. You can select more than one object at a time by holding the Shift key while you click each of the objects. You can also use the Select Objects button to click one drawing object to select it or to drag a box around multiple objects to select all of them.

Word has an invisible network of lines that covers the drawing area. That network is called a grid. You can display gridlines on the screen, but Word will not print them. The grid makes it easy to align drawing objects. By default, drawing objects snap to the grid. To temporarily override the Snap to Grid feature, hold the Alt key as you draw or drag an object. To turn off the Snap to Grid feature or to display gridlines, click the Draw button on the Drawing toolbar, and click Grid.

To "nudge" or move a drawing object a short distance, use the Nudge option on the Draw pop-up menu.

If you can't see an object you want to move to a different level, press the Tab key, or hold the Shift key and press the Tab key until the object is selected.

You can use the Group, Ungroup, and Regroup commands on the Draw pop-up menu when you want to group one or more drawing objects so you can treat them as one. Many clip art images are simply multiple drawing objects. You can use the Ungroup command to separate them—perhaps to change a color in one of the objects. Then regroup them to restore the clip art to one unit.

You can use the Free Rotate button on the Drawing toolbar to rotate a drawing object or group on its central axis or to flip it right to left or top to bottom.

When you click the Free Rotate button, small green circles appear at the corners of the selected drawing object. Drag any of these circles to rotate the object.

To rotate or flip a selected object, click the Draw button on the Drawing toolbar, click Rotate or Flip and then choose how you want to rotate or flip the object.

Adding Callouts

Callouts identify or comment on a feature of a picture or a drawing. The AutoShapes menu contains a Callouts option. There are a number of options available for displaying callouts.

Your document should look like this when you finish Step 13 in Step-by-Step 9.7.

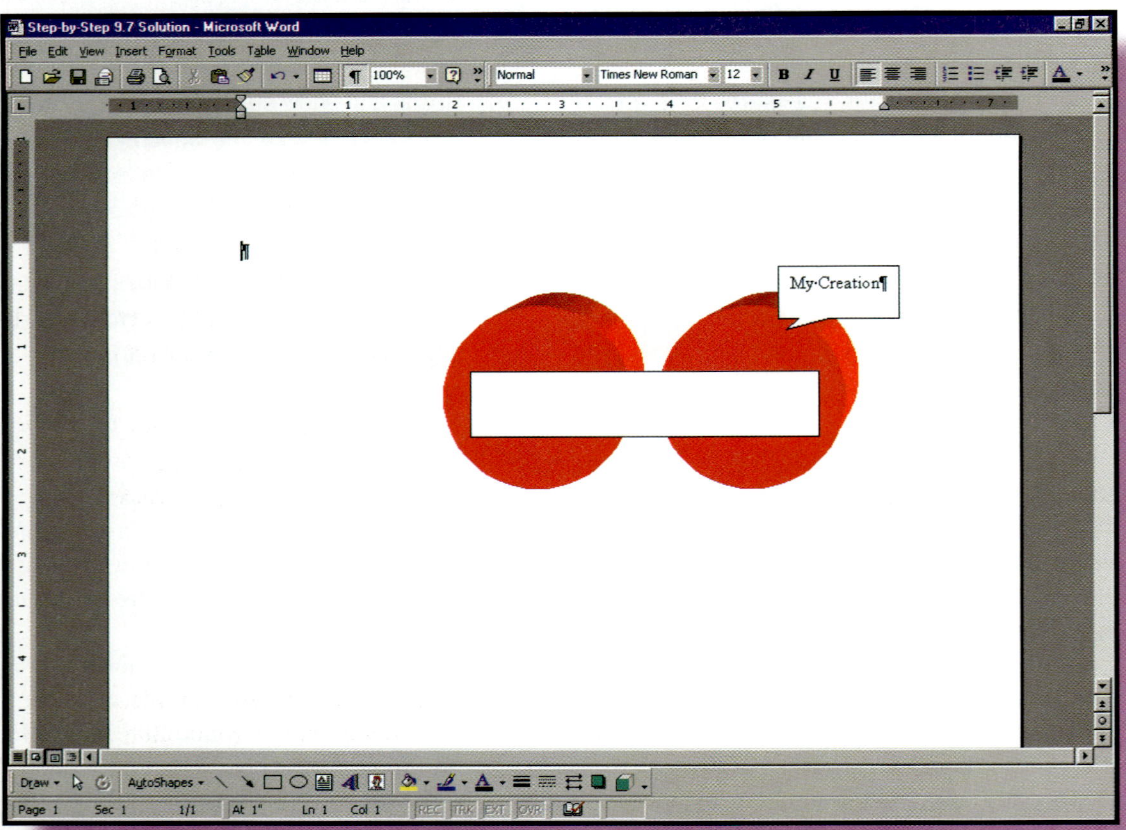

STEP-BY-STEP 9.7

1. To make a copy of the donut, be sure it is still selected, click the **Edit** menu, click **Copy**, and then click the **Paste** button on the toolbar. Notice Word pasted the donut on top of the original one.

2. To position the pasted donut to the right of the original, point to the selected donut until you see the double-crossed arrow, and then drag the copy to the right until it no longer touches the original donut.

3. To select both donuts, click the first donut and then hold the **Shift** key while clicking the second donut. Notice each donut has its own set of handles.

4. To change the fill color for both donuts, click the **Fill Color** button on the Drawing toolbar, and click a **red** color.

5. To group the two selected donuts so you can move them as one, click the **Draw** button, and click **Group.** Notice there is now only one set of handles for the two donuts.

6. To move the grouped donuts, drag them to the right. To return them to the original position, click **Undo.**

7. To draw a rectangle on the donuts like the one you see in Figure 9.11, click the **Rectangle** button, and drag to draw the

192

rectangle. Notice the rectangle is on top of the donuts.

8. To send the rectangle to the back, be sure it is selected, click the **Draw** button, click **Order,** and click **Send Backward.** Notice a bit of the rectangle shows in the donut hole.

9. To return the rectangle to the top, be sure it is selected, click the **Draw** button, click **Order,** and click **Bring Forward.**

10. To add the rectangle to the group, be sure the rectangle is selected, hold the **Shift** key and click the donut group, click the **Draw** button and click **Group.**

11. To rotate the group to the right, click the **Draw** button, click **Rotate or Flip,** and click **Rotate Right.** To undo the rotate, click **Undo** on the Standard toolbar.

12. To add a callout to your image, click the **AutoShapes** button, click **Callouts,** click **the Rectangular Callout,** click the crosshairs inside the image at the top right, and drag until the box is about the size you see in Figure 9.11, click on the callout, type **My Creation,** and click outside the callout.

13. If you like, experiment with the Drawing toolbar. Then print the document, save it as **Using Drawing Toolbar,** and close it.

Working with Text Boxes

Text **boxes** are invisible containers that allow you to position text and/or graphics. Text boxes can be especially useful for adding notes in the margins of a document but can also be used for keeping paragraphs and graphics together and for making text flow around other text or graphics (see Figure 9.12). Use the Text Box toolbar Word displays when you create a text box to link text boxes and use them, for instance, to continue an article from page one in a newsletter to page four.

Text boxes do not expand as you add text to them, so you must increase the size of the text box if your text does not fit.

You can use the Text Box command on the expanded Insert menu or the Text Box button on the Drawing toolbar to insert a text box. As you have done with other drawing objects, drag the crosshairs until the box is the size and shape you want. Then enter text at the insertion point.

FIGURE 9.12
You can see the text box.

To move a text box, click the double-crossed arrows on the hatched line when the box is selected and drag to a new position.

To delete a text box and all text within it, click the hatched or line border of a text box until the outline is made up of tiny dots, and then press the Delete key.

1. Open **Step-by-Step 9-8 Text.**

2. To add a text box to the rectangle in the graphic, click the **Text Box** button on the Drawing toolbar. Click the crosshairs, and drag to create a box almost the full width of the box within the triangle corners (see Figure 9.12).

3. To enter the text, type the following text at the insertion point. Press the **Enter** key at the end of each line.

```
Award Winning
Plain or Fancy Donuts
Fresh Every Day
Donut World
```

4. To change the font size, select the text, click the **Font Size** drop-down button on the Formatting toolbar, and click **16.**

5. To change the text color, be sure the text is still selected, click the **Font Color** drop-down button, and select a **deep blue** color.

6. Print, save, and close the document.

Summary

You have now learned how to insert a picture, edit and format pictures, use AutoShapes, use the drawing tools, insert a text box, and use WordArt.

Try the exercises on the following pages to test how well you remember what you learned. Don't be afraid to go back and look up answers or procedures, because that will help to reinforce what you learned.

LESSON 9 REVIEW QUESTIONS

TRUE / FALSE

Circle the T if the statement is true. Circle the F if it is false.

T F 1. You can use the Picture command on the Insert menu to find a picture file on your computer.

T F 2. When you want to resize a graphic proportionally, drag a middle handle.

T F 3. You can size a graphic to hide areas of the graphic you don't want to display.

T F 4. You can add borders and background shading to a clip art picture.

(T) F **5.** You must adhere to copyright laws when using clip art.

(T) F **6.** AutoShapes let you automatically create any of a number of common shapes.

T (F) **7.** Once you have created a WordArt graphic, you cannot modify it.

T (F) **8.** To draw a perfect circle with the Oval tool, hold down the Alt key.

(T) F **9.** OLE is an acronym for Object Linking & Embedding.

(T) F **10.** When you create a drawing object, it appears in front of text or other drawing objects.

COMPLETION

Complete the following sentences by writing the correct word or words in the blanks provided.

1. Choose _Picture Command_ on the _Clip art option_ submenu to insert a graphic from the ClipArt Gallery.

2. You use the _Layout_ tab on the _Insert Clip Art_ dialog box to control how text flows around a graphic.

3. Hold the _Shift_ key when using the Rectangle and Oval tools to create a perfect square or a circle.

4. Hold the _Ctrl_ key while dragging a drawing object to make a copy of it.

5. When you draw a number of objects, they are stacked in _Layers_ .

6. You can use the _Group_ command to move multiple objects as a single unit.

7. Use the _WordArt_ feature to turn text into a graphic.

8. _WordArt_ is a graphic made up of text you type.

9. You can use the _Rotate_ command to make mirror images.

10. The _grid_ is an invisible system of lines used to align objects in a drawing.

LESSON 9 PROJECTS

PROJECT 9A

SCANS **To practice what you've learned in this lesson, complete the following project:**

1. Open **Project 9-A.**

2. Use the Drawing toolbar to create something of your choosing. Use as many of the options available as you can.

3. Save the document as **My Graphic Image.** Print and close the document.

PROJECT 9B

To practice what you've learned in this lesson, complete the following project:

1. Open **Project 9-B.**

2. Position the picture below the first paragraph. Enlarge the picture until it is approximately 3.5 inches wide by 3 inches high.

3. Add callouts to label the following features: monitor, keyboard, CPU, and mouse. Then add a text box to the right of the picture and insert the following label: **Parts of Your Personal Computer.** Be sure the text box is well sized and formatted.

4. Save the document as **PC Labels.** Print and close the document.

Search Help for information about images that might be available on the Internet for downloading. Read and print the information.

PROJECT 9C

Search the Web for an image you might download for use in your documents. Access the Clip Art Gallery from the Picture command on the Insert menu, and then click the Clips online. Download an image.

CRITICAL THINKING ACTIVITY

SCANS

Create an invitation to a party to be held at your house at 8 p.m. on Saturday, September 23. Use the Page Setup command to change the size of the page to 6 by 4½ inches. Use some appropriate clip art and WordArt. Then print the document, save it with an appropriate name, and close it.

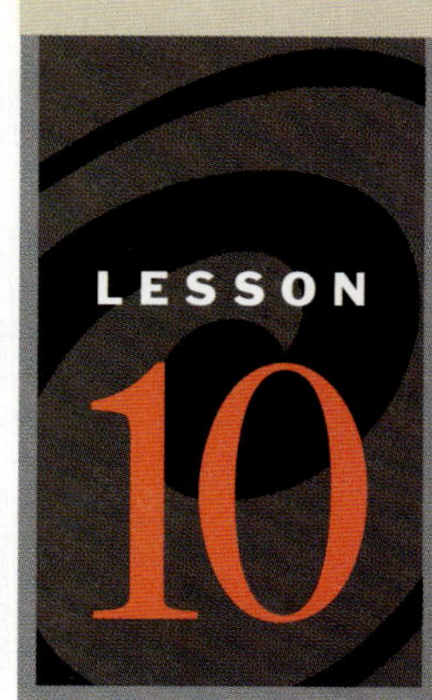

WORKING WITH LONG DOCUMENTS

Introduction

Word has many features that you can use to generate quite sophisticated documents and reports. In this lesson you will learn about several of them. Each of these features has many options that are not covered in this book, however. If you see a feature that you think will be helpful to you with your applications, be sure to use the documentation or Help to get information about all of the options available.

Using the Outline View

You can use Word's outline view (see Figure 10.1) to speed up scrolling, moving text, and changing the order and ranking of topics in a long document. Use the Outline View button at the left of the horizontal scroll bar with the other view buttons or the Outline command on the expanded View menu.

When you are in outline view, the Outlining toolbar (see Figure 10.2) appears at the top of the document.

Hot Tips

You will work with Master Document View later in this lesson.

This outline view shows headings and first line of each paragraph.

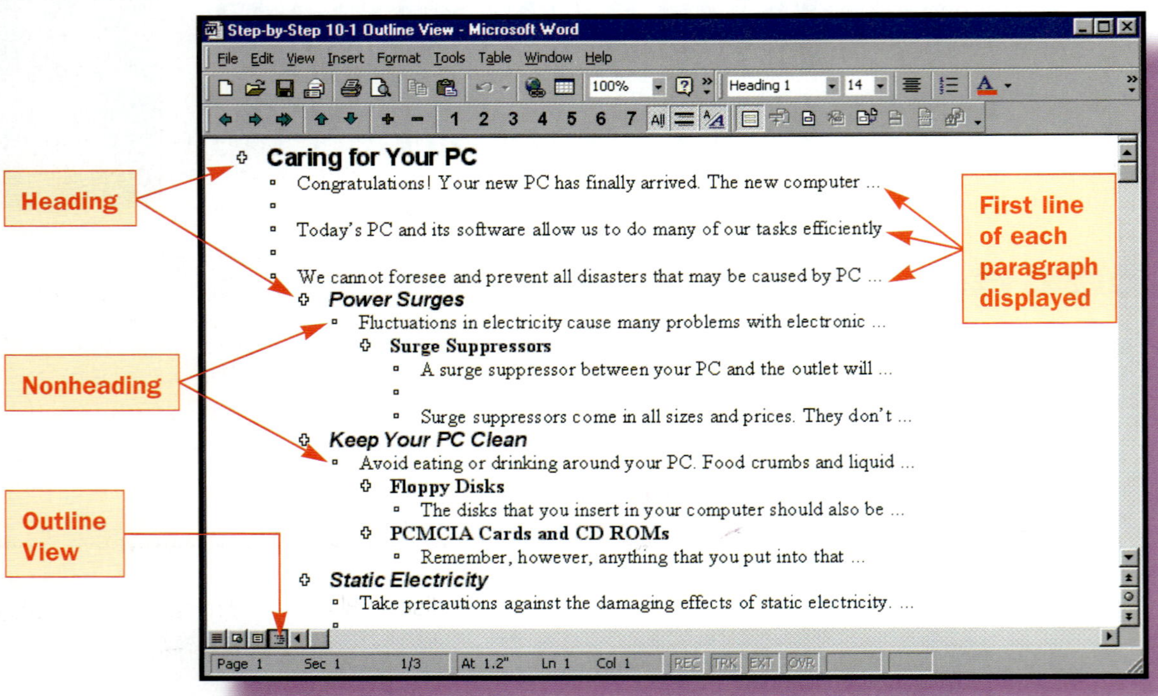

The Outlining toolbar appears at the top of the document.

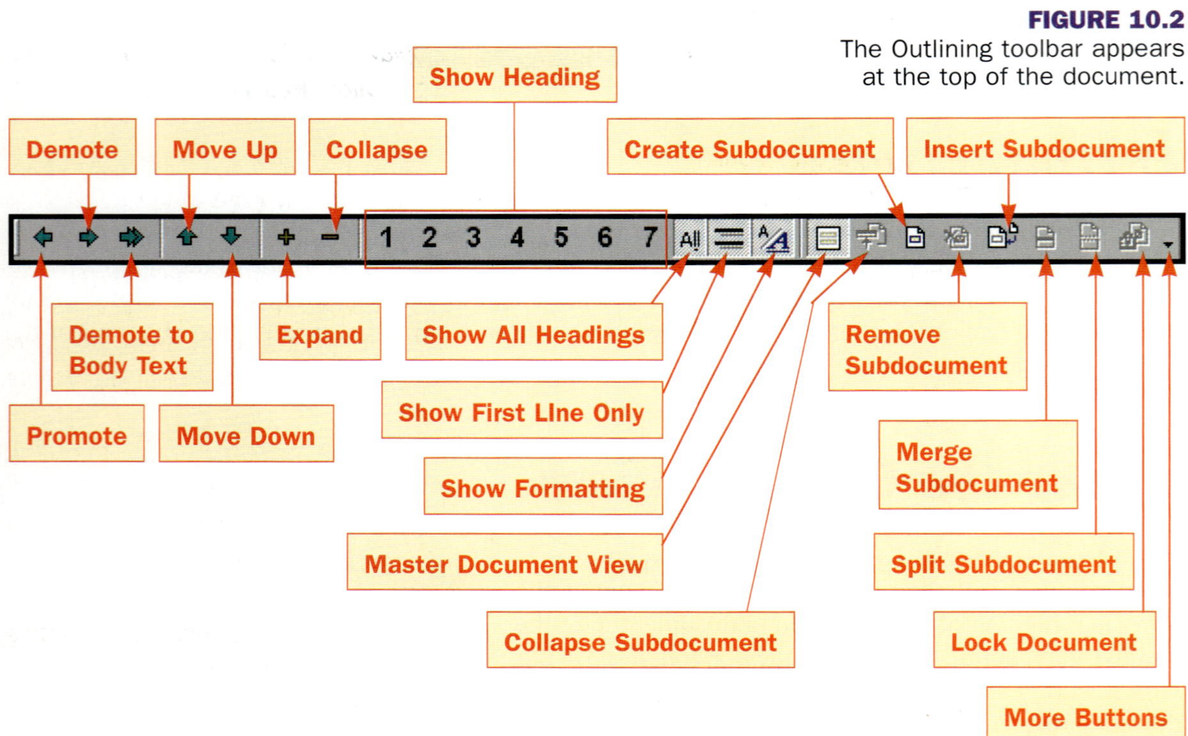

198

Displaying a Document in Outline View

When you display a document in outline view, text formatted with a heading style is displayed with a filled plus sign at its left. Each level of heading is indented under the level above. A heading with no subheadings or text below is displayed with a filled minus sign. Text that is not formatted with a heading style appears with a small square next to it (see Figure 10.1).

You can use the Show Heading 1 through Show Heading 7 buttons to display or hide as many subheadings as you like. The All button displays all headings and text. You can use the Show First Line Only button to show only the first line of body text in each paragraph under a heading. The Collapse button collapses a heading or hides its subheadings and associated text. The Expand button expands a heading or displays its subheadings and associated text.

You can use the Show Formatting button to toggle formatting on and off.

Concept Builders

When you print a document in outline view, Word prints the headings and body text indented as it is displayed on your screen.

S TEP-BY-STEP ▷ 10.1

1. Open **Step-by-Step 10-1 View.**

2. To see the layout of the document, click the **Print Preview** button on the Standard toolbar. Use the **Multiple Pages** button to display three pages. To return to the original view, click **Close** on the **Print Preview** toolbar.

3. To display the document in outline view, click the **Outline View** button at the left of the Horizontal scroll bar. You now see the entire document. Notice the filled plus signs to the left of headings and the small squares to the left of body text.

4. To display only the three levels of headings in the document, click the **Show Heading 3** button on the Outlining toolbar.

5. To display all of the document again, click the **All** button.

6. To display just the first line of body text in each paragraph beneath each heading, click the **Show First Line Only** button.

7. To display all of the document again, click the **Show First Line Only** button.

8. To display just two levels of headings, click the **Show Heading 2** button.

9. To display three levels of headings again, click the **Show Heading 3** button.

10. To print the outline displaying three levels of headings, click the **Print** button.

11. To display the text associated with the **Surge Suppressors** heading, click anywhere in **Surge Suppressors** heading, and click the **Expand** button on the Outlining toolbar.

12. To hide the text associated with the **Surge Suppressors** heading, click the **Collapse** button while your insertion point is still in the **Surge Suppressors** heading.

13. To display the outline without formatting, click the **Show Formatting** button.

14. To return to the original formatting, click the **Show Formatting** button again.

Moving Segments of Your Document

Very often when you are working with a long document, you will want to move large segments of the document from one place to another. Outline view makes that task very easy for you. To move segments of a large document, display headings to include the level of the heading you want to move, select the heading you want to move, use the Move Up or Move Down buttons on the Outlining toolbar, or drag the heading. The associated subheadings and text move automatically with the heading.

By displaying the first line of each paragraph of body text, you can easily move paragraphs within a heading.

Promoting and Demoting Headings

You can use the Promote, Demote, and Demote to Body Text buttons to promote headings and their subheadings and body text to higher levels, to demote them to lower heading levels, or to demote them to body text. **Body text** refers to paragraphs of text beneath the headings and subheadings in a document.

STEP-BY-STEP 10.2

1. To be sure your document displays three levels of headings, click the **Show Heading 3** button.

2. To move the **Passwords** heading and its associated text ahead of the **Floppies** heading, click anywhere in the **Passwords** heading, and click the **Move Up** button once.

3. To move **Security** and all of its subheadings and associated text ahead of **Power Surges,** click the **Show Heading 2** button, and point to the filled plus sign to the left of **Security** until you see the double-crossed arrows. As you drag the heading upward, you will see a line with a left-pointing arrowhead. When this line moves above **Power Surges,** release. Then click the insertion point in blank space.

4. To see the result of the move, click the **Print Layout View** button at the right of the horizontal scroll bar and scroll through the document.

5. To return to outline view and display all the heading levels in this document, click the **Outline View** button on the horizontal scroll bar and click the **Show Heading 3** button.

6. To move the **Passwords** heading below the **Screen Savers** heading and promote **Passwords** to a level 2 heading, click anywhere in the **Passwords** heading, click the **Move Down** button twice, and click the **Promote** button once.

7. Save and close the document.

Other Helpful Document Views

Word offers several other features that can make it easier to work with documents covering several pages: the Document Map and the split bar.

Using Document Map

The Document Map feature can help you find and move quickly to various parts of a long document. The Document Map command on the View menu displays a screen (see Figure 10.3) in which the document's headings appear in the left pane, called the **Document Map,** and the document itself appears in the right pane. To move to any heading in the document, simply click it in the left pane.

Concept Builders

Use the Browse tools at the bottom of the vertical scroll bar to access pages, sections, comments, endnotes, fields, tables, graphics, headings, or edits.

You can choose the level of headings to display in the Document Map pane by clicking the symbols to the left of the headings. An expand (+) symbol indicates that a heading has subheadings. Click the expand (+) symbol to display all subheadings below that heading. When a collapse (−) symbol appears, all subheadings are displayed.

FIGURE 10.3
Document Map gives you quick access to any part of your document.

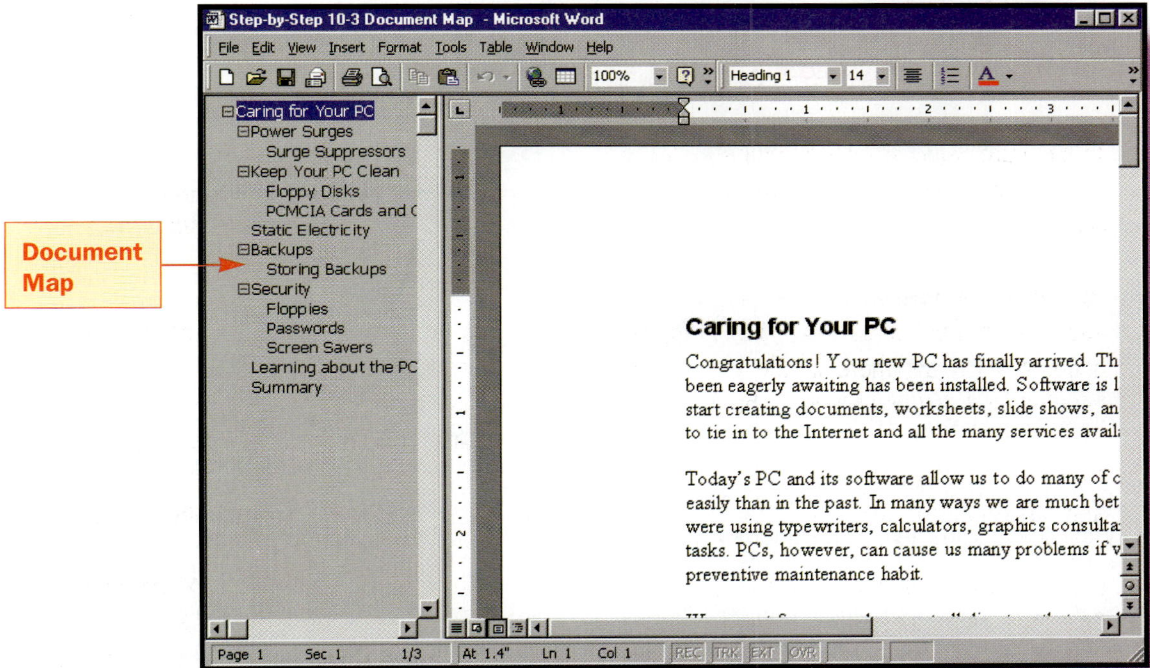

Using the Split Bar

Word's **split bar** makes it possible to split the document window into two panes so you can see two parts of one document (see Figure 10.4). Each pane on the screen has its own ruler and scroll bar so you can move to any location in the document in either pane. To split the screen, click the **split box** above the up scroll arrow at the top of the vertical scroll bar. When the double-headed arrow appears, drag the split bar down to any location in the window. To return to a single window, double-click the split bar.

Working with a split window makes it easy to copy or move text from one location in a document to another. Simply drag the selection across the split bar to its new location.

The split bar divides a screen into two parts.

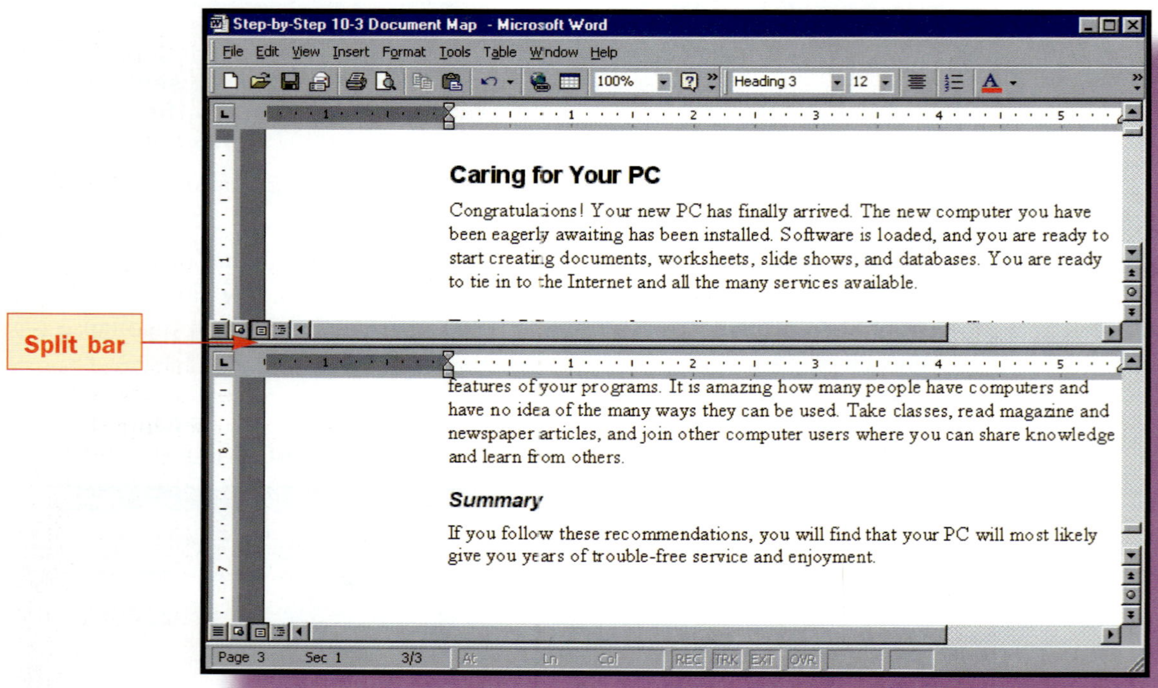

STEP-BY-STEP 10.3

1. Open **Step-by-Step 10-3 Map.**

2. To display the Document Map, click the **View** menu and then click **Document Map.**

3. To move to a specific point in your document, click the **Keep Your PC Clean** heading in the Document Map. Notice that positioning your insertion point in the right pane instantly displays that heading in the document.

4. To collapse the map structure, click the collapse (–) symbol next to the **Keep Your PC Clean** heading in the Document Map. Notice the heading now has an expand (+) symbol to its left.

5. To display the subheadings again, click the **expand** (+) symbol.

6. To close the Document Map, click the **View** menu, and then click **Document Map.**

7. To split the window into two panes, point to the split box at the top of the vertical scroll bar. When the double-headed arrow appears, drag the split bar down to the middle of the window.

8. To show the beginning and the end of the document on the screen at the same time, scroll in the bottom pane until the summary paragraph comes into view and scroll in the top pane until you see the **Caring for Your PC** heading.

9. To remove the split bar, double-click it.

10. Close the document without saving.

Creating Cross-References

A **cross-reference** tells the reader where additional information on a topic is located, either in the same document or in another document. You can also create cross-references to footnotes, endnotes, and captions created by Word or to items marked with bookmarks.

To create a cross-reference, do the following:

- Type the introductory text for the cross-reference, including the opening quotation mark if you want quotation marks. For example, type See ".

- Use the Cross-reference command on the Insert menu to display the Cross Reference dialog box (see Figure 10.5) and designate the type of reference (such as heading) and the reference text (such as heading text).

- Be sure the Insert as Hyperlink box is checked if you want to insert a hyperlink.

- To insert the words above or below, as appropriate, in your Cross-reference, check the Include above/below box.

- Insert the reference and type any following punctuation, such as ").

You can choose to display the cross-reference as a hyperlink, which allows the reader to jump immediately to the location containing the additional information. If the cross-reference item you want is in another document, be sure the reader has access to the other document.

FIGURE 10.5

You can use the Cross-reference dialog box to insert a hyperlink.

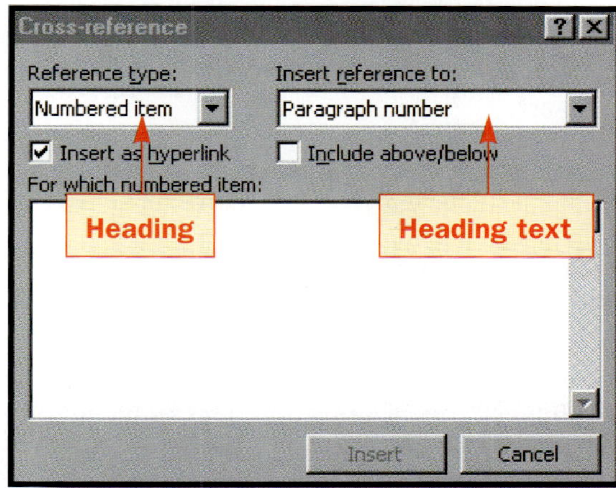

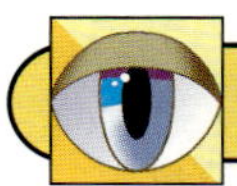
IMPORTANT:

Cross references should be used in documents that will be printed. The hyperlink is the most effective way of pointing to additional information in an online document.

S TEP-BY-STEP ▷ 10.4

1. Open **Step-by-Step 10-4 Cross.**

2. To begin entering the cross-reference, position the insertion point in the first paragraph of body text just before the word **You** at the beginning of the last sentence.

Type **(See** and a space, click the **Insert** menu, click **Cross-reference** and click Insert as hyperlink. Click the drop-down arrow in the Reference type box, and click **Heading.** Notice Heading text automatically appears in the **Insert Reference To** box.

(continued on next page)

Scroll down in the **For Which Heading** box, click **Learning about the PC,** and click **Insert.**

3. To add the page number to the cross-reference, click the insertion point after the words **Learning about the PC** that Word just inserted, and type a space, followed by **on page** and then by another space. In the Cross-reference dialog box, click the drop-down arrow in the Insert Reference To box, click **Page number,** click **Learning about the PC** in the For Which Heading box, and click **Insert.**

4. To close the dialog box, and finish the text for the reference, click the **Close** button in the dialog box and type **.)** and a **space.** Notice when you move the pointer over the cross-reference it becomes a hand with a pointing finger. This indicates the cross-reference is a hyperlink.

5. To jump to the **Learning about the PC** heading, click the hyperlink.

6. Save the document, and close it.

Inserting Captions

You can use the Caption command on the Insert menu to add numbered captions to figures, tables, and other items as you insert them. The figure number you see with each of the screen captures in this book is a caption. You can use the AutoCaption feature in the Caption dialog box (see Figure 10.6) to automatically add a label and a number to certain types of figures, tables, and equations as you insert them.

In the following exercise you will make copies of Word windows and place them in a document. You can copy a window to the Clipboard by pressing the Print Screen key at the upper right on your keyboard. You can copy just the active Word window to the Clipboard by holding Alt and pressing Print Screen.

Concept Builders

If you delete an item containing a caption, you must update the caption fields by selecting the document, clicking any field code, right-clicking your mouse, and then clicking Update Fields on the shortcut menu.

FIGURE 10.6
Use the Caption dialog box to automatically add a label and a number to a figure.

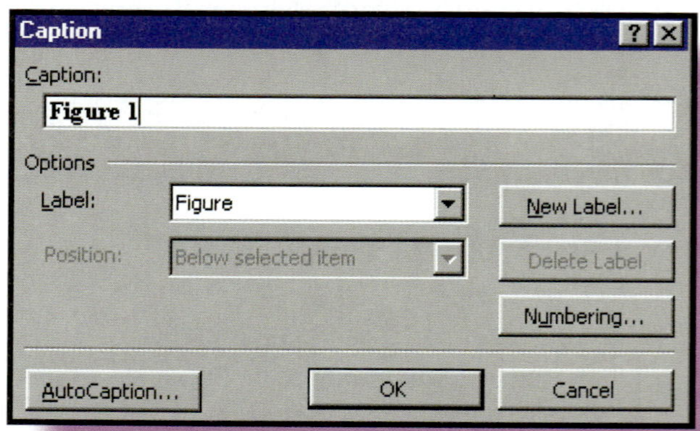

STEP-BY-STEP ▷ 10.5

1. To create a new document, click the **New** button.

2. To set up for the AutoCaption feature, click the **Insert** menu, click **Caption,** click **AutoCaption,** and then click the **Microsoft Word Picture** check box. Accept the default entries for **Use label** and **Position options** and click **OK.**

3. To capture the entire Word window and put it in the Windows Clipboard and then paste the picture in your document, press the **Print Screen** key. Then click the **Paste** button on the Standard toolbar. Notice the Figure 1 caption at the bottom of the screen capture.

4. To move down on the page, press the ↓ (down arrow) key, click the insertion point after **Figure 1,** then press the **Enter** key twice.

5. To capture a dialog box (the active window), click the **Insert** menu, click **Caption,** and hold the **Alt** key and press the **Print Screen** key.

6. To close the dialog box, click **Cancel.**

7. To paste the picture and automatically insert the caption in your document, click the **Paste** button. Notice once again your picture is labeled with a consecutive number.

8. Print the document. Save the document as **Using Captions** and close it.

Inserting Footnotes and Endnotes

You can use the Footnote command on the Insert menu to include footnotes and endnotes (see Figure 10.7). You can include both footnotes and endnotes in the same document. Footnotes and endnotes allow you to provide references for, comment on, or explain text in your document. Footnotes print at the bottom of the page. Endnotes print at the end of the document.

Word numbers your footnotes or endnotes for you and renumbers them when you insert or delete notes. You can also change the position of notes on the page, change the numbering format, and set other options.

To see an existing footnote, double-click the reference mark. In print layout view, the insertion point jumps to the note. In normal view, the notes appear in a pane at the bottom of the window. You can also see a ScreenTip for a footnote by sliding the I-beam over the footnote reference mark.

To delete a note, select its reference mark, and press the Delete key or the Backspace key. To move a note, select its reference mark, and drag it to a new location. To access the shortcut menu for notes, position the insertion point in the note text and click the right mouse button.

FIGURE 10.7
Use the Footnote and Endnote dialog box to add footnotes to the bottom of the page and endnotes to the end of the document.

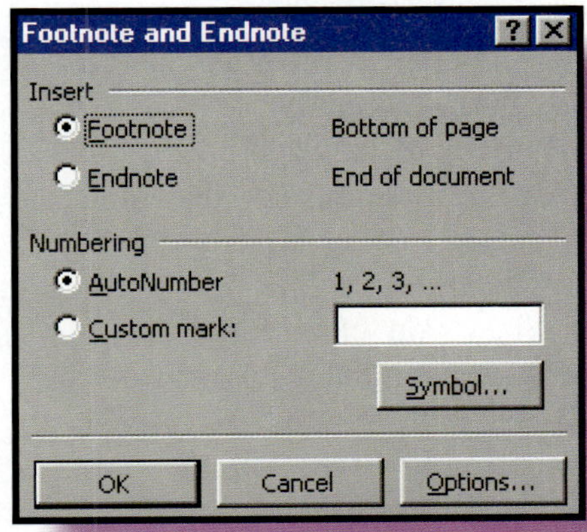

1. Open **Step-by-Step 10-6 Foot.**

2. To enter a footnote to explain **PC** in the first paragraph of body text, position the insertion point after the **C** in **PC,** click the **Insert** menu, click **Footnote,** click **Footnote** and **AutoNumber** if they are not already selected, and click **OK.** At the insertion point in the footnote area, type **PC is an acronym for personal computer.**

3. To enter another footnote, position the insertion point immediately after the last letter in the word **Software** on the second line of body text, click the **Insert** menu, click **Footnote,** and click **OK.** Type **Software consists of application programs** that contain instructions for the computer.

4. To see the text of a footnote at the reference point, slide your mouse pointer across the number **1** in the first paragraph until the ScreenTip appears.

5. To delete the first footnote, select its reference mark in the document (the number **1**) and press the **Delete** key. Notice the footnote reference is deleted and the reference mark next to **Software** is now number 1.

6. To print only page 1 of the document, click the **File** menu, click **Print,** click the **Pages** button, type **1,** and click **OK.**

Using AutoSummarize

You can create a summary of the key points in your document with Word's AutoSummarize command on the expanded Tools menu. AutoSummarize analyzes the text in a document and assigns a score to each sentence. Sentences that contain words used frequently in the document receive a higher score. You choose what percentage of the highest-scoring sentences to display in the summary.

You should always check the summary because it is not the whole work and may not accurately reflect the original work.

When you choose the Auto-Summarize command, Word displays the AutoSummarize dialog box (see Figure 10.8) after it completes the analysis. You can see an example highlighting the key points in the document in Figure 10.9.

FIGURE 10.8
Choose a summary option in the AutoSummarize dialog box.

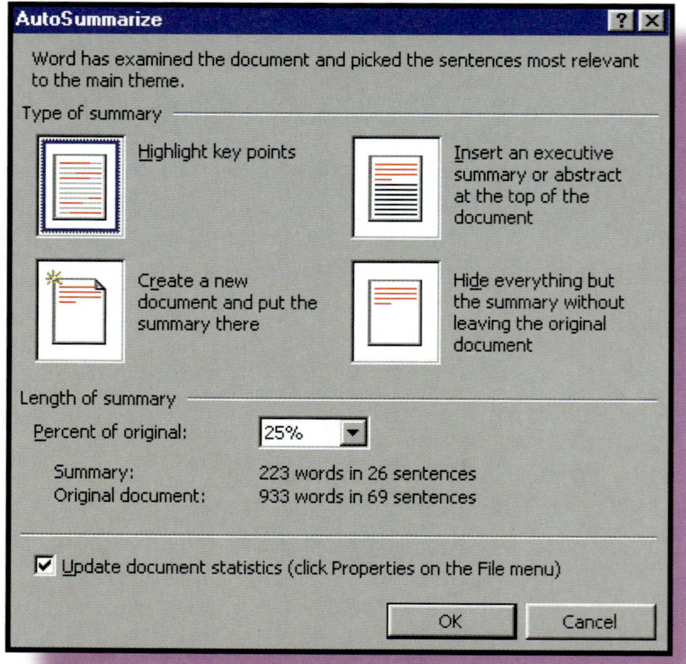

FIGURE 10.9
AutoSummarize highlighted key points in the document.

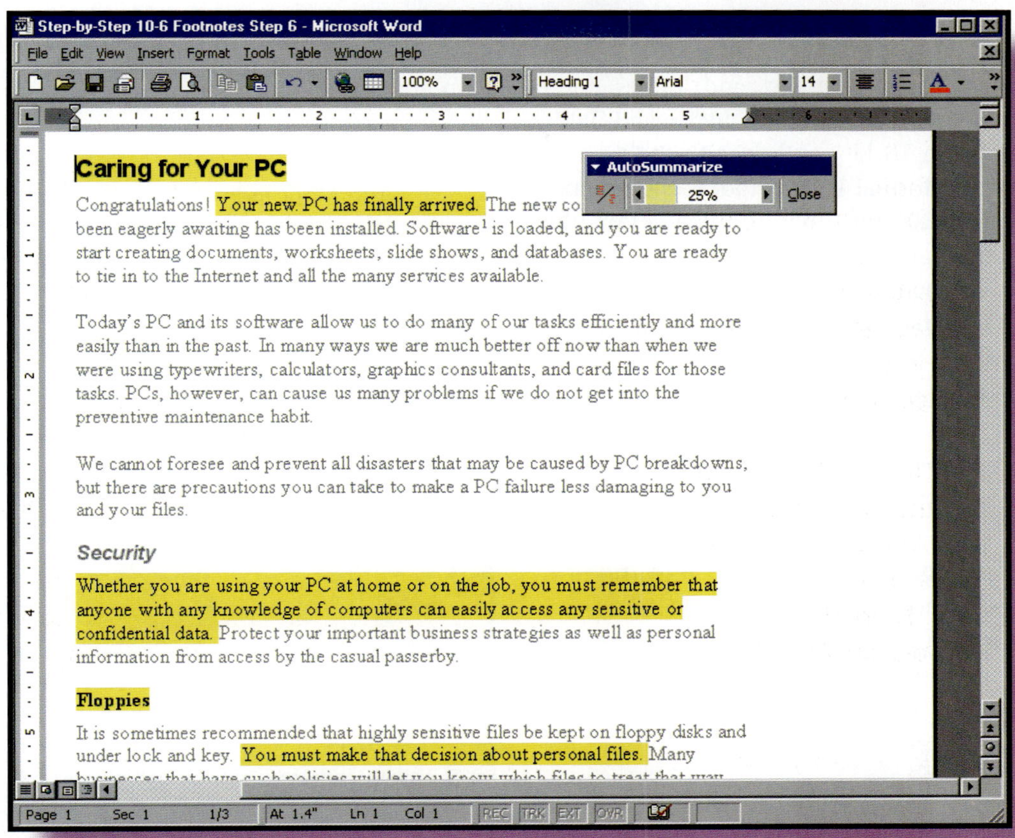

STEP-BY-STEP ▷ 10.7

1. To summarize the open document, click the **Tools** menu and then click **AutoSummarize.** Notice the progress of the summary operation on the status bar.

2. To highlight the summary material in your document, make sure the **Highlight key points** option is selected in the Auto-Summarize dialog box and click **OK.** Then scroll through the document and notice the highlighted text.

3. Close the document without saving it.

Creating an Index

You can use the Index and Tables command on the Insert menu to include an index that gives users page numbers for items they might want to look up in a document.

To mark the text you want as an index entry, select the text, choose Index and Tables on the Insert menu, display the Index tab, and click the Mark Entry button to display the dialog box you see in Figure 10.10. You can then edit the text and click the Mark button.

To build an index from the marked entries, position the insertion point where you want Word to place the index, choose the Index and Tables command on the Insert menu to display the Index and Tables dialog box (see Figure 10.11.) and specify the type of index and format for the index, the number of columns, and the alignment for the numbers.

To update an index, choose Index and Tables on the Insert menu, display the Index tab, click OK, and confirm that you want to replace the existing index.

NOTE:

To change index markers, use the Index and Tables command. Items changed in the index itself are lost when you update the index.

You can hold the Alt and Shift keys and press X to display the Mark Index Entry dialog box.

FIGURE 10.10
The Mark Index Entry dialog box is used to mark text you want as an index entry.

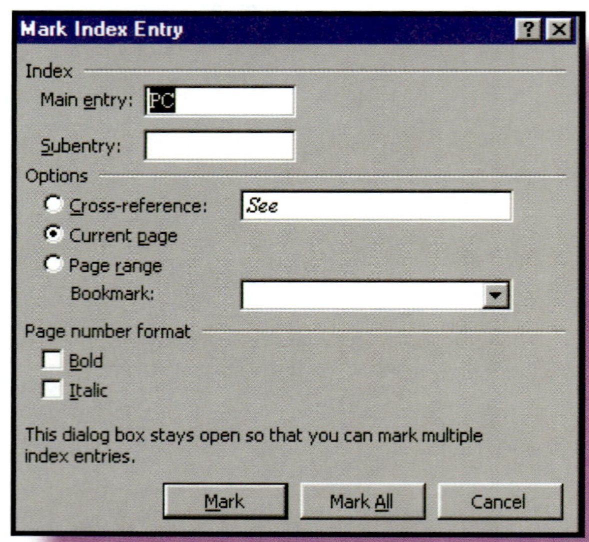

FIGURE 10.11
Use the Index and Tables dialog box to build an index from the marked entries.

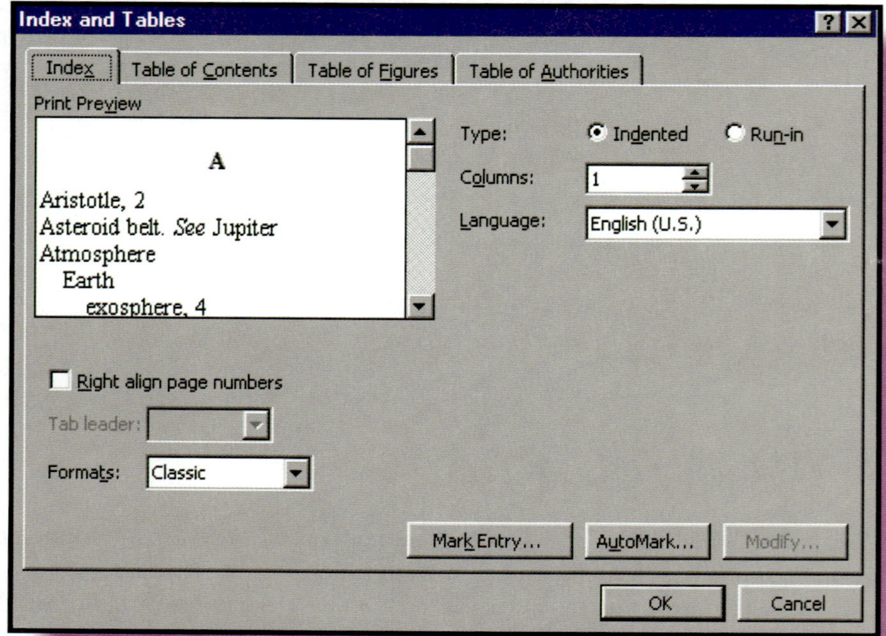

FIGURE 10.12
You will create this index.

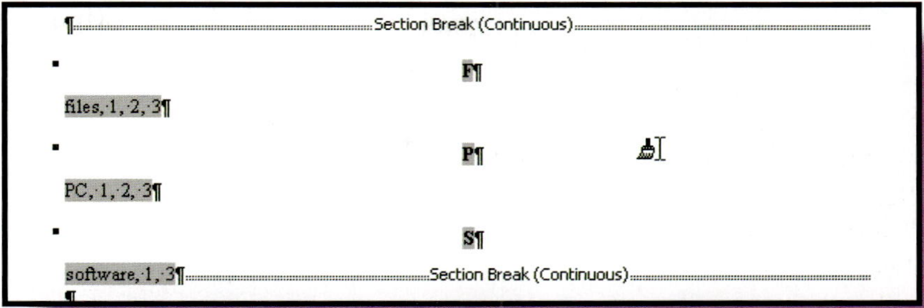

STEP-BY-STEP ▷ 10.8

1. Open **Step-by-Step 10-8 Index.**

2. To display nonprinting marks if they are not already displayed, click the **Show/Hide ¶** button. You may have to click the **More Buttons** button on the Standard toolbar.

3. To mark **PC** in the first heading, double-click **PC,** hold the **Alt** key and the **Shift** key and press **X** to display the Mark Index Entry dialog box, and click **Mark All** to mark all occurrences of **PC** throughout the document. Notice the field codes Word enters. You can leave the dialog box open until you finish marking index entries.

4. To mark **Software** (with a capital **S**) in the first text paragraph, double-click the word, click in blank space in the dialog box to activate it, edit **Software** to make the **S** lowercase for the index, and click **Mark All.** Use the scroll bars or the arrow keys to move through your document while the dialog box is displayed.

5. To mark the word **software** (it does not begin with a capital letter and therefore was not marked in step 4) on the top line of the second paragraph, double-click it, click blank space in the dialog box to activate it, and click **Mark All.**

6. To mark the word **problems** in the same paragraph, double-click it, click the dialog box, and click **Mark All.**

7. To mark the word **files** in the next paragraph and then close the dialog box, double-click **files,** click the dialog box, and click **Mark All.** Then click one of the **Close** buttons in the dialog box. Notice all the field codes for the index.

8. To create an index with those few entries, hold the **Ctrl** key and press the **End** key to move to the end of the document; hold the **Ctrl** key and press the **Enter** key to insert a page break; click the **Insert** menu; and click **Index and Tables.**

9. To see what the various formats look like, click the drop-down button in the Formats box, click on each, and notice each of the formats in the Preview box. Be sure **Indented** is selected in the Type box, **Classic** in the Formats box, and **1** in the Columns box, and click **OK.** Word inserts section breaks and displays the index.

10. To turn off nonprinting marks, click the **Show / Hide** button.

2 0 9

Creating a Table of Contents

You can also use the Index and Tables command on the Insert menu to create a table of contents, table of figures, or table of authorities (see Figure 10.13).

The easiest way to create a table of contents is to format headings in your document with the Heading 1 through Heading 9 styles and build the table of contents directly from the styles.

Did You Know?

A table of authorities is used in legal documents.

FIGURE 10.13
Use the Index and Tables dialog box to insert a table of contents, table of figures, or table of authorities.

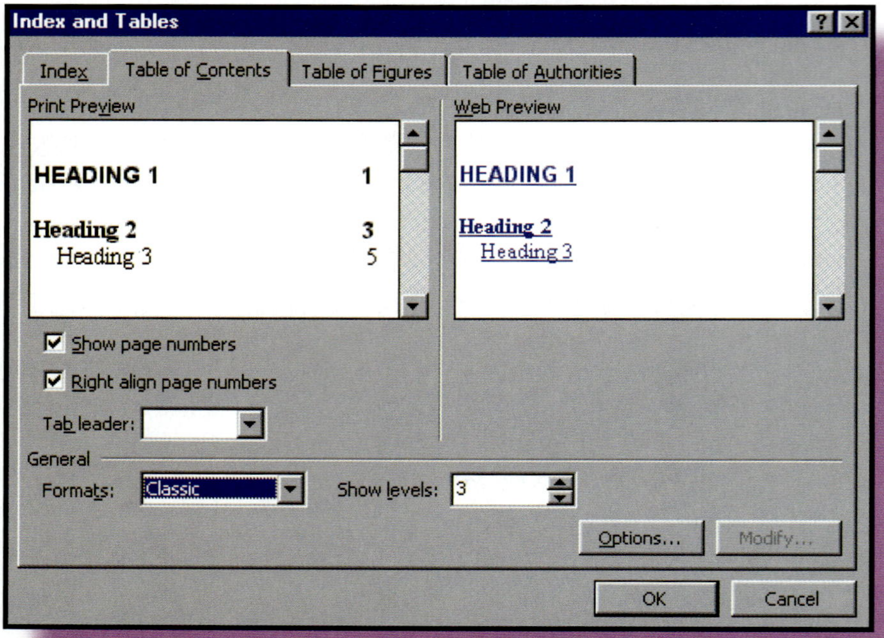

If you are planning to create both an index and other tables, such as a table of figures, in your document, you should create the index and other tables before the table of contents so that they can be included in it.

To create a table of contents like the one displayed in Figure 10.14 using built-in headings, position the insertion point where you want the table of contents to be placed, choose Index and Tables on the Insert menu, display the Table of Contents tab in the Index and Tables dialog box, and make decisions about the format for the table.

To update a table of contents, position the insertion point in the table of contents, press the F9 key, and choose Update Page Numbers Only or Update Entire Table.

Hot Tips

When you point to a heading or a page number in your table of contents, the mouse pointer becomes a hand so you can jump to a heading.

FIGURE 10.14
A sample table of contents.

CARING FOR YOUR PC	2
Security	**2**
Floppies	2
Screen Savers	2
Passwords	2
Power Surges	**3**
Surge Suppressors	3
Keep Your PC Clean	**3**
Floppy Disks	3
PCMCIA Cards and CD ROMs	3
Static Electricity	**3**
Backups	**4**
Storing Backups	4
Learning about the PC	**4**
Summary	**4**

STEP-BY-STEP 10.9

1. To create the table of contents at the beginning of the document, hold the **Ctrl** key and press the **Home** key, click the **Insert** menu, click **Index and Tables,** and click the **Table of Contents** tab.

2. To create your table, be sure **Classic** is selected and **Show page numbers, Right align page numbers,** and **Show levels 3** are the selected settings. Click the **Tab leader** drop-down button and click the **dotted** line. Click **OK.**

3. To enter a section break before the first heading in the document, click the **Insert** menu, click **Break,** click **Next Page,** and click **OK.** Then scroll up through the table.

4. To preview and print the document, click the **Print Preview** button, click the **Multiple Pages** button, drag over six pages, and release. Then click the **Print** button.

5. To move to the **Surge Suppressors** text and then move back to the Table of Contents, point to the **surge suppressors** in the Table of Contents, and click when you see the hand pointer. Then click the **Undo** button.

6. Print, save and close the document.

Using a Master Document

You can use a master document to make it easier to work with long documents. A **master document** is a Word document that takes some or all of its contents from one or more documents.

By working with a series of smaller documents, called subdocuments, and organizing them in a master document, you can save a lot of time. A master document also allows you to create cross-references to subdocuments and to generate tables of contents and indexes for a long document consisting of subdocuments.

With a master document, you can work either with the entire group of subdocuments or with any individual subdocument. Any Word document can be either a master document or a subdocument.

You use the Master Document View button on the Outlining toolbar that is displayed when you are in Outline View to access the master document. You can move between outline view, shown in Figure 10.15, and normal or print layout view at will.

A master document is helpful if several people are working on different parts of a document in different files. Use a master document to put all the parts together when it comes time to move parts of several documents into another document or to print the document.

FIGURE 10.15
Master document displayed in Outline View.

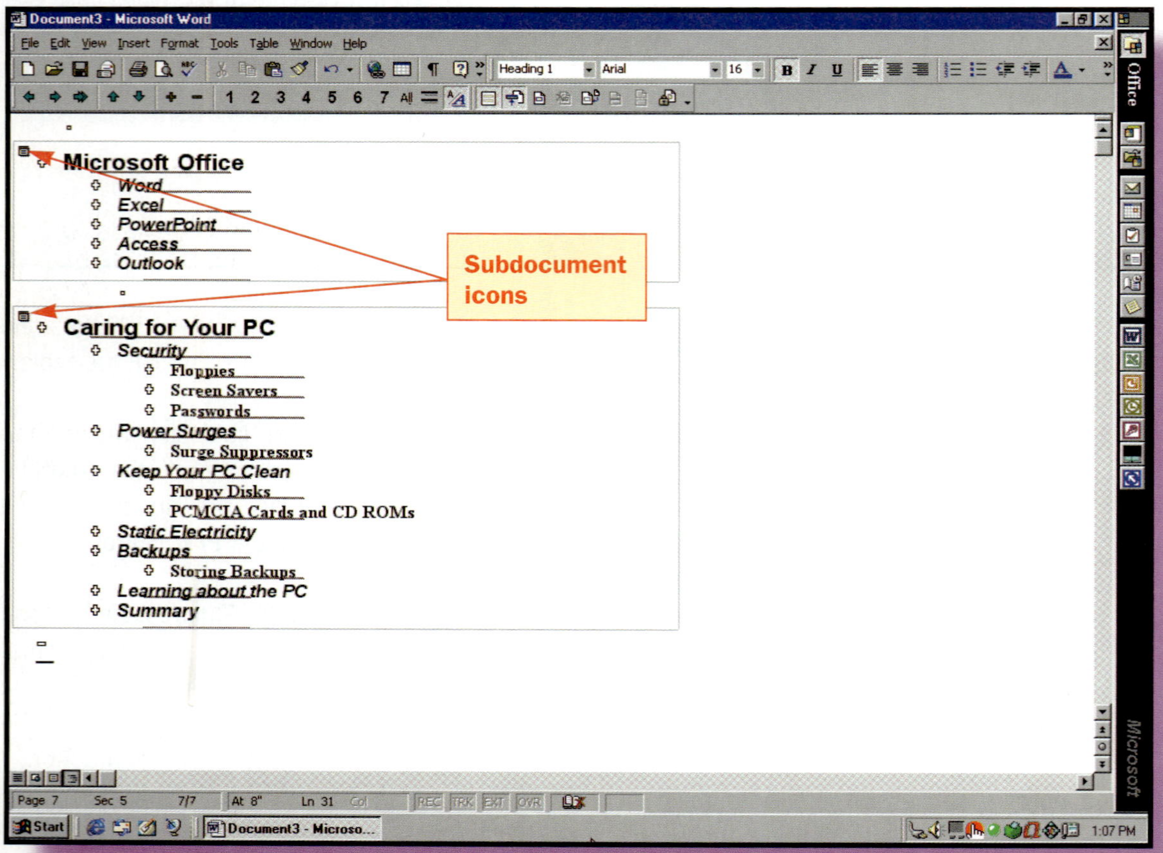

You can create a master document by typing an outline in Outline view, by converting an existing long document into a master document and create subdocuments, or by combining several Word documents to make a new master document.

When you open a master document, Word displays hyperlinks for each of the subdocuments (see Figure 10.16). To work with a subdocument, click its hyperlink, edit the subdocument in its own document window while the master document remains open, and then save and close the subdocument the same as any other document

Notice the hyperlinks to the subdocuments.

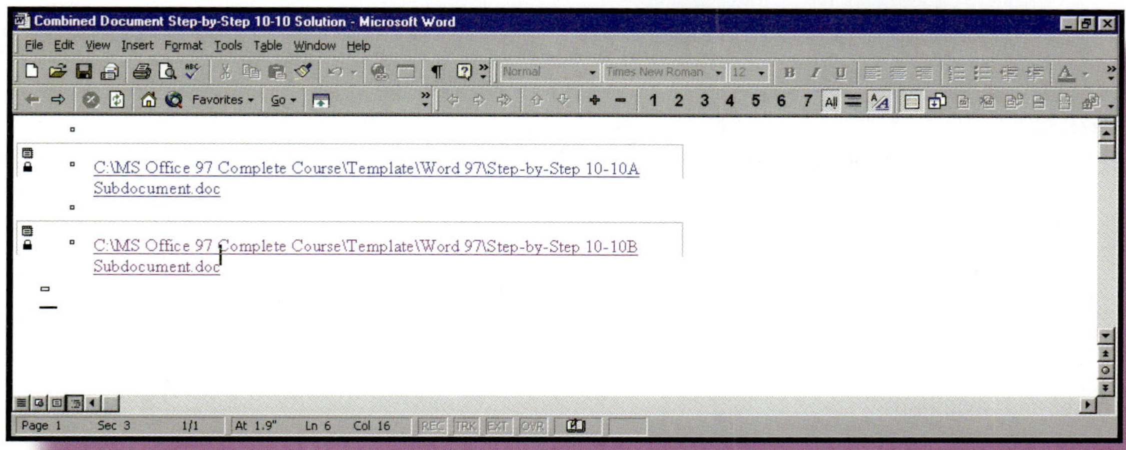

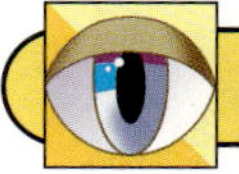

IMPORTANT:

Be sure you do not rename subdocuments or change their drives or directories unless you do so from within the master document.

Hot Tips

A master document is limited to 80 subdocuments, and the total size of a master document cannot exceed 32 MB (excluding graphics).

You can print a master document within the master document view with as many levels of headings and body text as are displayed. To print the entire master document, expand the subdocuments, switch to normal view, and print.

STEP-BY-STEP ▷ 10.10

1. To create a new file, click the **New** button.

2. To display master document view, click the **Outline View** button on the Horizontal toolbar and click the **Master Document View** button on the Outlining toolbar.

3. To add the first subdocument to the master document, click the **Insert Subdocument** button and double-click **Step-by-Step 10-10A Sub.** Notice how Word entered the document.

4. To add the second document, hold the **Ctrl** key and press the **End** key, click the **Insert Subdocument** button, and double-click **Step-by-Step 10-10B Sub.**

5. To display three levels of headings, click the **Show Level 3** button.

6. To display the master document in normal view and see the section breaks Word inserted before and after each subdocument, click the **Normal View** button at

(continued on next page)

213

the left of the horizontal toolbar and scroll through the document.

7. To return to master document view, click the **Outline View** button at the left of the horizontal toolbar.

8. To open a subdocument in its own window while the master document remains open, double-click the subdocument **icon** for the **second** document.

9. To close the subdocument, click its **Close** button.

10. Save the master document as **Combined Document.** Close the document.

11. To reopen the document to see how Word inserted a hyperlink to each subdocument and displays the Web toolbar, click the **File** menu and click **Combined Document.**

Working with Web Pages

You must have access to a Web server before you can create copy, save, or manage folders and files on a Web server. See your system administrator about putting your Web pages on the Web server or intranet.

To make a Web page available on the Internet, you must check with your Internet service provider, or else install Web server software on your computer.

You should find out from your Internet service provider or from your organization's Web administrator how Web pages, graphics files, and other files should be structured on the server. Find out, for example, whether you need to create separate folders for bullets and pictures, or whether you need to store all files in one location. Ask also about limitations on using those items because they require more server support.

> **INTERNET** When you create Web pages for international use, Word can save files with the appropriate text encoding so users can see the correct characters.

Creating a Web Page

You can use the Web Page wizard to create a Web page (Figure 10.17) and then save the document as a Web page. You can also create a Web page by saving an existing document as a Web page. When you use the Save As command save your Web page document as a Web page file type. Word then saves your document in HTML which stands for Hypertext Markup Language. HTML is a system of coding—marking up—text so that it can appear on the World Wide Web. Some aspects of your document may not be available as HTML codes, so the document may not appear on the Web exactly the same as it does in Word.

When you use Word to create a Web page, you can take advantage of Word's editing, formatting, spelling, grammar, and automatic text correction features. You can also create and format items such as tables, bulleted or numbered lists, and graphic objects the same way you would in any Word document.

Use the Web Page Preview command on the File menu to see how your Web page will look on the Web.

Different browsers display Web pages differently, so your Web page may not look the same when using Microsoft Internet Explorer as it looks when using Netscape, for example.

FIGURE 10.17
Create a Web page with the Personal Web Page template.

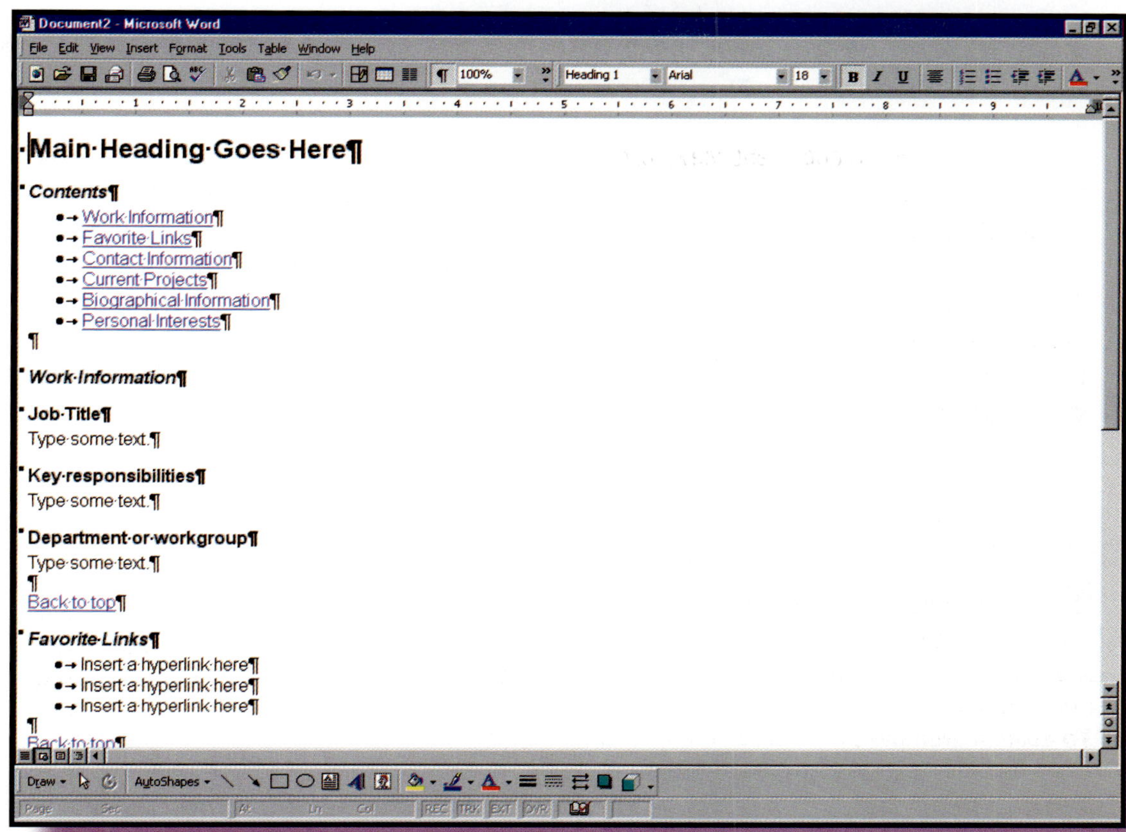

Tips for Creating Web Pages

Some tips that you should keep in mind when designing Web pages include the following:

- Content should be well organized. Deliver your ideas, and help the user navigate through your site.

- Text must be easy to read. Be careful about contrast with text if you add a background to a page.

- Large images take longer to download, and not all users choose to see images. Some Web browsers don't support all video formats. Be sure essential information is not confined to the images.

- Use tables as a layout tool.

STEP-BY-STEP ▷ 10.11

1. To create a Web page, click the **File** menu, click **New,** click the **Web Pages** tab, and double-click the **Personal Web Page.** Notice the hyperlinks to the subheads on the page and from the subheads back to the top of the page.

(continued on next page)

2. To add a theme to your Web page, click the **Format** menu and then click **Theme.** Click through the list of themes and when you see one you like in the sample box, click **OK.**

3. To enter your name for the main heading, select *Main Heading Goes Here* but *not* the paragraph mark, and then type your name.

4. To enter your personal information, go through the page, select each of the *Type some text…* paragraphs, and type the appropriate work information. If you are a full-time student, enter school information instead.

5. To preview the page, click **Web Page Preview** on the **File** menu. Click the browser's **Close** button when you finish.

6. To save the Web page, click the **Save** button, accept the name Word has chosen, notice the File type is Web Page, and click **Save.**

Using Word Features in Web Pages

Use the following Word features to help you design a professional and effective Web page:

- Hyperlinks for jumping from your Web page to other pages.

- Pictures and video clips for visual interest.

- Horizontal lines, picture bullets, and background color.

- Tables, scrolling text, and background sounds.

STEP-BY-STEP ⟹ **10.12**

1. To add visual interest, experiment with adding a picture to your Web page. You may have to use a table to position a picture exactly where you want it.

2. When you finish working on your Web page, save and close the document.

3. Be creative! Have fun!

Summary

You have now learned how to use the outline view, Document Map, and the split bar, create a cross-reference, insert a caption, create footnotes and endnotes, summarize a document, create an index and a table of contents, use a master document, and create a Web page.

Try the exercises on the following pages to test how well you remember what you learned. Don't be afraid to go back and look up the answers, because that will help to reinforce what you learned.

LESSON 10 REVIEW QUESTIONS

TRUE / FALSE

Circle the T if the statement is true. Circle the F if it is false.

T (F) **1.** When you are in outline view, you can see only the headings in a document.

T (F) **2.** When you print a document in outline view, it prints exactly as it would in normal view.

T (F) **3.** Images download very quickly for all users.

T (F) **4.** All browsers display Web pages exactly the same way.

T (F) **5.** You should not duplicate in text information in images.

(T) F **6.** You can have both footnotes and endnotes in the same document.

T (F) **7.** In print layout view, Word displays footnotes in a separate pane.

(T) F **8.** The easiest way to create a table of contents is to format your document with Heading 1 through Heading 9 styles and build the table of contents directly from the styles.

T (F) **9.** The split bar lets you see three or more parts of your document at the same time.

(T) F **10.** A master document lets you create cross-references to subdocuments.

COMPLETION

Complete the following sentences by writing the correct word or words in the blanks provided.

1. When you are in outline view, text formatted with a(n) _heading_ style is displayed with either a plus or a minus sign.

2. You can use _document Map_ to move instantly to any heading in the document.

3. You can use the _move up_ button in outline view to move headings to higher levels.

4. You can create a(n) _cross reference_ to another document if you are using a master document.

5. You can add numbered _captions_ to Word tables you insert in your document.

6. When you want to see a footnote in normal view, _double click_ its reference mark.

7. You can delete a footnote by selecting its _reference mark_ and pressing the Delete key.

8. Before you create a(n) _table of contents_ you should create the index and all other tables for your document.

9. You can use a(n) _master document_ to work with a group of documents and print them as one document.

10. You can open a(n) _sub document_ from within a master document while the master document remains open.

LESSON 10 PROJECTS

PROJECT 10A

To practice what you've learned in this lesson, complete the following project:

1. Open **Project 10-A.**

2. Print the document in outline format with three heading levels displayed.

3. Save and close the document.

Use Help to find information about using outline view to type a document. Read the information and print it.

PROJECT 10B

To practice what you've learned in this lesson, complete the following project:

1. Open **Project 10-B.**

2. Build an index and a table of contents. Be sure the index and table of contents are on separate pages, and add a title to the table of contents page (Table of Contents) and to the index page (Index).

3. Print the document. Save and close the document.

PROJECT 10C

SCANS

Search for information about a beach resort called Fripp Island in South Carolina. Print the home page after you've checked the site.

CRITICAL THINKING ACTIVITY

SCANS

You are the secretary of a a beach resort. Create a Web page for prospective visitors. Save and print the brochure. Use all your creative juices on this one!

A

Active document The document you can currently work on. Only one document can be active at a time.

B

Body text Paragraphs of text beneath headings and subheadings in a document.

Bookmark A marker placed in text so that you can access the text quickly.

Border A box, or combination of lines, that surrounds selected text, a paragraph, or a page.

Bullets Small symbols that mark the beginning of each entry in a list.

C

Callouts Labels that identify or comment on some feature of a drawing, picture, or text.

Characters Letters, numbers, symbols, punctuation marks, and spaces in a document.

Close button The button that you click to close an application or a document.

Command button A button in a dialog box that will carry out the options you have selected.

Clip art Pictures already created and available for use in a document.

Clipboard A temporary storage area in Windows memory. Material that has been cut or copied using the Cut or the Copy command or button is stored as items on the clipboard until you cut or copy additional text or until you shut down the computer.

Cross-reference A text reference that tells the reader where additional information on a topic, either in the same document or in another document, is located.

D

Datasheet The tabular window that allows you to enter data for a chart in Word.

Data source In a merge operation, the file that contains the information that changes for each form letter, label, and so forth.

Desktop The screen on which Windows opens applications and displays tools; the large area you see when you start Windows.

Destination The document or application into which you insert linked or embedded information.

Dialog box A box containing options to allow you to supply or change further information before a command is carried out.

Document Map view A split view that allows you to see a document's headings and text in side-by-side panes and to move easily to various parts of a document.

Document window The area on the Word screen where you create a document.

Drag-and-drop feature A feature that allows you to drag text to move it or copy it to a new location.

Drop cap A large or dropped initial capital letter or a large first word used to add interest, such as to the beginning of a document.

E

Ellipsis The three dots (...) that follow some commands, indicating Word will display a dialog box where you can change or supply more information.

Embed The act of inserting an object in a document. Embedding places a copy of source information in the destination document. The source and destination documents are not linked.

End-of-Cell mark The mark that indicates the end of a cell in a table.

End-of-Row mark The mark that indicates the end of a table row.

F

Fields Codes that tell Word to insert information of various kinds in a document; each piece of information in a data source record.

Fill Color or shade of gray that fills a bordered area or a closed drawing object.

Font The design of a set of letters and numbers with a specific name, such as Times New Roman or Arial.

Font styles The weight or appearance of a font. Common font styles are **bold,** *italic,* and ***bold italic.***

Footer Text or graphic material that print at the bottom of each page of a document.

H

Handles Small square boxes that surround a selected graphic object.

Hard page break A command that tells Word to begin a new page.

Header Text or graphic material that print at the top of each page of a document.

Home page The starting page for a Web site, or the page you choose as your starting page on the Web.

Hyperlink A link, shortcut, to an Internet site or to another document or file. Clicking a hyperlink takes you directly to the address or path embedded in the hyperlink.

HTML (Hypertext Markup Language) A system of coding text; text coded in HTML can appear on the World Wide Web.

I

I-beam The pointer shaped like a letter I displayed when the mouse pointer is in the text area.

Inline picture A picture that is positioned directly in the text at the insertion point.

Insertion point The blinking vertical bar that shows where text will appear when keyed.

Insert mode The default mode in which text is entered and in which new characters appear to the left of the insertion point.

Integration Using more than one application to create documents.

Internet A global network of computers that use a common language to communicate.

L

Leaders Symbols or characters used to fill the empty space between text and text appearing at the next tab stop.

Link The act of inserting an object in a document. The information about the linked object is stored in the source and updated in the destination document when changes are made in the source. Links are also created with hyperlinks.

M

Macro A recording of a series of commands that you can use to automatically carry out tasks.

Main document In a mail merge operation, the document that contains items that remain the same in each form letter, envelope, memo, and so forth.

Margins The white space surrounding text in a document that separates it from the edges of the page.

Master document A document in Word that contains a set of related documents.

Maximize button The sizing button that enlarges a document or application window to fill the screen.

Menu A list of commands grouped by category.

Menu bar The bar below the Title bar that displays the names of available drop-down menus.

Merge fields Field codes that tell Word where to insert information from the data source.

Minimize button The sizing button that reduces an open document or application window to a taskbar button.

N

Normal view A view that shows text formatting and a simplified print layout.

O

Object Information from another application that is displayed in the current document.

Object linking and embedding (OLE) A Windows feature that allows you to insert information from other applications in the current document.

Office Assistant Word's interactive help feature. The Office Assistant offers tips on tasks you are currently doing and allows you to type specific requests for help.

Office Shortcut bar A group of buttons that allows you to quickly access Office 2000 applications and features.

Orientation The direction that text is printed on a page. Landscape orientation arranges text across the length of the paper. Portrait orientation arranges text across the width of the paper.

Outline view The view that displays the structure of a document in classic outline format.

Overtype mode The mode of entering text in which new characters replace existing characters.

P

Print Layout view The view that displays the page, including headers, footers, footnotes, and graphics, as it will print.

Paragraph Any amount of text or graphics with a paragraph mark after it.

Point The unit of measure used for measuring fonts. A point is 1/72nd of an inch.

Pointer The on-screen symbol that reflects the movement of the mouse and the type of operation you are about to perform.

R

Record All the information about one person or thing in a data source.

Restore button The sizing button that returns a document or application to its previous size.

Ruler A vertical or horizontal measuring feature in the document window. You can use the ruler to set margins, tabs, and indents.

S

Scroll bar The vertical or horizontal bar that lets you move through a document.

Scroll box The box on the scroll bar that lets you move to a position in the document by dragging the box.

Section break A command that tells Word to start a new section. You can format each section in a document differently.

Shortcut menu A menu you access by clicking the right button on a mouse. A shortcut menu contains function-specific commands.

Soft page break A page break automatically set by Word as a page fills.

Source The document or application containing information on an object that is either linked or embedded.

Split bar A Word feature that allows you to divide the screen into two panes so that you can see two different parts of the document at the same time.

Status bar The bar at the bottom of the application screen that displays information about current document settings.

Styles Collections of formatting commands that define the appearance of various text elements of a document.

Submenu A menu that displays more commands to the right or left of a drop-down menu.

T

Tabs A word processing feature that allows you to align text on the left, the right, in the center, on a bar, or on a decimal place.

Taskbar The bar at the bottom of the Windows screen that allows you to start programs and switch easily between open applications.

Template A master copy for a certain type of document.

Text box An invisible container that holds and allows you to position text and graphics inserted in text anywhere in a document.

Title bar The bar at the top of the application window that shows the name of the application and the title of the open document.

Toolbar A collection of buttons that represent commands to perform common tasks or features. Click a button to access a command.

U

Universal Resource Locator (URL) The address of a home page at a site on the Internet.

W

Web Layout view The view that lets you see what your document will look like on the Web or on an intranet.

Wildcard A symbol (?,*) you can use in a search to represent a character.

Wizard A Word feature that takes you step by step through a complex procedure.

World Wide Web A graphical, easy-to-use interface for looking at documents on the Internet.

INDEX